Praise for *Wild at Heart*

Winner, Mountain & Adventure Narratives,
NZ Mountain Film & Book Festival, Wanaka, 2021

'Staying with a polygamous cult leader in Austria, avoiding bears in
Bulgaria and a terrifying escape from a deranged West A....
who was convinced their lifestyle i.
in Miriam's new
Mark Crysell, *Sunday*

'A compelling yarn of derring do. There's a
of Lancewood's focus, drive, determination   .... thirst for
adventure. She writes of the positive effects of this lifestyle on her body
and mind and describes in vivid detail the sharpening of her senses,
boundless energy and contentment. While not everyone will be
inspired enough to give away all their possessions and go bush,
this engaging memoir certainly serves as a vicarious thrill.'
Kiran Dass, *Kete*

'Another bestseller. For those who dream of casting aside
material possessions, walking off into the wilderness
and living off and in tune with the land.'
Alex Bligh, *Otago Daily Times*

'Gripping sequel to the international bestseller
Woman in the Wilderness.'
Professional Skipper

'*Wild at Heart* is a riveting story about life, death, and courage,
while exploring the wonders of wild places.'
Australian Wildlife

'Here's a dollop of armchair travel written by an explorer for
our times: a woman capable of confronting irritated Austrian
birdwatchers, deranged Australian desert dwellers,
and Teutonic gurus with impunity.'
Chris Moore, *Listener*

Praise for *Woman in the Wilderness: A story of survival, love and self-discovery in New Zealand*

'In the great tradition of *A Life on Gorge River* and all those memoirs of people who go off-grid to eke out a wilderness existence comes one that is distinguished by the author's talent for descriptive writing and her eagerness to tackle existential issues. Readers won't fail to be impressed not just by these qualities but also by Lancewood's courage, tenacity and resourcefulness in often harrowing circumstances.'
Paul Little, *North & South*, New Zealand

'Extraordinary.' *The Spinoff*, New Zealand

'*Woman in the Wilderness* is intriguing and mesmerising.
And Miriam and Peter are the freest people I have met.'
Ben Fogle, host of UK television series *New lives in the wild*

'It's an astonishing book.' *Libération*, France

'It's a most beautifully written book, it makes
you reflect on your own life.' Humberto Tan
(Dutch TV presenter of *RTL Late Night*)

'*Woman in the Wilderness* is a highly inspirational bestseller in which Lancewood delves into the boundaries broken, challenges faced and adjustments made since she started living off the grid.'
Savoir Flair, Dubai

THE DANGERS & DELIGHTS
OF A NOMADIC LIFE

WILD
AT HEART

MIRIAM
LANCEWOOD

ALLEN&UNWIN
SYDNEY·MELBOURNE·AUCKLAND·LONDON

First published in 2020. This edition published in 2021.

Text © Miriam Lancewood, 2020
All images from the author's private collection

Some names, places and identifying details have been
changed to protect the privacy of individuals.

All rights reserved. No part of this book may be reproduced or transmitted in
any form or by any means, electronic or mechanical, including photocopying,
recording or by any information storage and retrieval system, without prior
permission in writing from the publisher.

Allen & Unwin
Level 2, 10 College Hill, Freemans Bay
Auckland 1011, New Zealand
Phone: (64 9) 377 3800
Email: info@allenandunwin.com
Web: www.allenandunwin.co.nz

83 Alexander Street
Crows Nest NSW 2065, Australia
Phone:(61 2) 8425 0100

A catalogue record for this book is available
from the National Library of New Zealand

ISBN 978 1 98854 793 0

Front cover image: Murdo Macleod in Bavaria, Germany
Internal and cover design by Megan van Staden
Printed and bound in Australia by SOS Print + Media Group

10 9 8 7 6 5 4 3 2

MIX
Paper from
responsible sources
FSC® C011217
www.fsc.org

The paper in this book is FSC® certified.
FSC® promotes environmentally responsible,
socially beneficial and economically viable
management of the world's forests.

This book is dedicated to my husband Peter Raine,
who inspires many with the fearless decisions he takes in his life.

CONTENTS

PROLOGUE

I was born in 1983, and grew up in a loving home in the Netherlands. After my studies I worked for a year in Africa and then travelled to India, where I met Peter, a New Zealander, who had resigned five years earlier from his university lecturer position to live a free and nomadic life there. Together we trekked through the Himalayas, South East Asia and Papua

New Guinea, before arriving in New Zealand several years later.

After I worked as a physical education teacher for ten months, we gave away all our belongings, said goodbye to family and friends, and walked into the heart of New Zealand's South Island wilderness. We were curious what would happen with body and mind when living in a vast and undisturbed landscape. One year became two, and in the end we lived as nomads for seven years in the mountains.

With minimal food supplies, we survived mainly off hunting wild animals, and gathering plants and berries. I learned how to hunt with a bow, and later with a rifle, and Peter made tasty dishes of the goats, pigs and rabbits I brought back. We learned about medicinal plants, Peter taught me how to grow a garden, we trapped possums and I treated the fur to sew garments. We cooked on fires, were never far from fast-flowing rivers and on sunny days we climbed the mountains. Sometimes we didn't see another person for weeks on end, but we never felt lonely in the beauty and stillness of the Southern Alps. We found peace, clarity and happiness.

After seven years in the wilderness, we decided to take on a new adventure, leave New Zealand and walk through Europe . . .

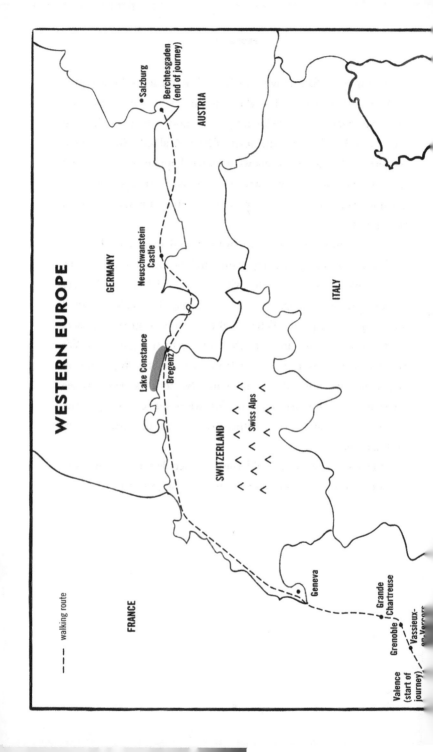

WESTERN EUROPE

- - - walking route

FRANCE

GERMANY

AUSTRIA

•Salzburg

Berchtesgaden
(end of journey)

Neuschwanstein
Castle

Lake Constance

Bregenz

SWITZERLAND

Swiss Alps

ITALY

•Geneva

Grande
Chartreuse

Grenoble

Vassieux-
en-Vercors

Valence
(start of
journey)

CHAPTER 1

FRANCE
WALKING INTO SPRINGTIME

We bade farewell to the snow-capped mountains and forested valleys, the clear rivers and pristine lakes, the icy glaciers and rugged coasts. We watched the embers of our fire fade, drank for the last time the pure water from a clear river. We whistled goodbye to the tūī and the bellbird, rolled up our tent, shouldered our packs and walked to the airport. We were ready to explore a new frontier: Europe.

'It's a big continent, something is bound to happen,' Peter had said. 'If I don't go now, I'll never go.'

We flew for twenty-four hours over clouds, oceans, deserts and vast areas of wilderness. In Paris we were shuffled out of the plane and directed through corridors and hallways towards Security and Customs. I had not seen so many people in one place for a long time, and looked at all the different faces while listening to the sound of many languages. Flashing screens told us where to go and what to expect next. Clocks everywhere showed us the time we had left for the day and in the distance, robotic voices were calling boarding times. But the dominant sound was suitcases on wheels going over the ridges of the floor tiles, tiggedee, tiggedee, tiggedee.

We moved down long halls towards the train.

We looked for a booth with a real person to sell us tickets, then noticed people queuing up for a machine. We stared at the yellow box for a while. Not wanting to risk a disaster, we decided to ask for help first.

A friendly-looking girl walked in our direction, but shook her head when I approached, and disappeared into a tunnel. Then a barefoot boy came by begging for money. He looked Roma, with his dark skin and his half-long uncombed hair. His blue shirt had turned brown, and his shorts were too big for his skinny legs.

'Ticket?' I raised my eyebrows.

'*Billet?*'

Without even looking carefully he punched some keys in a remarkably rapid sequence. He showed us the required money, and a ticket came rolling out.

'*Merci beaucoup, monsieur!*' I shook his sticky hand, and gave him a euro for his help. The coin went into his pocket, he said goodbye and off he went: the little master of the train station.

The ticket allowed us through the gates, and instantly we joined the mass of people moving with intense focus and speed.

We went with the flow, but instinctively I kept my back to the wall so that I could observe everything around me. For years I had hunted the forest, favouring shadows, often with my back against a tree or the rocks, watching for movement. The same instincts prevailed, even in the middle of Paris.

We moved through many tunnels and the smell was gloomy and greasy. It felt strange to be underground, invisible and devoid of fresh air. Inside the train we left our packs on and stood swinging in the middle, holding on to the oily poles as millions had before us. Everyone sat in silence.

When we made it to our stop, we rushed to the natural light of the station platform and felt grateful to be back among the living.

After a little wait in the beautiful old railway station, we boarded a train south.

We had left New Zealand in the autumn; in France, spring was bursting forth. From the train we saw everywhere blossoms and flowers, trees with fresh new leaves. There were gentle rolling hills, fields with hedges, strips of bright green forest, and often the distant spires of village churches.

Some years ago, my parents had sold everything in the Netherlands and immigrated to France. In the Ardèche, in the south-east, they bought an old house with a mill dating from the sixteenth century. In their back yard a beautiful stream flowed between rocks and boulders. It was a land of hills and forests, chestnuts and blueberries, and from the hilltops the French Alps were clearly visible.

I had not seen my parents for more than three years, and the reunion was joyful. Staying with them in their spacious house, Peter and I considered what to do. We knew the best way to see a country is by walking, and long-walking was a familiar way of life for us. We felt reasonably fit, we had arrived in France with all our gear and we were ready for a new adventure. Over the years in the wilderness we had reduced our belongings to the bare minimum. Any item that was not absolutely necessary—like a camera, phone or clock— had been discarded a long time ago. We had hiked three thousand kilometres from the top of New Zealand to the bottom the previous year. Trekking through Europe would be less wild, less difficult, but it seemed more romantic. It brought to mind images of roaming pilgrims, medieval rovers and gypsies with horse and carts.

We looked at long-distance routes in sunny countries, and discovered that Europe had dozens of pathways, called 'E1', 'E2', 'E3' and so on. The 'E4' ran from west to east, and seemed most suitable. It was actually a chain of existing shorter walkways. In France we would follow the 'Grande-Randonnée 9', in Switzerland the 'Jura Crest Trail', and in Austria and Germany the 'Maximiliansweg'. What would happen after Austria, we would figure out if and when we got there. Our ultimate goal, however, would be Istanbul. The old name Constantinople sounded so exotic; it also sounded very cool. Along the way people would ask, 'Where are you walking to?' And we'd answer, 'We are walking to Istanbul!'

I never learned how many kilometres it would be to walk the whole route, but we were going to start, and that was what counted.

The beginning of a journey is most important, because whatever follows is the adventure.

I t was already afternoon when my parents dropped us at the start of the route, in a small village near Valence. We thanked them for everything and hugged goodbye. We had spent a month together and didn't know when we would see each other again.

My father said he was glad I had found my own authentic way to live, and sad that I was leaving again. 'But most of all,' he said, while taking my face in both hands, 'I am just glad you exist.'

'The days together have been so full of joy,' said my mother with a smile. Then her shining eyes grew sad. 'Have I said everything I wanted to say?'

'Yes, I think you've said everything,' I said, and stroked her shoulder.

'You have moved far beyond the horizon. You've cut yourself a path through a thick jungle towards something you loved. But some of what you left behind, you loved most dearly.'

'Yes,' I said, and I felt the tears welling up.

'There are no two ways around it,' she said, and hugged me. 'For you, Miriam, freedom is a necessity. It is your inner fire, and without the flames there is only darkness.'

Peter and I shouldered our heavy packs and began our long walk. We set off down a narrow road. Every time I looked over my shoulder, my mother was still waving. Eventually she was only a figure in the distance, but I saw her determination to remain there until we turned the corner. I would be gone from her sight for years to come.

When I waved back for the last time, I realised what my parents had taught me over the years. They had encouraged me to be courageous but reminded me always to show a vulnerable side. Because, with vulnerability, they said, there is a connection to others.

I turned around and followed Peter around the bend. Some oaks were planted on the side of the track and I was glad for their shade. It was a hot afternoon, we had only walked fifty metres, and I was already sweating.

Then we reached the end of the road, where the serious ascent started.

'Are you ready?' I looked at Peter.

'No. You?'

'No,' I laughed. 'I'm already tired.'

'Walking to Istanbul sounds a bit ludicrous,' he said.

'Yes, it does.'

He turned to face the rocky mountain trail, and began to climb. All I could see was his big pack with two legs underneath. I looked at his muscled calves, covered in woolly blond hairs. Unlike me, he put his feet straight. He moved carefully and deliberately, with efficiency. He never wasted energy. Using his wooden sticks to transfer power to his shoulders, he steadily climbed the mountain.

We had cut four straight hazelnut saplings. Their light wood made perfect walking sticks. With a pocketknife Peter had peeled off the bark, except the bottom thirty centimetres. They looked authentic and we quickly grew attached to them. They were the symbol of long-walkers living in the forest.

The dusty track was steep, the vegetation dry and the soil had a yellow tint to it. With every step up through the scrubby bushes we were leaving one world behind, moving into another. We were walking towards freedom and independence.

It took us all afternoon to struggle to the top of the cliff where we wanted to camp.

'Look at this. Isn't it amazing?' Peter threw off his pack, turned around and gave me a hug.

After climbing for hours, he seemed less tired than when we started. And I too felt energised. Our home was here—once again, we were back in the wild.

We stood on top of an immense limestone cliff, looking out over a breathtaking landscape. We could see the lowlands with fields and forests, and in the far distance the city of Valence. On our left side was an even taller rock-face that curved around like a massive wall. It felt like being in an amphitheatre.

Peter walked casually to the very edge of the cliff and on to a little outcrop. One more step and he would crash a kilometre down. Sweat gathered in my hands.

'Peter, please come back here!' I shouted.

'Why?' There was a slight surprise in his voice. 'It's amazing to stand here! You should come over too!'

He had this habit of going to the very edge of everything—to the edge of security, to feel that touch of danger. To the edge of order, to meet chaos, and to the edge of finite life, to look at the infinite. I wondered what it was in him that resisted any boundaries in life.

When he walked back up to another outcrop that looked safer to me, I crawled towards him, and together we sat on top of a pillar.

'Why do you always want to go to the edge of everything?' I asked.

'Don't know,' he smiled. 'I guess living without security means you sometimes end up in heaven and sometimes in hell. But for me, that's still better than living a bland and mundane life, where I feel more like a robot than a human being. I am goddamn happy to be out of the house. Your folks have been very nice to us and the place is really beautiful in the forested hills. A few weeks are good, but God . . .' He patted the ground. 'I am so glad to live out in the wild again!'

I smiled, took a deep breath and laughed quietly. I felt like we were two kids who'd packed their little bags and were off on an adventure, not even knowing where they were going.

'Why you laughing?' he asked. His left hand cupped my right knee.

I put my arm around his shoulders. 'I have never been more content. I just love this so much. You, and your fearlessness. Adventure. Being in France. Sitting on a cliff . . .'

L ife, since I met Peter eleven years ago had never been boring. We climbed the Himalayas without a guide or cooking gear, slept under the stars or in caves for the lack of a tent. We had travelled by boat through Indonesia; Peter nearly died of malaria in Papua New Guinea; and we had walked for seven years through New Zealand with a rifle to catch food. Apart from one year in which I had a job, we'd had one long adventure, always changing shape, never going home—never even seeking a home. Our life was out in the open, naked before a blinding sun and a cold moon; exposed to darkness and dangers; vulnerable to thunder and lightning, ice and snow, floods and storms; always touching the soil. To sleep at the base of a huge tree, hearing the river, the wind and night animals felt the most natural way of living.

I pitched the tent among the flowers underneath some trees, just five metres from the edge of the cliff. There was a wiry bush between us and the crevice that offered some sense of security. I thought it was a great spot to spend the night because we had a brilliant view of the evening sky with all its sunset colours.

With some dry leaves, Peter lit a fire. Flames crackled up among the twigs and soon it was strong enough to add some bigger branches. By using three of our four walking sticks and a piece of string, I made a tripod. At the end of the string was a long metal hook that carried our cooking pot, black with soot from years of cooking over fires. Peter carefully poured some water from a bottle in to the pot, and I added a cup of rice, lentils and some yarrow and plantain that grew around the tent.

'Within one month of living in a house, my body has forgotten how to squat,' he said. 'Can you believe it?' He stood up straight to stretch his legs. 'It surprises me how quickly the muscles and tendons become stiff again.'

We needed to squat, because everything was on the ground. We had to reach for a spoon, add a bit of wood to the fire, or get out of the way of the swirling smoke. The body was always in motion.

'How long, you think, before you're supple again?' I asked.

'A week maybe. It'll also be a shock to sleep on a thin mat again! My back is going to be painful for a few days.'

When the food was ready, we sat down on the edge of the cliff to watch the sun set. The limestone rock-face was changing from moment to moment, from a broken white to soft crimson to almost orange.

A blackbird sang in a tree not far away, and within a few seconds another bird joined it in the distance. The pink in the sky was caught by fluffy little clouds moving slowly towards the north. There was stillness in the air, a sense of peace. This place had seen humans for thousands of years. People had perhaps fought and died here. People must have gathered on top of this cliff, celebrating a full moon, equinox or solstice, worshipping their gods. Good things and bad things had happened, yet the place itself remained unaffected and always returned to its natural state. One of peace.

The next morning, and many mornings after, we followed a narrow track through the forest. Up mountains, through rolling fields. We walked under a roof of blossoms and bright green spring leaves, through clearings with high grass, in the perfume of endless meadows of wild flowers. We walked in a land without fences that made us feel free.

This was a part of south-east France called Vercors, dominated by fantastic limestone ranges of many scarps and cliffs. It was very impressive but also very dry. Rainwater found its way into cracks and caves, and disappeared. To be on the safe side, we often had to carry five heavy litres of water each.

After a week we walked into a charming village with winding streets and Roman bridges. An old man smoked a cigarette on the steps of his house. From the open window we could smell meat being cooked in the kitchen. Further down, an old lady sat on a chair next to her door. A black cat walked ahead of us, sometimes looking back.

The village shop was closed. A sign said it re-opened at three o'clock. A man and a little boy walked past and we asked the time. He showed us his watch: ten past twelve!

We sat down on a bench in the shade under a big old plane tree with smooth bark. Peter was studying the map, learning names, observing the contours, deciphering the clues for what mattered to us: the steepness of the terrain, forests for firewood, good creeks to wash in, where the villages were, where to ask for water.

'It doesn't matter if we have to wait,' he said. 'Have a look around if you like, I'll stay with the packs.'

Walking without the rucksack was so easy, I felt as if I was floating. The village dated back to medieval times, with streets barely wide enough for cars to pass. The houses were linked cosily together. Their doors were rounded at the top; most of their windows had shutters, some crooked and weatherbeaten, others painted sapphire blue or cherry red. These dwellings had been built with big river stones, shaped in to squares, packed together with cement. People had carried these stones from a nearby river to the site, and each one of them had a place in the structure where it fitted best. And slowly, carefully, the house had been completed and made to last. The people who lived in these houses also had a secure place within their family and community. They carried out their duties, passed their values on to the next generation and so, over the centuries, this culture was built to last.

The door of the church was open. It was surprisingly cool inside, and there was a faint musty smell. Little light came in through elongated windows. My eyes slowly adjusted to the darkness. It felt like being in a very dense pine forest, with only a few stripes of sunlight on the ground. I sang a little melody that filled the empty space. The echo faded when I stepped back into the light.

There was an important-looking council building opposite the church. '*Liberté, égalité, fraternité*' had been engraved on its front. A reminder of the French revolution—lest we forget to rebel against an unjust system.

In the corner of the square was a café with a few people sitting at tables and chairs in the shade. I wandered over and shyly asked the price for coffee.

I ran all the way back to Peter.

'Peter! There's a little café near the church! Shall we have a coffee there?'

'But we can't afford to drink coffee in cafés,' he said when I stood panting beside him.

'No, I asked what it cost, and it's only one euro. We are now in France, where the coffee is only one euro. Even wine is only one euro! Do you want a glass of wine?' I laughed. 'And we can sit on a terrace and play chess at the table. We can sit there all afternoon if we like!'

He chuckled, and I quickly handed him his sticks and lifted his pack, before shouldering mine.

'This way's a shortcut,' I said, pointing with my walking stick towards a narrow street leading up the hill. 'You'll see flower boxes on tiny balconies and grapevines in people's gardens. They spend a lot of time making things beautiful here!' I looked over my shoulder to see if Peter was listening. 'Just for aesthetics! In New Zealand a lot is just practical, a farmer mentality, quite useful and easy-going. But here! Everything is made to be pretty. And look, not everything is neat and tidy—this old ruin here in the middle of the village has probably been like this for years. The whole thing is charming, isn't it? Look at all those trees growing through the roof!'

I led him across a little stone bridge, through a narrow alleyway made for people and horses, and up a flight of ancient stairs. Finally, we came out at the church. We crossed the square, and at the café we took our packs off and sat down.

'Nice, eh?'

Since it was Peter's first time in France, I was constantly hoping he would like it.

He smiled. 'Well, it's very different from those big glacial river valleys in New Zealand, isn't it?'

The waiter came, and we ordered two coffees. When he elegantly placed two cups on the table, I sat up more straight. I kept my elbows off the table, crossed my right leg over my left, which felt very awkward, and lifted my right toe into the air.

'What are you sitting so rigid for?' Peter grinned. 'You never cease to amuse me.'

'We're drinking coffee on a terrace,' I said, and suddenly the whole scene looked like a theatre. It felt as if we were playing a little king and a queen, and the waiter was acting as a servant. We are paying money for the role-play, I thought.

We put up the chessboard, drank our coffee and enjoyed ourselves in the sun.

At three we stood in front of the shop. A man came out and casually put a sign saying '*Ouvert*' on the pavement.

'Let's buy something we've never tasted before,' said Peter, and he put local goats' cheese, sweet tomatoes and *crème de marrons*, a chestnut purée from the Ardèche, in our basket.

'Do you know what this is?' he asked, holding up a packet with a black sausage.

'*Boudin noir*,' I read from the label. 'No idea, never seen it in my life.'

I had grown up vegetarian, and the meat we ate in New Zealand was from wild animals that I had spotted, stalked, shot, skinned and gutted, carried back to camp and butchered. I was completely familiar with meat, yet knew nothing about names and products wrapped in plastic in the supermarket.

'Black pudding we used to call it. It's made from blood, fat and barley.' He put the package in his basket. 'And look at these potatoes! They're weirdly shaped! As if all the malformed ones are put together. What are these? Can you ask?'

'*De la ratte*,' said the grocer.

'Little rats?'

'Yes, I've heard of them,' said Peter. 'They have a nutty flavour.' He took one in his hand, polished it up as though it was something precious. 'Freshly dug, I bet, still got the dirt on them. We'll have some tonight.'

Peter had a surprising passion for potatoes. In his younger years he had planted thousands of them on the hillsides in New Zealand and could instantly tell the difference between one type and the other. When I saw him admiring the potatoes, I wondered how many people of my generation shared his passion for something so simple.

We left the village, and walked for days through a national park. Flocks of sheep were allowed to roam the clearings between the forests, and a shepherd was living with them. We had seen warning signs for the sheep dogs, the *patou*.

We were hiking up a steep hill when we saw a mob of sheep in a clearing and on the path. In the middle of the mob sat a big white dog.

'Watch out for the guard dog! Walk slowly, don't run, don't show fear and don't wave sticks,' I said, remembering the text we had read on the signs. 'These guard dogs attack humans who come too close to the sheep.'

The dog spotted us from a distance and sat upright. He got up and walked threateningly to the edge of the flock, all the while watching every move we made. Once we were in his territory he started barking fiercely.

We moved nervously away from the dog and went towards the shepherd, who sat under a big oak with two small black dogs. He was dressed in hiking boots, shorts and singlet, and greeted us cheerfully. He spoke English well and told us he had grown up in Paris but escaped the rat-race in the city.

'Is the white dog really dangerous?' asked Peter. His father was a sheep farmer, and he had never seen a really dangerous sheep dog.

'Well, he is a *patou*,' the shepherd said. 'This dog thinks he is a sheep instead of dog. Since he was a puppy he was put with the lambs, so he grew up among them. Nobody pets him for the first years, so he bonds with sheep. His name is Remi, but he only listens to sheep!'

'But what is he protecting the flock from?' asked Peter.

'Mostly wolves. Conservationists are re-introducing wolves and bears. There should be around five hundred wolves now.'

'There are no dangerous animals at all in New Zealand,' Peter said. '*Patou* dogs wouldn't be much use there.'

'No snakes either?'

'No, nothing. No bears, crocodiles or snakes. It is totally safe.'

'Aren't you lonely sitting here all by yourself?' I asked.

'No, I have my two dogs.' He patted one of them and the dog immediately curled himself on his back while wagging his tail, looking up at his human friend.

'In the Himalayas,' Peter told him, 'shepherds live out in the mountains for months on end. They take their sheep and goats over five-thousand-metre passes to get better grass and get away from the monsoon. They are amazingly tough people, and they move across those mountains as agile as mountain goats. When Miriam and I crossed the most dangerous passes, we waited for the shepherds to turn up, because they always knew the way.'

'Maybe I will join them one day, for a summer. Do you think that is possible?'

'Yes, that would be an amazing thing to do! But you might have to learn the language.' I started laughing.

'Which language?'

'They mainly speak Gaddi—a dialect of Hindi—but also have a special goat language. The sounds the shepherd makes could be repeated by the goats!'

'This is a joke, *non*?'

'No, it is true! We have witnessed it.'

'Yeah, we have,' said Peter. 'Goats are quite intelligent, so they always lead and the sheep follow. The shepherds have about fifteen to twenty different commands for the goats. Weird sounds like "ahê, ayê, wêge", which mean go left, or go right, go up, or go down.'

'It's true, we watched them,' I said. 'The goats listened!'

'And the goats answered?'

'Yes,' I laughed.

We chatted some more, and when the dusk gathered we left the young man to seek shelter in the forest. We always camped under the biggest tree we could find. The long branches above us were like a big hand over our heads, shielding us from the outside world. We slept between the roots that held us like a mother carries her baby. At night we almost felt we were part of the tree's consciousness.

We hiked and hiked. We followed our trail towards the east. Up the mountain, and down the mountain. Our packs were our home. Like snails we crawled over the earth. The physical demand of long-walking is indescribable. Lifting a twenty-five-kilo pack on my back was so hard that I would think twice before taking it off. Walking uphill was gruelling, walking downhill dangerous and strenuous. It was a hot spring and we were sweating heavily, our shirts stuck to our backs, always thirsty and hungry.

But after two weeks on the journey we became fitter. By the time the first crickets began to chirp, and the spring leaves had turned into a deep green summer colour, we were into the swing of things. We lost weight and our muscles became strong, and being very fit brought its own joy. The rucksack gave me the feeling of independence. We were equipped to camp anywhere we liked. We slept well, and in the morning I felt refreshed. Once we were back in the rhythm, it was hard to imagine anything better than this way of life.

The most rewarding moment was when we climbed a high hilltop and saw for the first time the snow-capped Alps, with Mont Blanc piercing the clouds. It was sheer exhilaration. The tops were touching heaven; they were unpolluted and untouched by humans.

We were glad to be walking and sleeping in the forests and mountains, for this was the living world, where everything was growing and blossoming, slowly rising upwards towards the sun. To be underneath the swaying branches, cooking on a fire, walking through forest where every animal was living without the slightest difficulty made me feel part of an eternal rhythm.

We came to a village named Vassieux-en-Vercors. It was a strange, eerie sort of a place. We learned that it once was a base for the Maquis, the French resistance movement against the German occupation during the Second World War. It had been bombed to smithereens. In the museum we looked at pictures of rows of citizens being shot by the Nazis for supporting the partisans.

'Imagine if you are living in this village,' I said to Peter. 'You know where the partisans are hiding, and you fully believe that the Maquis will save France in the long run. Then the Nazis come, and they give you the choice: either you die, or you tell them where the partisans are. What would you do?'

There was a pause. 'I guess I let myself get shot, but it would be better if I never had to make that choice. With this long-walking, I would have the confidence that I could walk away from anything. I could even walk out of big cities. I would take my pack, and walk away from war, lawless chaos and so forth, and keep on walking and walking . . .'

We studied the information and pictures on the signs.

'What do you think would be the best thing to take if we had to leave at short notice?' asked Peter.

'I wouldn't go anywhere without a hunting rifle,' I said. 'I would have to find one somewhere, and ammunition, as much as I could possibly carry. Then something to light a fire, matches and a flint. Then some rations like flour and salt, and a pot to cook. Then I would head for the forest. I could hunt and defend myself, and if I didn't have a tent I'd build a shelter.'

'A lot of people wouldn't want to leave on their own,' said Peter, 'but groups are an easy target.'

'Yes, to be able to do this alone is a good skill, but one day we should try to live completely off hunting and fishing,' I said. 'In the past we always had some supplies, but I'm curious to know if I've learned enough skills in the last seven years to survive just with a gun and bullets and no food.'

'Just a rod and rifle? That would be tough, but we would have to try that in New Zealand, since you can't get a firearms licence in Europe.'

'Yes, I'd like to,' I said, and a little idea was born.

O ur trail mostly went through the forest and the occasional village, but one day we navigated Grenoble. We came down a steep slope in the morning, walked through the entire city, and in the late evening we found a small place to camp in the forest.

Peter lit a tiny fire, just big enough to boil some potatoes and fresh corn. We listened quietly to the evening chorus of the birds while eating our dinner. The flickering light of the fire made moving shadows on the trees as it slowly grew dark around us. Down below us in the valley we heard the trains, snatches of highway noise, police sirens and cars hooting. We could hear the machines of civilisation, yet it felt as if we were right in the wilderness. All around us were trees and signs of animals. It was quite astonishing how close animals lived to a city.

During the night we experienced angry roe-deer—small deer with little spiky horns. They didn't like being invaded and they tried to chase us out. They circled the tent for hours. They kept barking and barking very loudly: humans belong in the city at night, not the forest.

F rom Grenoble we entered the Chartreuse region. We walked for two days through the forest before we came to a small village. In the golden afternoon light, the flowery fields and the surrounding forested mountains were especially beautiful. We bought some bread in a shop and began to look for a suitable place to camp. It had been a hot day, and only in the evening did the temperature come down a little.

We followed our path up a mountain, over little bridges, along a river, and eventually entered a forest with big old trees, where it was nice and cool. We looked everywhere, but it was hard to find a flat space big enough to pitch the tent. When the sun had left the valley and birds started their evening songs, we considered camping on an overgrown four-wheel-drive road. We put the packs down, and stamped the grass flat, only to discover big hollows and humps. With a sigh we shouldered our packs once again and continued on the track.

And so it was that we entered the 'silence zone' in twilight. This zone, surrounding an ancient monastery, was a specified region on our map. We had spotted the monastery in the distance two days earlier. It was like a fairytale walled palace, with pointy towers and spires amid the steep, forested mountains. Now, a sign in English told us that the Grande Chartreuse monastery, dating back nearly a thousand years, was the head of the Carthusian Order. There were dozens or perhaps hundreds of dedicated monks living there in complete silence. They could pray, eat and sleep, but not talk. Another sign, in French, said 'silence' and something would be punished with a 135-euro fine. We assumed it was for making any noise.

I pointed at the steep route ahead. 'The markers say we are going this way.'

Peter looked at the map. 'Yes, but we have no chance of finding a camping spot up there. Let's go through the valley past the monastery. Looks a lot flatter.'

'But we can't go in there,' I said. 'If talking is illegal, freedom camping certainly will be.'

Peter smiled. 'They won't see us, smell us or hear us.'

I grinned.

We walked right towards the ancient monastery over a cobbled road. The colours of the sunset lifted from the mountaintops and dusk came into the valley. When darkness crawled around the old oaks on the side of the road, I became anxious about where we would find a place to stop.

We walked on towards the castle. The only noise was the loud 'tick tack' of my wooden sticks on the cobbled road.

'Your sticks!' whispered Peter. He carried his sticks in his hand and slid stealthily over the road.

We proceeded silently until we saw a person in the distance. A dark figure was walking in our direction. Peter shuffled towards the cover of the trees on the side of the road. I followed him into the shadows. He turned around to face me and slowly put his finger on his lips. 'Shhh.' We waited anxiously for some minutes, until the man disappeared down another path.

With every step we came closer to the high walls of the monastery. If you didn't know better, you'd think that everyone had left a long time ago. It seemed eerily silent; even the birds were quiet.

Then we heard running water. Right next to the big wooden door, which was settled into a big stone wall, was a running fountain. It felt as if we had walked into the Middle Ages.

I looked at Peter, and made a water-drinking signal. He looked up at the tower to see if we were being watched. He moved back into a dark spot near the wall and pulled my water bottle off the side of my pack. I rolled my eyes when the crackling plastic seemed to make an almighty noise.

'Hush!'

I quickly filled up the bottle, while Peter hid behind a tree and studied the map in the last of the light. We were still only twenty metres from the monastery, and here the path climbed steeply up the mountain again.

'Unless you want to climb to the tops to find a flat spot,' whispered Peter, 'we have to pitch the tent right here.'

'So close to the monks?' I looked over my shoulder at the dark walls.

'There?' He pointed towards a place among huge trees. The creek was not too far away, and all around us were scattered boulders the size of cars. When we came closer, we found a flattish stone and a little bit of soil. It was quite clear that one of us would be sleeping on that big boulder. That person would undoubtedly be me.

For me, the hiking was challenging; for Peter, this journey was very hard. He was now sixty-three and his body did not recover as quickly as mine. He sometimes had so much pain he had to take painkillers to get to sleep. I tried to help him wherever I could. I carried all the food, so that his pack was lighter, and I gave him the flattest place to sleep, for he needed his rest the most. In order to continue this way of life, each of us did the best we could.

I pitched the tent, and Peter cut a baguette lengthways and filled it with tomatoes, cheese and some wild thyme and other herbs we had picked along the way. We drank water instead of tea—we could not risk lighting a fire.

Then we lay down. I had a little air mat to sleep on, but I felt the big boulder right through it.

I n the middle of the night we were woken by small chiming bells. It was as if we were right in the monastery, so clear was the sound. Within the silence of the valley, this sudden music was a surprise, almost a miracle.

'Prayer time,' said Peter softly.

I imagined the monks getting out of bed to pray. It was incredible to sleep so close to these men who lived in a totally different reality. Their bells called us into their religious world. The night and the whole valley was enchanted.

We went back to sleep and, just before dawn, the bells rang again. With the first light, we got up and had some breakfast. We were almost finished packing our bags when we saw movement between the trees. A monk was walking over the cobblestone road. A flawless medieval monk in long white robes with a white hood over his head.

'A monk! A monk!' I whispered to Peter. 'Look!'

In the atmosphere of absolute stillness, it was very moving to see this man walking through the gloomy trees. His gait was purposeful, yet at ease. He seemed at home and secure. We watched him until he was out of sight.

W e took our packs and sticks, and sneaked away from the monastery without leaving a trace. The track climbed quickly up the side of a mountain. The pack felt very heavy again that morning.

'To live together, and not be able to speak, is surely some sort of torture. On top of that, the obligatory praying at those unearthly hours is even more tormenting,' said Peter. 'The church has invented this idea that suffering is good for you. Somehow you will become enlightened, or in this case "one with God" if you suffer enough. What total nonsense . . .'

I burst out laughing. 'One could argue that we are suffering, dragging ourselves up the side of a mountain with a twenty-five kilo backpack, after sleeping all night on a rock . . . and we don't even receive enlightenment in the future!'

Peter laughed.

We came to a viewpoint. Through the pines we could see a valley far below us. Sounds of a fast-flowing river came up with a little breeze. We sat down on massive roots of a tree.

'I'm quite fascinated by monasteries,' I said. 'To be totally devoted to the so-called higher consciousness is an extreme way of living . . . But in a way, just as intense as long-walking.'

'Yes,' said Peter, 'I guess writing a PhD is similar to living in a monastery. I hardly went outside, always writing or doing research. I lived for years like an academic monk. It was hard and disciplined work but it really is an exciting journey, you know. You discover amazing concepts and want to go further and further.'

After his doctorate, Peter worked for some time as a lecturer, until one day he thought, I have to live this stuff, not just write about it. He sold everything and emigrated to India. He wanted to find out what freedom was. Not the concept of freedom, but actual freedom. He said he had to face all attachments—to people, things, concepts and life itself—and let them go.

'Over the years,' said Peter as he slowly got to his feet, 'I discovered you have to give up comfort and security in order to live intensely.' He picked up his walking sticks and carefully placed them against the tree. 'But there is a price to pay for living on the edge,' he added.

'What's that?' I asked.

'You can fall off.'

He lifted his pack, and within the same movement, dropped his shoulders underneath the straps and took a stick in each hand.

'Shall we?'

After three weeks walking through the high country, we arrived at the mighty Rhône river, which flows from the Swiss Alps, through Lake Geneva to the Mediterranean Sea. The entire landscape was influenced by the river. It had carved a valley through the mountains, and brought life to the fields and crops. People had wandered here for thousands of years, and once upon a time Celtic tribes had lived along the river's banks.

Following a narrow pathway, we meandered through long grass with many flowers. At our side, the river ran slow and smooth and deep. The air was thick and humid, and little clouds of insects hovered over the surface of the water.

The temperature had finally dropped a little when we came to a small village with cobbled streets surrounded by vineyards. An ancient church stood on top of a hill, and we filled up our water bottles at the communal pump.

Not far out of the village, we noticed a long stretch of poplars between the river and a huge cliff. In between the trees the ground was flat and grassy. It was a good place to camp. Only after we had thrown our packs down did we notice a very graphic sign—something like a sea with big waves, and a man among the trees with his hands high up in the air, his face showing true terror, his mouth and eyes open in panic. Whoever did the design had made a good job of it. We could not read the text, but it was pretty obvious that somewhere upstream some kind of dam was operating to regulate the water level of the Rhône.

If we had not been so dead tired, we would have most certainly walked back to the village, and taken the road that led up and over the cliff. Instead, we looked around: here and there were piles of debris from former overflows. The flood level seemed about three metres at its worst. We concluded that it had been dry for some weeks and decided to risk it. It was midsummer, we said to each other, how many floods could we expect?

We pitched the tent, lit a good fire with all the driftwood, and sat on a log to eat our meal of couscous, beans and boiled stinging nettle that grew nearby. In the daytime it all seemed very dry and benign, but I knew that the darkness would bring more fear and anxiety.

When we went to bed I put our money, passports and important papers in a little waterproof bag. I carefully knotted a string onto the bag, and tied the other end to my wrist, like surfers with their board. I figured that if a flood came, I would scramble out of the tent, swim upwards and hang on for dear life to a tree. If we lost everything else, then at least we had our passports.

I visualised the procedure: getting out of the tent would be the worst part. You could easily drown trying to find the zips. (Luckily, ours lit up in the dark.) We went through the scenario several times before trying to sleep.

'Doesn't this river come from Switzerland?' I said after a few minutes. 'What if it rains right up in the mountains and brings a flood to this area? Will they open the barrages?'

'I hope not,' said Peter.

Then it was very quiet, apart from the wind in the poplar leaves that sounded just like rushing water.

'When my mother was a baby,' I began, 'there was a huge flood in the south of Holland where she lived. Most of that area was reclaimed land below sea level. My grandfather used to talk about it. More than eighteen hundred people drowned. The combination of a spring tide and a huge storm broke parts of the dikes and floodgates.

'In the days following, many men, including my grandfather, went in rowing boats to the disaster area to save people from the tops of their roofs. He said that being in a boat in the village was like being right out on the open ocean with choppy and foaming waves. It was hard to know where you were.

'The storm went on for days. It was the first of February and midwinter, so it was cold and wild. By pushing tiles out of the way, people had climbed from their attics to their rooftops. My grandfather could hear people screaming for help. Dead cows, horses and sheep were floating around. He saw babies floating by. Not everybody could swim, many drowned. There was so much panic, so many were screeching and screaming for help, he said.

'He had to identify a dead woman who was heavily pregnant. He always remembered her, for she had a smile on her face. She was pregnant and dying, yet she died with a smile. Unbelievable, isn't it?'

'Well, that's a great bedtime story,' said Peter. 'The timing is priceless.'

I laughed. 'Well, I had forgotten about it until now.'

We didn't sleep well because of the worry, but the next day we were elated. We had survived. Nobody had pushed the button to flood the Rhône.

We were not seeking thrills or danger, but sometimes we happened to be in the middle of it. Surviving perils made me feel stronger. A touch of danger allowed me to test my abilities, and every time I had handled a thunderstorm, a freezing night or some other precarious situation, I felt a little more confident.

W e packed our bags, left the flood zone and continued on our trail. In the afternoon we zig-zagged up a steep cliff and came out at a hamlet that overlooked the valley. There was a seventeenth-century stone *lavoir*, a place where women used to wash their clothes. It had a roof and only one wall; the rest was open. We had seen these communal *lavoirs* in almost every village. They were built near a natural spring or river.

We washed our clothes with a bar of soap, and while the T-shirts were drying over a bush in the sun, we ate a bag of wild cherries we had picked on the way. Below us was a house with a garden full of flowers. Two women were sitting at a small table. We waved, and the younger woman greeted us in English: 'Come down, come down!'

We walked via a little cobbled path into her garden.

'My name is Aimée,' she said. She had long, curly, reddish hair and a pretty, delicate face with high cheekbones. She wore a summery dress with elegant sandals. We chatted a little before she led us to the table where an old lady was seated, a cup of tea untouched in front of her.

'*Bonjour,*' I said, and we sat down. Above us grew a brilliant, strongly scented wisteria. It was an amazing feeling to be in the shadow of such flowers.

'*Maman*, these are New Zealanders and they are walking to Istanbul,' Aimée told her.

The old lady looked at her daughter but didn't answer.

'She is ninety-five and doesn't speak English.'

Aimée explained to us that she lived in Canada for part of the year, with her daughter in South America for a few months, and with her old mother in France in the summer. 'Living in one place kills you,' she said, quite matter-of-factly. 'It's important for me to keep on moving. Because every time you move you re-invent yourself in a way. You become somebody different. *Enfin*, not totally different, but you can't help feeling different if you are in the winter in an apartment in Montreal, or in the summer in an ancient village in France or in subtropical Brazil. I relate to all kinds of people and I adjust. I have to. It keeps me flexible, psychologically speaking.'

Aimée spoke quickly, as if she had no time to lose and wanted to say as much as possible in one afternoon.

'Where did you come from today?' she asked eventually.

'Down the valley! We nearly drowned in the Rhône. We were sleeping in the flood-zone,' I said with a laugh.

'*Quoi*?' She looked at us incredulously.

After we told Aimée the whole story, she said, 'Let me get you a cup of tea, it'll only take one minute.' She disappeared inside.

We watched as her mother slowly reached out to her own cup. She appeared not to know why it was there. With her index finger and thumb she turned the base of the cup around, bit by bit, until the handle was facing her. She looked up at Peter.

'*Bonjour*,' he said softly.

She looked again at the table. Her face was white and covered in very fine lines. Her wrinkly, big-knuckled hand moved slowly to a teaspoon that had a tiny oval picture of a little church at its end. She touched it ever so slightly, before leaning back. For a moment she sat completely still. Time seemed to slow right down. Her eyes seemed lost in the void. Slowly she wiped some invisible crumbs off the table. Then she clutched the table, shifted forward, and with great effort stood up.

'What are you doing, *Maman*?' Aimée had come out again, and everything seemed to come back to life. She carried a tray with a teapot, cups and a bowl with raspberries from the garden. She put the tray on the table and gently helped her mother back in to the chair.

We chatted, had a cup of tea, ate some raspberries. Aimée's story appealed to us. Shifting from continent to continent was a great way of being nomadic, in a worldly sort of a way.

'But we don't have relatives who live in three different continents,' I said.

'No, but you could buy or rent a place,' she said. 'Look carefully, there are cheap properties in the countryside. Like Greece or Italy, for example. The south of Italy is great—a friend of mine bought a house for ten thousand euros. She has to fix it up of course, but even so. Avoid the cities, look for places nobody wants to live, where there is no work. If you have an independent income, you don't need a job. If you get tired of walking, you might want to have a base somewhere, but don't settle in one place. Because if you live too long in one place, then the world will become smaller and smaller. Terrifying in a way.'

'Yes, I like the idea of living in different places all over the world,' I said.

'*Oui, oui,* keep your eyes open!' said Aimée. 'You're wandering through many semi-deserted places here in Europe, you just might see something you like.'

We finished our tea and said our goodbyes. We walked out of the village and back into the forest. The beautiful sweet smell of pine moved gently through the trees. The track was flat and easy, and since we didn't need to use our walking sticks, we took both of our sticks in one hand. We talked about the countries we'd like to live in. Maybe we'd meet someone in France who offered a cottage for sale for a good price. It was exciting to think about, but the image of Aimée's mother weighed on my mind.

'Did you see the old lady?' said Peter.

'I was just thinking of her. My goodness, ninety-five!'

'I wouldn't want to get so old.'

'No?' I said. 'I'd like to get to hundred.'

'Not in that state, no. If you live long enough, the body slowly deteriorates. First your sight will fail, then you go deaf, then you can't walk, might have to live with pain, and then your mind goes. No, no, I'd rather die before all that misery starts. You can live too long. I don't want to be so old that I don't even know where I am.'

'No, but I would like to be old and healthy.'

'My worst, most horrific image of old age is being kept alive by machines. I hope they will change the law in New Zealand in favour of euthanasia. Isn't it ludicrous that they can keep you alive against your will? Life is not a prison, you know.'

'No,' I said, and took his hand.

On our last day in France, just a few kilometres from Switzerland, we camped on the edge of a beech forest. We found a flat spot in the grass to pitch the tent, looking out over a clearing with many yellow flowers. We washed in the forest creek and found plenty of dry wood for a fire. A little breeze made the leaves whisper. A red glow lit the sky and illuminated the long grass. As we sat on a log with our plates of rice and brown lentils with fresh herbs, we became aware of a rustling noise, little snorts and loud trampling. We stood up, and there before us was a mob of twenty or more wild pigs trotting up the hill. They were determined in their course and had no fear for us. It was a breathtaking sight. Big boars with their hefty bodies and strong necks, and the smaller sows with all their tiny piglets— whole families were on the move.

The sight brought such joy. If wild creatures were allowed to live freely, we could survive too.

After almost three hundred kilometres and one month walking, we had come to like France very much. We had been surprised to see so much regenerating forest. In the last decades, many people had moved to the cities and much of the countryside was now inhabited by trees. We also liked the *laissez faire* attitude, the slight chaos, a choice of a siesta over commercial gain, the lack of traffic rules, the lack of fences, the cafés, the good food and the appreciation of life that people seemed to have. To experience all this in slow motion was the best way to enjoy the essence of France.

CHAPTER 2

SWITZERLAND
THE LAND OF PRECISION

'I guess it's because I come from an island that I cannot for the life of me understand the concept of land borders,' Peter said. He sounded genuinely astonished. 'Especially when there is no geographical barrier or different language.'

We had followed a zig-zag path down a little hill. At the bottom was a road. According to the map, the other side of the road was

Switzerland. We crossed the asphalt, went through a gate and into a paddock—and found ourselves in Switzerland.

'And how *incredible* that we can just cross it without seeing anyone! Once upon a time people would have died to cross this border!' He pointed at France. 'Over *here* your life is in danger.' He pointed at Switzerland. 'But *here* you are safe! Can you understand it?'

We walked from the paddock into the forest, and deep within the trees we saw the first sign of Switzerland: stacks of firewood. Each was an absolutely meticulous piece of art. The identical pieces of wood were precisely one metre long and cut at a proper ninety-degree angle. The firewood was stacked on a decent pallet for airflow. The structure was topped off with a sheet of iron, and held there with a reliable piece of rope tied to the logs in a neat and orderly pattern. These seemingly inconsequential stacks of wood suggested much about what we might expect of the Swiss: this was the land of precision.

Our French trail linked up with the Jura Crest Trail. We were going to walk for a month over the Jura mountains, a limestone range between the Rhône valley and the Rhine, complete with spectacular gorges, cliffs and canyons. Jura meant 'forest' in the old language of the Celtic Gauls, and today the area is still mostly forested. The trail is a 310-kilometre path from Nyon to Dielsdorf, well made with good gradients, and all of it well signposted. Getting lost would be impossible.

Wild camping for one night was allowed in France, but the rules in Switzerland were not quite clear to us. To be on the safe side, we would try to be invisible and leave no trace. Our first day took us on a small forested mountain path. The area felt remote, but when it came time to camp we crept as far as possible into the forest so that nobody could see us. It had begun to rain and we lit a small fire with wet wood that smoked terribly. We dried wood next to the fire to have something to burn for breakfast, and we slept restlessly for fear of being discovered.

We saw the characteristic white-cross-on-red flags in the distance as we neared our first village the next day. My Swiss pocketknife was clipped onto my shorts, as always. 'How do you feel being in your fatherland?' I asked it.

'You're talking as though it's a person,' said Peter.

'Yes, it's the only item I've had since . . .'

He laughed. 'Yeah, yeah, I know: since you were ten.'

'It has buttered thousands of slices of bread, peeled a million apples, skinned countless animals, and it's still going. It's *unbelievable* what a good knife it is!'

'There's a reason why those knives are famous,' said Peter. 'Everything is built to last a hundred years here.'

Grey clouds were hanging overhead when we came to the first houses. Compared to France, the village seemed bleak, empty and lifeless, and much too neat and tidy. It was as if the streets had been cleaned with a toothbrush and the grass trimmed with scissors. We had grown so used to the vibrancy of France that we had to resist the desire to run back across the border.

Just before going to the bank to get some local currency, we stopped at a little vegetable shop with some melons on display. The owner approached with a box of strawberries.

'How much is the melon?' I asked, and held a small one in my hand.

'Seven francs,' he said.

'More than six euros! Twice the price of the same in France!' I put the melon back.

The shop owner laughed. '*Bienvenue en Suisse!*'

'What are we going to do for food?' asked Peter in despair.

'I have heard most people shop across the border,' I said. 'Even the locals do.'

We looked on the map and saw that our route was never far from the Swiss border. It would be possible for me to hitchhike every week to France for shopping, and in a few weeks we would be close to Germany to do the same there. With that solution, we didn't need to exchange euros to Swiss francs, either.

We followed the trail up into the hills and along the crest, often looking out over the breathtaking snowy Alps towards the east. It was a stunning route and relatively quiet. Almost every day we found berries, fruit, herbs or edible plants along the way to add to our basic meals.

One evening I was drinking water from an old-fashioned pump in the middle of a village while Peter was studying the map. 'You see that hill there?' he said. 'That's where we're going.'

I looked at the incredibly sharp ridge in the distance, and could vaguely distinguish a path that seemed to climb straight up.

We crawled up the spur with ten litres of water. As the sunset filled the sky with red and pink, we saw a clearing amid some big old trees, their bases covered in moss. The air was filled with the smell of pine. The wind in the tops brought about a particular rushing sound, almost a tune. We pitched our tent on top of a thick layer of needles.

As we sat quietly around the campfire, a little mouse appeared. It came out of a hole, raced over the needles and disappeared into another hole. Soon after, another mouse popped up. Then a third mouse jumped out and started cleaning the entrance of one of its holes. We were eating peanuts and threw the crumbs towards them.

'We're in Mouse-town!' Peter seemed delighted. 'There's a whole tunnel system underneath here, an entire town!'

In the middle of the night we were woken by gusts of wind and distant thunder. When I went out for a pee, I could see the treetops swaying back and forth. I placed a pan underneath the tent flap to collect rainwater, and crawled back in time to hear thunder, closer this time. I felt very vulnerable on top of a hill, jammed between two huge mountains. The thunder moved precisely over our heads. Without rain it felt eerie and ominous. All my senses were directed to the next flash and thunderclap. There was a waiting silence— until the boom hit, so deafening that I blocked my ears. And even with my eyes closed the flashes of light were blinding.

It was a relief when it finally started to rain. The air cooled down and the storm blew over. I tried to go back to sleep, but then the wind increased and howled through the treetops, snapped at the guy ropes, flattened the tent. I worried about falling branches and stiffened every time a big gust hit the trees. When the wind died down at last, we heard the thunder coming back! Again, we had to go through the fear of being struck by lightning, again the thunder shook the ground underneath the tent, and again it passed. As it always does.

The next morning, it was still raining and we stayed in the tent.

By afternoon it had cleared, so I walked down a steep track with a packful of empty water bottles, then followed an asphalt road for several kilometres until I saw a house. It was some sort of restaurant, quite empty by the look of it, a big space with tables and chairs and a bar. On the walls was a whole collection of cowbells of various sizes. The proprietor, dressed in a white blouse and a traditional apron, let me fill my bottles at the tap outside.

With the full water bottles my pack was a lot heavier and the track seemed incredibly steep. I was exhausted by the time I had climbed back to camp.

'Did you find water?' asked Peter. He was reading our one book in the tent—Nietzsche's *Thus Spake Zarathustra.*

I told him about the cow-bell restaurant, and sat down with my back against a pine tree. Slowly the drizzle stopped, and some rays of sunshine came through the clouds. My eyelids felt heavy and I closed my eyes. A serene stillness came over me that was like a kind of fragrance. It soothed my brain. Then I heard a little rustle that made me open my eyes. A tiny mouse came out of its hole, not more than a metre away, and looked curiously at me.

'Hello, Innie Minnie,' I whispered.

The mouse sat very quietly in a ray of sunshine. The world seemed to become slow and languid. The sun had warmed up the ground and the bushes, the trees and the air. Some of the bigger trees were steaming, and puffs whirled their way through the branches. A pigeon soared between the trees, never touching any branch at all. Then it was still again. So still and so beautiful that the whole world seemed to rest.

The little mouse sat motionless, until the shadows fell over the mountains. When that spot lost the sun, it went inside its house.

'Bye bye,' I said.

A few weeks later we were camping in a canyon and it was raining.

'Do you think you'll get the fire going in this rain?' shouted Peter. He had just found the pot and the cups, and stood under a huge beech. We were camping on the side of a mountain, near a river that flowed fast through a gorge. It was a stunning place, but the rain made everything difficult.

'Don't know!'

I was squatting near the fire in my raincoat, sheltering the space underneath me with my upper body. The rain on my hood was so loud we had to shout to hear each other.

'Do you need better wood?'

'Maybe some more kindling!'

Peter put everything on the ground and walked into the wet forest with the hunting knife to scrape pieces of bark from under a fallen tree. I focused again on my hapless little fire.

For every meal and every cup of tea we had to start a fire. It was an essential part of our lives. We spent hours around the flames and everything smelled of smoke: our clothes, body, hair and all our gear. The pots and pans were black with soot and our fingers were often marked with black stains. We were always thinking of where to collect wood and how to keep the packet of matches dry.

When Peter came back with the resin-filled bark, the fire became big enough to boil water. Finally, we were able to make some flatbread for breakfast. I put one cup of flour and a pinch of salt in our big plastic plate and mixed a little water with it. I kneaded the lot into a ball. Using the honey jar as a rolling pin, I rolled small balls into pancakes, then roasted them in the frypan. After so much cooking effort, the chapatis seemed tastier than ever.

When at last the rain stopped we packed up the wet tent and made our way into the gorge. The pathway through the forest was wonderful. Huge rocks and cliffs stood on either side; big old trees enjoyed a natural sanctuary.

I loved walking into a brand-new day, feeling curious about what might happen. We never knew in the morning how the day would end. The unknown kept my brain alert and gave me energy. Adventure was unfolding in front of us. This way of life was so intense, so all-consuming, there was no space to miss anything. Every minute of the day we were busy with living.

We were following a section of track that was quite popular with other hikers, but when the sun lowered the place became beautifully quiet again. In the early evening we found a spot underneath some fir trees, just below a ridge. After pitching the tent, we rested on the soft grass. A pigeon was cooing in a tree and the place seemed suddenly extraordinary. We didn't talk, we just felt the peace. There was a deep silence, so unusual that I made note of it in my diary. The surroundings weren't spectacular, yet the feeling of exquisite stillness was remarkable.

Then, not too far from us, we heard the warning call of a roe-deer. We looked up towards the ridge, saw no movement.

A few minutes later, I looked again. And there it was. My first thought was 'Tiger!' I wasn't at all afraid, even though the animal looked huge.

Of course it wasn't a tiger, it was a lynx—a breathtaking lynx. He was the size of a large dog, light coloured, with soft hair on his back, white around the chest. His eyes were focused on us. Intense, alert and calm. His big ears were pointing forward. He was curious, and stood looking at us for some time. He seemed to feel quite safe, standing about twenty metres above us.

Eventually he left us. He leaped away up the hill and over the ridge to the other side. He was so light-footed, so agile and so aware. This was the most beautiful wild animal I had ever seen. It felt almost otherworldly. The lynx had a presence that seemed to have influenced the whole area.

We sat still for a long time, enchanted and humbled by our brief encounter with an endangered animal.

The Jura trail led us through forests, often coming out in grassy fields with cows. The cattle lived up in the mountains in the summer and elsewhere in winter. We could hear the cowbells long before we came to their fields. They were loud enough from a distance; once we were close to the animals, the racket was so deafening we had to block our ears. We looked with pity at the poor animals. With their sensitive hearing, they must suffer unbearably.

We carried on past a village called Prés de la Montagne, and after just a few kilometres came out in Stierenberg where people spoke only German. I gave away my French dictionary and bought a little German one. From now on I would practise new words and slowly improve the language I had learned in school, years ago.

Every week I hitchhiked to Germany to do shopping. Returning from one such trip, I walked back to the edge of town and waited on the road that led back to Switzerland. After half an hour, I was very happy to see an old red car stop at last.

When I opened the door, I saw that the front passenger seat was already taken by a large teddy bear and two small sofa pillows.

'*Gutentag, Ich heiße Johannes,*' the elderly driver said. He sounded friendly enough. I made to get in, and he put the teddy bear on the back seat, murmuring: 'This one can sit over there.'

It was perhaps in the way he handled the bear that I understood it was not meant for a granddaughter but for his own company.

'Where are you going?' he asked.

He wore a wrinkled shirt and slightly faded Colbert jacket. He had little white hair left on his head but still plenty on his bushy eyebrows; there were tiny red lines of broken blood vessels on his cheeks.

When I told him where I was going, he kindly offered to take me all the way back to Switzerland.

'It's quite a long way. Are you sure?' My German practice was proving even more useful than I'd thought.

'Oh, yes, I have nothing to do all day, I'll be more than happy to drive you home. Where are you from, my dear?'

'Holland originally,' I said, 'but I have immigrated to New Zealand.'

'I have been in the Netherlands,' he said. 'Yes, Magdalena and I, it was in 1989, we went to Vlissingen.'

'Oh, to the beach—did you enjoy it?'

'Yes, we did. It was a nice summer's day.'

He talked for some time about Vlissingen. I could not quite follow the full story, but that didn't matter; to meet a stranger, to have some connection despite the different languages, was what counted. That's the beauty of hitchhiking—meeting the unexpected. The fact that this old man was slightly odd didn't worry me in the least.

We were driving out of town when he turned to me and asked, 'Is this the right way?'

'Yes,' I said. I had come in this way, so I recognised the route. We had to go a few kilometres over the highway to get back to where I'd left Peter.

'How long have you been living there?' I pointed at the town behind us.

'Since 1984,' he said, and began telling me about the history of the town.

Just when I was about to ask something more, he asked, 'And where are you from, my dear?'

I felt the blood drain from my face. For a second it was as though the world froze. My mouth felt dry and I could feel myself tense in every limb. My eyes shifted from his hands to the rear vision-mirror, the traffic, his actions, the road signs . . . We were now well out of town, among the grass paddocks, almost getting to the highway. It was too late to get out.

We arrived at a big curved ramp which led towards the autobahn. We were supposed to accelerate here so that we could merge with the Porches, BMWs and Mercedes that raced along ahead of us. To my horror, the old man didn't gather speed, but slowed right down. At the point we should have joined with the other traffic, he stopped altogether!

He was looking left and right, as though we were at a normal village junction. 'We need to go there!' He pointed left, the direction we had come from.

'No!' I said in a panic. 'We're going *this* way.' I pointed right. 'This is a highway!'

'No, no. I am living *there*!' He was shaking his head with tiny movements.

Two cars went past at tremendous speed, and I started to feel almost nauseous with fear.

He turned his wheel to the left, towards the approaching traffic.

In a flash, I leaned over, grabbed the steering wheel and pulled it towards the right.

'*This* way!' My hands were trembling. Surely I wasn't going to die such a stupid death.

He turned right. Luckily, nearby cars made space. But he was driving at fifty kilometres an hour now. Other drivers were racing past at what seemed like two hundred. Relative to them, we were standing still.

'This is a highway, we have to go a little faster,' I said, while nervously looking over my shoulder. Anyone could hit us from behind at any time. 'Since you live there—' I pointed behind us— 'you will take the first turnoff, and turn home.' I needed to get out of the car as fast as possible.

'*Das ist eine Autobahn, we müssen etwas schneller fahren.*' I kept repeating this mantra every two minutes while watching all the mirrors for traffic. I was ready to steer us off the highway onto the roadside. If he did anything stupid, I could direct us towards the grass.

He managed to increase his speed to eighty kilometres an hour. I felt my heart beating in my throat. Repetition calms the mind, I told myself.

'This is a highway, we have to go a little faster,' I kept saying, while Johannes kept silent.

After ten debilitating minutes, the first turnoff finally came. I closed my eyes for a second and sighed with relief. I pointed to the turnoff.

'Here we go,' I said, keeping my finger in the air, pointing in the right direction. No space for errors now. He drove off the highway, and approached a roundabout. 'You are going back this way,' I said in my calmest voice, 'and perhaps you can stop there, so I can get out.' I pointed towards a safe stopping place.

He stopped in the middle of the road, right on the roundabout, with four cars behind us. But it was enough. Without thinking more, I pulled open the door and stumbled onto the grass, signalling an apology to the drivers of the other cars.

My heart was thumping, I was short of breath and my knees felt weak. I squatted down and considered crying.

While Johannes drove off, I realised I should report him to the police—a driver with dementia was a danger to himself and others. But in my rush to get out, I had forgotten to memorise the registration plate. All I knew was his first name, old red car, and a teddy bear on the front seat.

I was picked up again, this time by a friendly woman who dropped me off at the edge of the forest. I got out, left the road and walked into the trees, following a small trail until I spotted our creek. When I climbed up the rocks, I could already smell the familiar scent of wood-smoke. I went through the water in my sandals and turned towards the big old fir tree that was growing on a boulder. Peter stood on top of the stone, as though he had been expecting me. Behind him I saw wisps of smoke curling through the branches.

'Your tea is ready. I thought you'd be back about now.' He offered his hand to help me climb up. 'How did it go?' There was some concern in his voice.

'I survived!' I took off my pack and sort of fell into his arms. I shook my head. 'Bit of a close call, this one.'

One day we were camping under a big oak. The tree had dropped many leaves over the years and provided a soft bed for us to lie on. At daybreak I quietly crawled out of the tent and sloped off down the mountain. In my pack were eight empty bottles, a few pieces of dirty clothing and a bar of soap. If I could find water this morning, we could have a rest day. The earlier I came back, the more rest I would have.

I figured from looking at the map that there was a farmhouse down the track where I could ask for water. The forest path was all downhill, the pack was light and I felt quite cheerful, until I felt something warm in my pants. I retreated to nearby bushes, and saw that I had soiled myself. I was horrified. Thankfully I had some toilet paper in my pocket and I could clean myself off a little. But where was the next water supply? If I came to a house, I could hardly ask the farmer to wash my underwear! I felt so miserable, I cried. Last time I shed tears about shitty pants was when I was five years old. I couldn't stop crying as I carried on down the path. I felt so sorry for myself. We had been walking for six weeks, I was more tired than I thought, and this embarrassment seemed the last straw.

At last I dried my tears, and came to some paddocks. I looked around for a water trough. But there was nothing; I would have to go to the house.

There were three dogs behind the gate. One was loose, the other two were tied up. All of them were growling and snarling. I looked at them anxiously for some time.

'Anybody home?' I called out. No answer.

My eye fell on an outside tap right next to the door.

I looked at the border collie right behind the gate.

'Nice dog,' I murmured. My heart was in my throat.

I was frightened, but looked over my shoulder, and at last I slowly opened the gate. The tied-up dogs barked viciously, jumping up and down. They jerked their chains and were instantly snatched backwards, which only increased their fury. The loose border collie ran a circle around me, barking. I forced myself to squat down and offer the back of my hand for him to sniff. If he wanted to, he could bite me very easily now. I had to risk it because I needed to get to that tap.

'Good dog, calm down,' I said in the way Peter would have.

The dog approached and sat down. When I patted him, the other two dogs fell silent.

I hastily filled up my bottles at the outside tap, hid behind the bushes, and washed all my clothing with soap. When everything was clean again, I felt immensely relieved.

I walked an hour back uphill to the camp, and put the washing out in a tree to dry. The fire was burning, and I sat down with my back against the tree.

Peter handed me a cup of tea and a hot chapati with slices of tomato and melted cheese. I quietly ate my 'pizza' and looked out over the valley below. There was a cuckoo in the distance and I softly imitated the call. The forest looked wonderful with its dark green foliage. The sun was shining through the leaves, which made lovely moving patterns on the ground. Everything was warm and dry.

We were following a cattle track over a grassy hill with lots of wild flowers and blackberries. It was warm, with a few wisps of clouds high in the sky. I had a small stone in my sandal, which I couldn't dislodge, so I stopped to take it off. Peter kept on walking, and my pack squeaked like a nest of chickens when at last I ran to catch up with him.

He was about twenty metres ahead of me when, out of nowhere, came a terrifying loud noise, so close that a rush of adrenaline ran through my whole body. I instantly dropped my sticks to protect my head with my hands.

Right over the top of us flew a very sophisticated and super-fast jet fighter. The sudden blast and vibrations were overwhelming. I had never seen or experienced anything like it.

'Woo-hoo-hoo!' I yelled.

Peter turned around as I ran to join him. 'Un-be-lie-vable! It was so close! He flew right over our heads! But,' he said in a more sober voice, 'this is made for war. Imagine if it were to drop bombs on us.'

In the weeks after, we learned that Switzerland puts a great deal of value on its military capability. All able-bodied male citizens must do military service and Switzerland has one of the highest rates of gun ownership in the world. Often we heard the sound of ordnance in the distance, presumably soldiers shooting at targets.

On one quiet afternoon, we followed a forest path that climbed gradually up a mountain. The sky was clouded, and in the distance were the now familiar fields of cows. The sound of their bells floated upwards with a cool breeze. Then we spotted an old concrete structure covered in moss tucked into the side of the hill.

'That looks like a bunker to me,' said Peter.

'Let's look inside!'

He walked to the door and tried to open it. 'It's locked.'

'Would that be a bomb shelter or a nuclear bunker?' I asked.

'No idea, but the whole country is full of them. They passed a law during the Cold War that every Swiss citizen has a right to bunker space.'

'Imagine,' I said. 'There's a nuclear disaster, and you make it to this bunker in time. They let you in and close the door behind you. And for days, weeks, months and maybe years, you're stuck with dozens, maybe hundreds of others.'

'Sounds like prison,' said Peter.

'It's either that or die from nuclear radiation.'

'Hmm,' said Peter. 'I read about this famous bunker in Lucerne. When it was built in the seventies, it could protect twenty thousand people. A whole city under the ground, with seven floors! They had everything in there, even some prison cells. A prison in a prison! That's a very Swiss joke, you'd think.'

Later that day we must have crossed an old border, because we saw concrete blocks as big as cars dotted among trees in the forest. These were anti-tank obstacles dating from the First World War.

A week later, I learned a bit more about this aspect of Switzerland. I had hitchhiked to a supermarket again, and on my way back caught a lift in a jet-black Mercedes Benz racer. The interior, including the steering wheel, was clad in fine leather. The driver was a Swiss clock-maker who spoke perfect English. He was small-built with a narrow face, sharp cheekbones and clear green eyes.

He wore a watch, expensive no doubt, and my eyes fell on his classy leather gloves.

'What are those gloves for?' I asked with a laugh.

He kept his eyes on the road, turned on his indicator and smiled. 'Comes with the car.'

'Do you live around here?' I asked.

'Yes, I live in a small village near here, and I work in Zurich. I drive about fifty kilometres each day, which is a lot. But it's quite common; most Swiss people stay in the village they were born in and drive to work. People change jobs every few years. I think it's pointless moving each time you get a new job.'

We talked about this and that, and eventually I moved the conversation to the military.

'We heard some army practice in the forest. Why is there so much military in Switzerland?' I asked. 'Who's the enemy?'

'Germans,' he said with all seriousness.

'You're joking? That was seventy years ago.'

'Yes.'

I was waiting for an explanation, but nothing came. So I asked, 'Do you have a bunker somewhere too?'

'My cousin has one. Well, he inherited it from his father, but I have never been there. I visited a public bunker, though, about three years ago, on 15 July.'

'Really? What was it like?'

'Fascinating indeed.' He paused for moment to recall the details. 'The walls are one-and-a-half metres thick. It has air ventilators and special showers to get the nuclear waste off the people who enter. People wouldn't have their own bed, because there's a rotation system. Since no daylight comes in, you can sleep eight hours, then the next one will sleep eight hours. It's very well thought out. It's the best system in the world, in fact. There's a lot of fuel stored to keep the air filters going, with safety vents and hatches to stop contaminated air from entering. The communication system remains traditional, since satellites might be destroyed and cellphones or internet wouldn't work. Then there's a huge water reservoir. There used to be great stores of food in every shelter, but the perceived risk of a nuclear disaster has diminished. Many bunkers have been converted to other things like hotels or private safes. Those sorts of things.'

'How many bunkers are there?'

'I couldn't tell you exactly, but something like twenty thousand nuclear bunkers, then another three hundred thousand or more private and public fall-out shelters. But some of them are out of order now.'

When we arrived at my junction, I almost had to crawl out of the car, the seats were so low.

'Sorry,' I said. 'I've left some mud on the floor.' I felt bad about dirtying his pristine vehicle.

'That is not a problem, I can vacuum it.'

While I shouldered my pack I saw him looking for traffic in the rear-vision mirror. He turned on his indicator and drove carefully on to the road. Within fifty metres he was at full speed, zooming over the smooth asphalt towards Zurich.

I waited until it was silent, and slipped into the forest. I followed a walking path for half an hour until I found the white stone that I had left on the track. This stone was my cue to look for the empty stream-bed further in the forest. I climbed up the gully and moved to a spur. I saw the big tree, found the holly shrub and I whistled, imitating a New Zealand owl. From the distance I heard a reply.

The Jura Crest is a beautiful walkway, with deep gorges and impressive panoramas. Every day we climbed up forested mountains and descended into lush green valleys. We felt fit and strong, but after hiking nearly two months we were both in need of a few rest days.

In the midst of a forest we came across a remote car park with a tap. Half an hour further on, we found a flat spot that was ideal for camping. We pitched our tent, intending to stay there for a few nights. Every day we filled our water bottles from the tap, sat around the fire, ate, played chess, read Nietzsche and did as little as possible.

On the third day we saw a tall and skinny man with a hat, standing above us in the paddock.

'Vhen. Are. You. Leafing?' he shouted in broken English. He made no attempt to climb over the fence to walk down to our tent.

We looked at each other with big eyes.

'Tomorrow!' shouted Peter.

With that, the man went away. Next morning we left, grateful that we'd at least had three days of rest.

T he Swiss trail officially finished in Dielsdorf, but we continued a few days onto the banks of the Rhine river, which forms a natural border with Germany. The river was slow and steady. There were many trees on the banks and it was clear that it didn't flood much. It seemed dependable and stable—a bit like the people who lived on either side of it. We camped in the willows, and followed the river for some days.

After walking along the shores of Lake Constance, we crossed the border into Austria. We found ourselves on the edge of the city of Bregenz. We tried hitchhiking to the other side, but nobody stopped. So we kept on walking. The roads were hideously busy. The roar of cars and heavy trucks was so persistent that it felt almost like a form of torture, and I could feel the tears coming.

In the evening we reached the centre of town, where we blended with people celebrating a Saturday night in midsummer. We asked around for a youth hostel, but were told that everything would be full. 'Next time book ahead on your phone,' a young man advised us.

We kept on going. I had been so energetic in the morning, but we had been hiking for ten hours and with every step I felt more exhausted.

'Where, for heaven's sake, will we sleep?' I said, and leaned for a second on my sticks.

'We will just keep on walking,' said Peter without slowing down, 'and we will find a place to camp. Even in the dark we can pitch the tent with our headlights. There's no problem.'

It is just a matter of endurance, I told myself. Forget for a moment that there's nowhere to camp in the middle of a stinking city.

Just before twilight, we saw a strip of forest that looked a little more wild than anything we'd seen so far. When we looked closer, we discovered it was a swamp. I could not take one more step, and waited on a park bench while Peter walked into the muddy swamp. He came back to tell me he had found a tiny dry clearing, just big enough for one tent, right on the edge of a river running into the lake.

We went to the site and finally took our packs off.

'Let's hope the river doesn't flood,' he said. He was washing his muddy sandals in the water. The river was flowing just twenty centimetres below the grass. I was too tired to worry about a flooding river and a flooded tent.

Peter gathered firewood and while the river reflected the sunset colours, I pitched the tent. In the half-dark, we sat around our tiny fire to eat our meal of rice and lentils.

After such a long and deafening day, it felt as if the trees repaired my fragmented, frazzled brain. Everything around us was soft and loving. I felt my body relaxing and my mind rejuvenating.

When it was completely dark, we covered the remnants of the

fire with sand and went to bed with the boom of music in the distance.

'*Hey, was machst du hier? Es ist verboten zu campen!*' we heard at the crack of dawn. The low male voice sounded angry and irritated.

Jerked out of sleep, I looked at Peter. 'Police?' I whispered.

Peter pointed at me—I was the one who could speak German. I nervously zipped open the tent.

In front of us were two men with binoculars. They told us that this was their bird-watching position and that wild camping was not allowed. They had a camouflage cover that they wanted to erect as soon as possible in the place our tent was standing.

'We will go away,' I said, and we immediately started stuffing our sleeping bags in to their covers.

The men waited impatiently. The space was so cramped, they stood on top of last night's fire without noticing.

'Welcome to Austria,' I whispered as I rolled up my mat.

Peter looked up at me and chuckled silently.

CHAPTER 3

GERMANY
IN THE
FOOTSTEPS
OF THE KING

Maximilian II was a Bavarian king. He was told by his subordinates about the pretty lakes that were hidden in old forests, waterfalls from cliffs, and mountains with peaks so steep and narrow they looked like church spires. Some of his men had seen thunderstorms on the tops, with lightning that could split the rocks. Some had witnessed the torrential rain that turned little creeks into raging rivers. Everyone had admired the beauty and the grandeur of the high rocky mountains—except the king himself. So, one summer in 1858, the king decided he would like to see his land.

He appointed a group of strong men and began a long journey, starting at Lake Constance. They marched up and over the mountains, always on the border with Austria, and from the tops he could look far and wide over his beloved Bavaria. But the king grew quickly tired, and more often than not he had to be carried by his entourage. Through wind and rain they climbed up, down or along the ridge, and after 350 kilometres they arrived in Berchtesgaden.

The people remembered where the king had walked, marked the route and called it the Maximiliansweg.

fter 650 kilometres in France and Switzerland, we were now going to follow the footsteps of the king and his men.

From Bregenz, we walked into Germany, into the forest and up the wild mountains. We lit countless fires and found places to sleep under the trees. We listened to the woodpeckers, saw squirrels running up and down trees, and fish in the calm lakes.

One day we climbed to a high pass and followed the track down into a valley. It was as wild as anything we had seen in Europe. The forest air was cool and fresh, the sound of the roaring river came floating upwards on a breeze. A falcon was soaring in the blue sky and there was no sign of civilisation. Finally we came to a beautiful, fast-flowing river.

There was a tiny beach with white sand. We unloaded everything and used sand to scrub ourselves clean. I stood in the river and washed my hair in a pool with a bar of soap. The water was clear, yet pleasantly warm, and it was wonderful to feel its power. The river had flowed for thousands of years through this landscape, carved mountains and supplied life to all animals. Every day more pure water was flowing down. It was a symbol of the regenerating power of Earth. The source was always pure, no matter how it would find the sea.

We bathed, and washed our shirts and shorts. While the clothes were drying in the sun, we lit a fire with willow-wood that didn't smoke. Nobody saw us. I picked some nettles and chickweed to eat as spinach, fried an egg, rolled some chapatis, and Peter boiled water for tea. We were delighted: it was a glorious afternoon, and this was a wild and beautiful spot with plenty of pure drinking water.

We walked through this valley for two sunny days until we found a place in the forest to rest. Everything around us was covered in a thick layer of moss. There was a small side creek and nearby was a little opening from where we could view the entire valley. All afternoon, we sat on a soft log, sipping our tea. We collected firewood before we went to bed and slept well on a carpet of moss. We decided to rest here for a week.

At dawn I woke to the sound of rain, and looked at our wood supply in the vestibule. We would light a fire using some dry branches and add wet wood later. We could survive quite a few rainy days this way. Then the noise started: chainsaws, high-pitched, revving; the crashing of branches; a mighty boom as a tree fell to the ground. We were lying in our sleeping bags, staring at the tent fabric, listening, appalled. The loggers were not far away— there must have been three or four of them.

I tried reading a book while the chainsaws kept cutting the forest around us.

'Imagine,' said Peter, 'that you're living for generations in the forest, like Native Brazilians, and then one day the dreaded white man comes with his machine and cuts the trees down around you. Off you go! they'd yell. Out, out, out! Leave the forest, go to the reservations, go to the towns, live in buildings. Do what you're told!'

His words were sharp as a knife, and tears welled up in my eyes. Never had the situation felt so real or so dreadful.

The chainsaws kept revving, and over the days I could feel anxiety rising. As though my core was being drilled and modified into a shape that was not me, and could not possibly ever become me. I closed my eyes and waited. This was the most beautiful place we had been, and the most horrible place we had ever camped.

On the fourth day the clouds disappeared, and the loggers didn't turn up. We lit a big fire and cooked a lot of food. We looked at the sunshine reaching the forest floor. Steam was curling upwards. The little bundles of pine needles hanging from the branches lit up and moved softly in the wind. Two falcons were flying high in the sky. They were far apart, yet they seemed to circle each other. Big and wide circles. They were gliding upwards, moving effortlessly in great spirals.

The moment we had arrived in Germany, Peter talked excitedly about a certain castle. As a child, he had seen pictures of Neuschwanstein and never forgotten it.

King Maximilian had a son whose name was Ludwig. He was born to rule, but unfortunately his heart was not in politics. Expected to produce an heir, he became betrothed but never made it to a wedding. Some people said he was more interested in men.

After Germany became united in 1871, the Kaiser became the official ruler. Ludwig retreated into his fantasy world of knights and castles. He built several lavish castles, ran out of money, and borrowed fourteen million marks from other European kings to continue building more. His debt became an embarrassment to the Bavarian government, and his ministers declared Ludwig insane. Three months later, in 1886, the king was found dead in a lake. Nobody knows what had happened, but many speculate murder.

All his castles look like something from a fairy tale, with many towers, turrets, frescoes and throne halls. But the most breathtaking aspect of Neuschwanstein is its setting. To the north are rolling hills and two lakes; on the other side are the Alps. The towers mirror the surrounding peaks, cliffs and rock faces.

'Precisely as I imagined,' said Peter when he first saw it. His eyes were glistening.

Then we walked over the asphalt road towards Marienbrücke. This was a spectacular bridge, built ninety metres above the river. It gave the impression that lightning had split a rock in half and the king had built a bridge between the spikes.

Further up the valley, it was surprisingly quiet. None of the tourists ventured past the bridge. We looked for somewhere to camp but we were surrounded by vertical rock faces. Forced to climb up and up and up, we left the last traces of civilisation behind and arrived at a pass in twilight. From the tops, the sky was wide and far, giving an enormous sense of space. Orange and red clouds were smoothed by the wind and streamed in one direction. We could see many peaks of the Ammergau Alps.

We found a flat spot and pitched the tent. Although it had been a long day, we felt energised. It was as if we were back in the real wilderness. I felt I could run forever here, living off fresh air and drinking clean water seeping from the rocks. The rawness, the altitude, the untamed powers created a different kind of energy. There was a joyous fire inside of me that made me feel very vulnerable yet courageous at the same time.

Next morning, we hiked towards a higher pass. We were surrounded by gravel and rocks, and the last bit we had to climb with hands and feet. We rested on top, looking out on the eastern ranges stretching far into Austria. After some food, we walked and slid down the mountain. The terrain was steep, with some parts angling down a rock face. It was hot—we had sweated a lot coming up. We still had a way to descend and were completely out of water.

Then we saw a distant cliff glistening in the sun. While Peter rested, I took the bottles and climbed towards the waterfall. It was much further than I thought, and on the way I spotted a large group of mountain chamois. These brilliant creatures, related to the antelope, are not much bigger than a goat and have brown fur and small white faces, with a stripe of brown running from the nose to the ears. They have pretty, spiky horns that curl backward at the tips. We had seen them occasionally in New Zealand, where they had been introduced from Europe. They are now classified as a pest and the New Zealand government spends a lot of effort keeping the numbers down. To see them in their natural habitat was wonderful. They were grazing so quietly. They saw me but were not afraid. Some of the leading animals seemed to look up at the sky, and the flock was slowly moving down the valley. Clouds were building up in the distance and the wind seemed to increase.

'I think there's a storm coming,' I said to Peter when I got back. 'We'd better find shelter in the trees for tonight.'

I didn't want to go too far down the valley. I wanted to stay as long as possible in the wildest places. I wanted to feel the full force and immensity of the storm in the mountains, to strengthen my heart. So we made a camp at the first bit of forest we saw.

The big, old, gnarly trees were at the bottom of an ancient rockslide. They were bent down and shaped by wind and lightning storms, floods and stone avalanches. They had been here a long time and we felt protected.

While a strange glow of purple and green inhabited the sky, we lit a fire to cook our meal. When the shadow overtook the valley, the temperature plummeted. Wearing all our clothes, we sat on a rock to watch the immense dark clouds slowly floating towards us. The open tops of the rocky peaks were waiting for the fury. It was eerily silent, with not a sound of even a bird. I felt tension building up and had to resist an urge to hide in the tent.

It began with a distant rumble and flashes on the horizon. When it moved towards us, we saw huge, jagged lightning strikes. They filled the sky and created a strange yellow light. Some were directed to Earth, but some jumped from cloud to cloud. It was frightening, yet exhilarating. As the storm came closer, the thunder and echo became continuous; the lightning flashes were so constant, they had a stroboscopic effect. My head felt strange, as though I was lifted towards the sky by invisible hands. My body and mind were completely part of the lightning storm. My sense of self ceased to exist for a moment and I received a huge charge of energy.

In the days after, we saw downed trees and flooded rivers, all caused by the great storm's passage. It looked like one big ravage, but as soon as one tree went down, a new sapling had a chance to grow. New seeds had been waiting in the soil for this destruction. Death meant life in the wilderness.

We often came across hunting hide-outs—simple platforms built in trees overlooking clearings. Feeding bags were suspended nearby to attract deer and pigs. The hunter sat in his spot and waited; when he saw an animal, he would line up and shoot. This was a different kind of hunting from what I was used to in New Zealand—going off in the late afternoon with the lowering sun, looking, looking, looking, searching for movement or a colour that belonged to an animal and not a plant or stone.

I was part of the natural world when I was hunting. I felt fearless and alert, like a tiger seeking out her territory. Hunting was in my blood, in my genes and my ancestry. It felt the most natural thing to do. There was stillness and tension in the air that increased awareness. The golden light would shine on every tree and slope and grass clearing, but I would stay in the dark shadows and make no sounds. I would watch everything patiently, listen so carefully that my thought ceased. With the fading light, more animals would come out. I would walk softly, move towards viewpoints or climb onto a tree branch. With the first star, the animals would begin grazing and roaming, and I would stay on the edge of the forest, until it was too dark to see movement.

I missed the hunt, and I missed eating the wild meat that gave me so much energy, but as a foreigner it was difficult to obtain the legal hunting documents. Our journey through Europe was a very different experience from our years in the New Zealand wilderness. This was not as remote, but the Bavarian Alps with their high peaks and spires were equally as impressive as the Southern Alps.

It was the end of August, and after a thousand kilometres and three months' solid walking, all we could think of was where we could rest. By the time we reached the end of the Maximiliansweg in Berchtesgaden, near Salzburg, I was tired and Peter was exhausted. We didn't even think of what we would do next, and stopped talking about Istanbul, for Turkey was another two thousand kilometres away.

We desperately needed a place to recover for a few weeks. More than ten years ago, when Peter lived in India, he had befriended a man whose mother was Indian and his father Austrian. They had kept sporadic contact over the years, and Peter knew he was back in Austria. We went to a library for Peter to send him an email and thankfully Simon sent a warm reply with an invitation to stay.

From the end of the trail, it was an hour's drive east to Simon's place. The bus was huge and empty. It took us along winding roads, up and over the mountains, past lakes and orderly towns. But the beauty wasn't quite the same. Inside the vehicle we suddenly felt a bit isolated. We couldn't feel the fresh air or the steepness of the mountain slope. We couldn't hear the silence or a bird singing. We couldn't fill our lungs with cool mountain air. But it was faster than walking.

The bus left us in a village with neat gardens, surrounded by tidy fields and looking out over rugged, forested mountains and an impressive white cliff.

Simon had told us we were welcome any day—but it had to be after 3 p.m. When we arrived at his house, he told us he had just woken up. He was about fifty years old and looked very Indian, with long, black, silky hair, elegant fingers, a quiet smile with voluptuous lips, and soft, brown eyes set into a round face. He also had a great big stomach and two skinny legs sticking out beneath it.

He welcomed us, laughed heartily, gave us a hug and said his new name was Chunmay. This name was given to him by his old guru in India, he said, and it meant supreme consciousness. When he turned around to lead us to the living room, I looked at Peter. He rolled his eyes. I grinned.

We sat down and chatted about our journey, then I casually asked what he did for a living.

'He didn't tell you?' Simon looked surprised for a moment, but recovered quickly and said, 'I'm what they call a teacher of Advaita Vedanta. I don't like the name guru, because life itself is a guru, a person is never a guru, but I teach *satsang*, which is Sanskrit for being with the truth. I ask people to be one with everything; to be in the moment and not to identify with anything or anybody. Because that is total freedom.'

I listened attentively, because he had obviously read much about the topic.

'Truth opens your heart and quiets your mind. But thought, fear and so forth cause the heart to contract and consequently the mind gets busier, you follow?'

'Yes,' I said, and Peter nodded.

'We do a lot of silent retreats too,' said Simon.

I told him that we had slept right next to the Chartreuse monastery where the monks were also silent. Then Peter told him about the lynx, and I about hitchhiking with the old man with dementia. Then we talked about the wilderness in New Zealand and all our experiences there.

'I still remember those great conversations we had in India,

Peter,' said Simon. 'Peter was reading the ancient Indian scriptures, the *Mahabharata*, at the time.'

'I like Yaksha's questions,' said Peter. 'What were they again? Ah, yes. What's faster than the wind?'

'The mind!' Simon grinned.

'Who is truly happy?' asked Peter.

'A person free from debt of any kind,' answered Simon.

'And in Dutch, guilt and debt are the same word,' I added.

'What's the greatest wonder?'

'Man sees death all around, yet he himself believes he will never die,' said Peter.

Simon made us a cup of tea, and asked, 'When you're sleeping right underneath a big tree, do you feel its energy?'

'Sometimes yes,' said Peter, 'and when there are other big trees nearby, you feel that the roots are connected. Nothing stands truly alone.'

'It is so nice you are here,' said Simon. 'My friends from the wilderness.' He leaned over to take my hand in his left hand, and Peter's hand in his right. 'You, like no other, would know what oneness is.' He took a big breath and exhaled slowly, while smiling at us. 'You would have practised satsang with every particle of your body, without thinking about it. The only sound in the wilderness is the whisper of truth.'

I nodded ever so slightly. 'Yes, I guess.'

'Did you have any moments of non-duality, or what they call mystical experiences, in the wilderness? Did you ever take any psilocybin when you were out there, because this is a great teacher too. My moment of breakthrough was with the help of ayahuasca.'

'No, we never took anything like that,' I said.

'But things happen when you live quietly in the forest. It is timeless, without a clock, without technology and distractions,' Peter told him.

We talked a while longer, then Simon asked if we'd like to stay in one of his ashrams.

'Ashrams?' said Peter. 'Where?'

'About half an hour's drive from here,' said Simon. 'Suhina will come and get you.'

S imon apparently had five ashrams. The one we were to stay in was, we discovered, an apartment owned by one of his followers in the middle of a small town. The owner was a young woman who was the sole parent of two little boys. She told us she used to be called Else but was now called Suhina, which meant beautiful. Because I couldn't remember all these unfamiliar names, I just called her Beautiful. She was certainly pretty, had long blonde hair, a slim and athletic figure and joyous eyes.

She showed us the bedroom for satsang guests. She did not want us to pay rent, but we insisted on making a contribution to her bills. For the first time in three months we could sleep without worrying where we would find drinking water. After emptying my pack I had a hot shower and found the water pressure almost scary. Back in our room, I suddenly smelled all the smoke we'd brought with us from the campfire. Beautiful showed us how to use the washing machine, and soon we were quite presentable to the human world.

While the boys were playing in the living room with their wooden train, we sat chatting around the kitchen table. Peter was cooking a vegetable curry, and Beautiful was chopping some red onion. With her thin knife, she cut the onion in to minuscule pieces. While I was cutting up some tomatoes for a salad, I caught myself trying to figure out whether Beautiful had a boyfriend somewhere, or whether she was into spiritual celibacy.

'Well, we are totally devoted to Chunmay.' She smiled briefly. 'As you can see.' Behind her was a table with a framed photograph of Simon. 'I feel completely at peace when I am around him. He teaches us to overcome all our conditioning, to throw away all the stuff that doesn't serve us, like private property, private husbands, private egos.'

'Are you saying you're Simon's lover?' Peter asked.

She grinned. 'I'm sort of his lover.'

'Sort of? How many does he have?'

'He has five at the moment. But there are no particular limits.' She shrugged. 'I don't own him.'

Five? I thought. Where are they all? 'And you, do you have five lovers too?'

'Oh, I'm nowhere near as enlightened as Chunmay. It would be too confusing for my mind. I am not totally empty yet. It is important at this stage to focus on one teaching. Chunmay is my guide. He has the clarity to see.'

Over the next few days we bought food for all of us, cooked, cleaned, shared meals, played with the children, and every so often other men and women would gather at our ashram for a visit from the guru.

He came on his Moto Guzzi. The first time I saw it, I couldn't help wondering how much it cost. While Simon was taking off his helmet in the hallway, I asked after the motorbike.

'Oh, it cost a lot,' said Beautiful. 'A small fortune, I can tell you that.'

'Isn't it strange that Chunmay would have such expensive

material things?' I asked, while placing the cutlery and napkins on the table.

'For us, yes. Because we would identify with it and get attached to it. But Chunmay is not attached to anything, certainly not material things like a motorbike. He can have property or not, it doesn't affect him. That's freedom.'

'Where does he get the money from? Just from teaching satsang?'

'From anywhere and everywhere.' She laughed as she lit a candle. 'He never worries about money and he always has enough. When he wants to buy something, the money seems to come miraculously. The universe provides.'

Then Simon and his six followers moved from the hallway to the living room, and we took our places around the table. Everybody spoke English very well and the conversation was pleasant. While Simon was talking, I searched for signs of enlightenment. I was curious to discover whether it was something genuine or manufactured. Apart from his soft voice and little smile, which could be cultivated if you put your mind to it, he did seem to have another quality to him. He could sit back and watch, psychologically speaking. It was as if he was always sitting back in a chair, observing the world around him with amusement. It was difficult to tell if he was always like that, or only in the company of others. Nevertheless, during those evenings there was an air of equanimity about him.

Simon treated us like royal guests, but he commanded his followers. He'd call out, 'Wine!' and even snap his fingers. Then someone would jump up and pour him more wine.

'Why do you do all this?' Peter asked one of the young men.

Not mockingly, but out of genuine curiosity.

'Enlightenment!' said the young man, as if it was obvious. He had a broad forehead and a ginger ponytail, and moved like a rugby player. 'The longer I am around Chunmay, the more I learn and the sooner I will get enlightened. Life is not worth living without nirvana. I have consciously taken the position of a servant and I will observe the arrogance of my ego. Slowly, over time, it will dissolve.'

'Will it not affect the person who is served?' I asked.

'Not if he is enlightened,' he said, and looked at Simon.

'Once you have abolished the ego, it cannot be affected by insult or compliment, or people serving him,' said Simon with a grin.

We got to know the five girlfriends quite well. All of them were very pretty blonde women, no older than thirty-five. Most of them had small children and the father was off-stage. Chunmay's newest girlfriend, however, was only twenty. He had named her Madhuri, which means Sweet One.

One day I found her crying in the kitchen. 'What's the matter?' I asked, patting her on the shoulder as I quietly took a seat.

It took a while before she said anything, but eventually she sobbed, 'I'm not so certain any more what I want. I am really happy with Chunmay, but maybe I want a boyfriend just for myself and that is such an egotistical thought.'

'Well,' I said. 'You don't have to be his girlfriend, you don't have to live here. You can leave any time you want, you know. Go back to your friends and family in Frankfurt, if you like. This is not a prison.'

'My family in *Frankfurt*?' she said suddenly in a very normal voice.

For a second I thought I had named the wrong city, but then she said, 'No, they have no idea about me. My father is so conservative. He would have a heart attack if he knew I was a guru's girlfriend. No, seeing my parents wouldn't do me any good. They would drag me right back where I started.'

'Well, your old friends then, they might understand you better?'

'No, they're studying business and marketing or something equally trivial. No, I love the spiritual energy here and living in an ashram. Chunmay says that this chaos in my head is just the ego trying to create havoc. My conditioned self is bringing up all kinds of arguments why I should leave. But I should not listen to this, because that only strengthens the ego.'

'But how could you ever make a decision of any kind, if you cannot trust your thoughts to be true?'

She stared at the kitchen table. 'That's the problem. I cannot trust my own thoughts, but I can trust Chunmay. I love him so much. While I am in a chaotic state, he can guide me. He will steer me towards a spiritual path. Not everyone can handle it, he says. You have to be persistent. There are many obstacles on the way.'

'The obstacle being the ego, you mean?'

'It's always the ego. It's trying to escape into superficial things, creating distractions in cunning and clever ways . . . So this is one of the many difficulties that I will face. We all have to sit through this. And then we will learn. And eventually—' she glanced up for a second—'I will come to nirvana.' She smiled for a moment before she lowered her eyes again.

It had been raining all day, but now a soft breeze came through the open kitchen windows. The sun was about to set, and I could see a bit of pink in the sky.

This, I thought, is starting to sound like a real cult. Simon had explained the world as if it was a maze. He had told these young women that salvation lies in the centre. And if you walk long enough, try long enough, you will eventually get there. The problem was that nobody quite made it to the centre. Once you were in his maze, he had very cleverly erased the exit.

Simon would come for a meal, and would stay until three in the morning. Nobody dared to go to bed before he decided to go home. It was exhausting, because the children woke up every morning at daylight. So Peter and I did not recover from our walk as we'd hoped. If anything, we deteriorated. I became physically tired and then mentally exhausted. I medicated, like the other women, with an overdose of coffee to get through the day, and felt unbalanced in every sense of the word. On one hand, I could not wait to leave. On the other, I was intrigued. I had read books about cults, yet never seen one with my own eyes. This wasn't the most extreme cult in the world—it was in fact very mild—but in the end, it was curiosity that kept us staying in the ashram a little longer.

We had been there a little over a week when another of Chunmay's girlfriends approached me. Her name was Divine Energy. We chatted about this and that, then suddenly she said, 'We went to Sweden for a retreat, and the Swedish girls there really loved Chunmay. They are so open and affectionate; they just want to touch Chunmay. It is so lovely to see.'

Instantly I smelled a bit of a rat. This seemed a message directed at me personally. Indeed, a few days later, she mentioned the topic again, this time adding, 'Have you noticed that if you touch him you receive a special feeling?'

'Uh, yeah kind of,' I muttered.

'His energy is so pure, so light. I feel this when I touch him. You can also be affectionate with Chunmay if you like.'

No way, I thought.

Between showers of rain, Peter and I put on our warmest clothes and walked to the supermarket. On the way we saw a child dragging something behind him on a string. It could have been a rag, maybe an old doll.

'You know that joke about a dog called Bobby?' said Peter.

'No?' I started to smile.

'There was a man called George living in an asylum. Every day he walked up and down the hallway with a brick on a leash. He was convinced the brick was a dog. A dog he named Bobby. One day he had to appear in front of a committee, to see if he was still insane.

'"And how is your little dog going today?" asked one of the men at the end of the assessment.

'"My dog?" George looked surprised. "That's not a dog! That's just a brick!"

'As George left the room the psychologist said, "Well, that is a very good sign, George is improving."

'George went out with his brick and piece of string. As he left the meeting he mumbled to the brick: "Fooled them this time, didn't we, Bobby?"'

I laughed. 'He knows it's a brick, and he believes it's a dog. It's a bit like that question in the *Mahabharata*, that we know we're going to die, but we believe we won't. I wonder how much that is happening in daily life.'

'People in dysfunctional relationships know that they detest the other, yet still want to believe that they love their partner,' said Peter. 'Done it myself in the past.'

'Do you think Simon also believes he is enlightened?' I asked. 'Yet somehow, deep down, he knows he is not?'

'I think he wants to believe it, acts accordingly, and makes it a reality. It works until the bubble bursts for some reason or another.'

The next day Simon came to visit and, without saying it out loud, indicated that I should sit next to him on the sofa. The couch material was so soft, I couldn't help but touch him. I sort of slid into the middle, and to my dismay he put an arm around my shoulder. On the other side of him sat Beautiful. Simon had the situation nicely under control. I looked at Peter, who smiled at me with amusement.

'What happens with your consciousness when you are always in the forest and mountains?' Simon asked him.

'You realise how small the mind is,' Peter said. 'How insignificant we are. We are tiny compared to the huge mountains.'

'And our thoughts and worries are even tinier,' I added. 'So much so that all those things seem to dissolve, rather than being solved.'

Conversation carried on, but I was aware that Sweet One was sitting stiffly on the other side of the room. She didn't speak and looked very unhappy. I had the feeling she normally sat on Simon's right side and I felt guilty for making her sad.

The following evening, we learned more about Simon's influence. We went to a satsang session. He went on his motorbike, the rest of us went in a van to a beautiful old building in the city centre. His followers had decorated the room with flowers, opened the big windows, put down mats to sit on, and in the front were two chairs. There were about twenty people of all ages and nationalities in the room. We all sat in lotus position and were supposed to meditate until the guru arrived.

He came in, took his seat. His big stomach heaved up and down. For a few minutes he looked around. His head moved from left to right as he observed us all.

'Now please relax,' he said slowly. He spoke in English. 'Relax, totally. And listen to the silence.'

There was a lot of noise outside. An ambulance sped past with its siren, cars drove by, kids were calling out . . .

'Just for the time being, leave everything outside. Your mind, your thoughts, your past and ideas of the future. Leave everything. Now go to the core of your being. In this state, can there be a creator?'

I looked nervously at the others. Were we supposed to answer this question?

'No,' Simon said at last. 'There is no creation or creator. There is nobody creating anything. It is thought that creates a virtual identity. What does the creator make?'

He answered his own question. 'All that you desire,' he said. 'We create happiness, wonderful romance, successful business and so forth. And the creator gets attached to the outcome. But this creation is an illusion. You have created an imaginary sunny side, and with the sunny side comes automatically the dark side. And after a while we come to loathe that dark side, and spend all our time trying to avoid it. But we cannot. We can't keep the sunny side and destroy the darkness.'

The session took two hours, and in the end we witnessed a naming ceremony. The ten-year-old son of one of his girlfriends was to become officially part of the ashram. He sat excitedly in the big chair, waiting for his Hindu name. Simon said that the boy was innocent, strong and would go far, as long as he followed his inner light. He named him Tejas, which means Light.

After ten days in the ashram, Peter and I were anxious to move on, and discussed what we should do next. The weather had turned from warm and summery to wet and cold. The leaves on the trees were turning yellow; it felt like autumn would not be too far off. It did not appeal to us to keep on walking through Austria, so we talked about taking a train to warmer places.

Then I received an email from a Dutch woman. She had read my book *Woman in the Wilderness*, and invited us to her family's yurt in Bulgaria.

'Where is Bulgaria again?'

'South of Romania, north of Greece, west of Turkey, east of Serbia,' said Peter from the couch. 'I would have thought you'd been taught this in school—you know, coming from Europe and all?'

'Yeah, a long time ago. Now there's a Dutch family in Bulgaria who has invited us to stay in their yurt. They've stepped out of the Dutch system and they don't want to send their children to school. They want to live in nature and with other like-minded people.'

'Are these like-minded people forming another cult?'

I laughed. 'I don't think so, but I can't be certain.'

'And the Bulgarian education system doesn't mind the non-schooling?'

'I don't know—they're travelling in Romania right now but back home next week. They say that there are tons of grapes, wild mushrooms and berries, and apple, pear, cherry and walnut trees. The fruit trees were planted for everyone in the Communist era.'

'Did you mention grapes?' said Peter. 'Because that means a fantastic climate. I'll go anywhere they can grow grapes. Do you think they'll mind us staying in the ashram for another week?'

'They want us to live here, as long as we believe in Chunmay.'

'Yes. We totally believe in Chunmay!' grinned Peter.

T hat evening Simon came again. This time he suggested that we should receive an official name so that we could be part of the ashram. When Peter hesitated, Simon focused on me. I couldn't think of how to say no.

At the beginning of the next satsang we sat in silence. Instead of meditating, I was practising what I should say during my naming ceremony. Simon first spoke about truth, and several people went to the chair to ask him questions. Then his fifth girlfriend stood up. Her name was Shrijani, which meant Creative. She lived in one of the other ashrams, and we didn't know her so well.

Creative walked to the chair. Her voluminous hair flowed behind her like a cape. She had angular cheekbones and a Roman nose. She crossed her slim, long legs, and her hands rested in her lap. She said she had been very confused lately. She had gone with her sister to another form of treatment or counselling, called Hellinger Family Constellations.

'We went last week, and I discovered . . .'

'What do you mean, you went last week?' Simon spoke with a slow tone of superiority, still with a smile on his face.

Her hands went to the armrest, and she moved back into the chair.

'Well, we went to discover the psychodynamic . . .'

'How come you go *there*?' he interrupted. He never looked at her, but gazed calmly into the audience.

When she started to stumble, he said, 'So why did you go there?'

I felt a wave of anxiety coming over me.

She began to talk, but he interrupted her again and said: 'You are getting entangled in too many different things . . . You are like a woman who sleeps with everybody, not knowing where her deep love lies. This is a sign of total ignorance and confusion.'

It was embarrassing to witness this. It sounded like a domestic row.

'Why did you go there? Huh?'

'I am exploring different methods to . . .'

'No, you're all over the place,' he said, still looking into the audience. 'This is not devotion or loyalty, this sounds like betrayal.'

'No, it's not betrayal,' she said, and clasped her hands in her lap.

He was silent for a second.

'No? What is it?'

She hesitated. 'I don't know.'

'No, you don't know. If you want to continue with the truth, remain in your seat. If you want to continue living in chaos with a fragmented confused attitude, then go. This is your chance. Now see who is so smug and brash to run all over the place.' He paused. 'Just go! It is really simple to go now. Go!' He flicked his hand towards the door.

It felt like watching a reality TV show.

'No.' She remained seated, her shoulders falling slightly forward.

Peter looked at me and moved his eyes quickly to the door, indicating that he wanted to walk out. I wanted to stand up but hesitated. If we left, we'd be showing support to Creative, but we would have an argument on our hands with Simon. Also this was not our business. All these people were adults, making their own choices.

The argument went on for a long time. Simon's voice remained calm, but his words were persistently pestering. It looked more like a quarrel about power than a search of truth.

'This is what I would call betrayal,' Simon continued. 'Not betrayal towards me, but towards the truth. You have left satsang, the truth, behind. You can go any time you want.'

I wished the girl would stand up and go, but she didn't.

Nobody said anything.

'What is it that you want, Srijani?' This was the first time he looked at her, and he had changed his voice to a more gentle tone.

She looked at her hands, her head fell forward and then she started crying. Her fingers pressed on her eyes.

'Don't know.'

'Now, Srijani, that is the best position to be in.' He moved forward on his chair. 'To admit not to know is to be able to look clearly. But if you think you know, you are lost. The usefulness of a pot comes from its emptiness. Empty yourself of everything, let your mind become still. You follow?'

'Yes,' she sobbed submissively.

'Now look at me.'

She looked at him. He now smiled in a very friendly manner.

'Feel yourself becoming quiet. Very calm.'

She closed her eyes. We waited for what felt like a long time.

'You are tremendously loved here,' he said at last.

She looked up at him. She took a deep breath and seemed to relax a bit.

'Be here a hundred per cent. Enter this moment. This is your opportunity to take it in completely. This is the truth: you are tremendously loved.'

They sat in silence, locked eyes and smiled at each other. After what felt like ten minutes, she slowly stood up and walked back to her place.

How often had this happened before? It seemed to me an awful humiliation. But I was up next—the naming ceremony—and I had received a quick lesson in what not to do. I decided to play the game, or at least restore the atmosphere to something more positive.

Simon looked at me, nodded, and I walked to the chair.

'Welcome,' he said. He looked as if he had forgotten the argument with his girlfriend already.

I took the seat. We looked each other in the eye. I felt my heart beating in my throat. Relax, for God's sake, I told myself.

'Why did you agree to take a name?'

Here we go, this is the test, I thought. It's about the right words. Use the symbolic language.

'We don't live in a house,' I began. 'We live in a tent. We live in the forest, in the mountains, in nature. We know the wind, and how to be flexible and agile. We know the sunshine, and how to be warm from the inside out. We know the thunder and the lightning, how to endure, to wait. We know the mountains and how to keep still. I don't mean the knowledge from the head, but the knowing from the core.'

This at least was true. These words took me away from the horrible argument, and made me drift into the natural world where everything is indifferent, where you could die in a lightning storm but you could not be hurt and manipulated by words.

'We know the divine within the natural world, but not the divine within the human world.' I paused. Did I sound convincing? 'I will carry the name you will give me. And with the name I will carry your divine energy from here—to there.' I pointed outside. 'In that way, we carry your blessing. So the forest and the waterways will be blessed, wherever we go.'

Simon nodded slowly and took a deep breath. Our eyes were locked for what felt like five minutes.

'Your name will be Diana,' he said. 'The goddess of the hunt. She knew how to take life to nourish herself and others. She understood the principle of life and death and the cycle of nature. Everything that lives has to die. Because she was the huntress, she understood the animals more than anyone, so she was also the guardian of all wild animals and the forest. She was pure and talented—and sometimes unpredictable. Would you be able to receive this name?'

'I would be very grateful.' I said. I folded my hands in the Hindu greeting posture. Then I turned to the audience. 'And thank you, my dear friends.' I bowed.

The room was radiating with smiling faces. There was only one exception, and that was Peter. His smile was of a different nature. His eyes were twinkling and he seemed to be grinning . . . no, laughing. He made no sound, but I could see his tummy moving. I winked, and took my place next to him.

'Fooled them this time, didn't we, Bobby?' he whispered.

L ater that night, I reflected on what I had witnessed. Simon's girlfriend had questioned his authority. He had punished her by shaming her, threatening her with rejection. He tried to ostracise her, make her a social outcast. She fought back but in the end she repented. She was made to feel lonely, then allowed back in—as long as she promised to behave.

I thought about a book I had once read about breaking in horses. Monty Roberts had developed his 'join-up' method by observing herds of wild horses. When a young horse misbehaved, the maternal leader would push it away aggressively. The youngster would suddenly feel isolated and scared, and do anything to be allowed back in the herd.

The more I thought about it, the more it seemed obvious that any group requires obedience in order to function. I had experienced a similar thing in school, families, groups of friends, and even my relationship with Peter. Any misbehaviour is punished by the threat of becoming an outcast. It suddenly occurred to me that we comply with the rules because of the fear of being alone.

If I didn't have that fear, I wondered, what would my life look like? How much of my life is influenced by this fear? The question lingered for a long time in the back of my mind.

A few days later, we thanked Simon for his hospitality and said goodbye. Divine Energy, Beautiful and her son Aksel took us to the station, from where we would take a train to the city and then a bus to Slovenia. I swung the little boy for the last time onto my shoulders and gave him a hug while his feet were dangling from the ground.

On board, we stood by the window and waved. Aksel ran along the platform as the train slid away. When he ran past the end of the platform roof, he found himself in the rain and stopped. He waved with both hands, then he dropped his arms sideways to imitate a flying bird.

We were heading for Bulgaria.

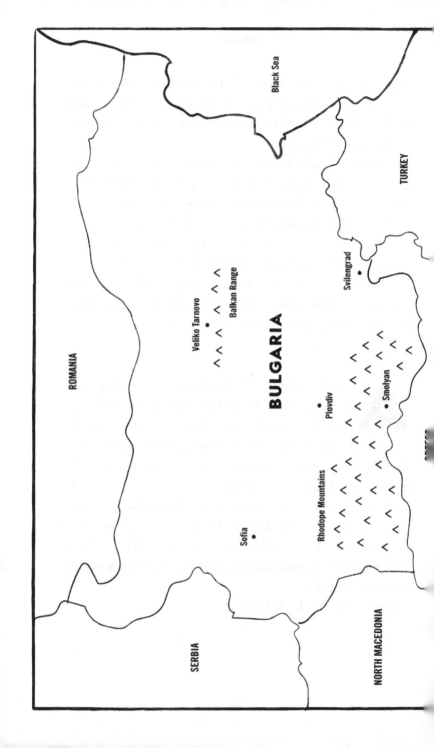

CHAPTER 4

BULGARIA
UNEXPECTED
MEETINGS

I t rained all the way through Austria. As the bus cut straight through the mountains, we disappeared into long, dark tunnels and re-entered the world to more depressing drizzle. Mist seemed to settle in the mountains, announcing the beginning of a wet autumn.

The moment we crossed the border into Slovenia the whole

atmosphere changed. The sky was blue. It was dry and pleasant. I sighed with relief when I felt the warm sunshine on my skin. It was as if we had moved into a land where people were more important than the law. We were suddenly feeling relaxed and free. For some reason it felt as if we had escaped a sort of prison.

After a couple of days' bus travel, we arrived in Belgrade, the capital of Serbia. We had expected to be instantly reminded of the war that raged here twenty years ago, but we found the city far from threatening. Grass here was allowed to seed, wild flowers were left alone. Traffic was chaotic, cars swirling around holes in the asphalt, but it felt vibrant.

We asked directions to a campground, and a young woman walked us to a bus station. With our packs and walking sticks, we took up much space in the full bus.

'Where do you want to go?' asked a friendly older man. We told him, and he looked on his cellphone for directions. A woman joined in. While she searched on her phone, two other young men right in the back of the bus checked too. In the end we counted five different people trying to give us directions. When at last we reached our destination, we stepped out and waved goodbye to the entire bus. Because of the lack of streetlights, we walked the last kilometre in the pitch dark—but were welcomed at the campsite with a sip of *rakia* by the owner.

Next day we woke up to a blue sky and saw that we were on the bank of the Danube—the third great European river we had camped beside. How different each one was. The Danube was enormous, flowing through great plains.

We felt like we had landed on our feet. We could afford the campground, we made friends on the first night, found a wild apple tree, and were allowed to light a fire in the dry grass to cook.

We were busy peeling a bucket of wild stewing apples when the campground owner came by. He was a tall, lanky figure with short dark hair and a generous black moustache. He squatted next to us. We chatted for a long a time, and in the end he asked where we were going.

Peter pointed east. 'Bulgaria.'

'Bad choice.' The man shook his head. 'You will be disappointed there. Compared to Serbia, people are distant and unfriendly.'

'Doesn't everyone say that about their neighbours?' I laughed. 'That's why they made a border in the first place, no?'

'There used to be eight million people in Bulgaria, there are only five million left. Everyone is leaving for jobs in the West and Russia. That says something, doesn't it? They call it the fastest shrinking country in the world! I haven't been there, but I've heard the stories.'

We took a bus across the border, and were unimpressed with what we saw. The place looked run down, towns were ugly, and large parts of Sofia, the capital, were degraded and in decline. EU money had built an expensive metro system, and from the bus we saw flash-looking buildings with Citroen, BMW, Toyota and other big names emblazoned on them. The big companies had nestled themselves next to the new highway, as if waiting for Bulgaria to become developed.

'What shall we do here?' asked Peter.

'Don't know,' I said.

We were not very enthusiastic about Bulgaria. Maybe the Moustache was right.

After two days' travel, we arrived in the city of Veliko Tarnovo, where we were picked up by the woman who had contacted us by email in Austria: Susan.

She was tall, with a tanned face and high cheekbones, dark hair that reached her shoulders and a fringe. Like me—and many other Dutch people—she talked loudly, laughed loudly, and was very well organised and enthusiastic. She drove us out of the city into the countryside. We saw rolling hills, fields of crops and a lot of what seemed to be barren land. Towards the south we could see the forested Balkan mountains.

Our destination was a small village on the banks of the Yantra river. There was an old factory, now closed, with all its windows broken. Some of the houses were empty and half fallen down. The streets were quiet and weeds had overtaken the village square, but the trees had grown and the grapes were thriving in people's gardens. Fruit and nut trees were everywhere. If New Zealand was the place for hunting wild animals, Bulgaria was going to be the land for gathering wild food.

Susan explained many things, while pointing out trees and places of interest. We came to a house with a big garden. 'A young Bulgarian couple with two toddlers live here,' she said. 'They know so much about gardening, bottling fruit, gathering mushrooms, making jam, distilling rakia. Their knowledge is extraordinary! I'll introduce them to you tomorrow! Or would you like to meet them right now?' She put her foot on the brake and we came to an instant halt.

'Tomorrow will do,' smiled Peter.

Susan lived with her husband and three children in a yurt on a small plot. We camped around the corner in the large garden of her Bulgarian friend, Galya.

After we pitched the tent under the oaks, I lay down in the dry leaves. Apart from some birdsong, it was silent. We were in a country with hardly any people—every day there were fewer. I closed my eyes and the weight seemed to fall off me.

The air was dry, and smelled of leaves and wood and grass. The treetops were moving slowly in the breeze. I heard a rustle and saw a black squirrel running to the top of a tree, jumping from branch to branch, tree to tree. A little later, a second one followed.

I felt as if I could truly rest for the first time since we had arrived in Europe. What is the price we pay, I thought, for relentless busyness and background noise?

In the afternoon we met with Galya, who lived below us in a picturesque stone house with her four-year-old daughter Rada. Galya was twenty-nine, and an English and Hindi teacher. She had travelled a lot, and was familiar with different cultures. After she had Rada, she decided to leave the capital and move to the countryside to give her child a very different upbringing.

We chatted with Galya, and I ignored her little girl for some time, thinking she would not speak English. Eventually, I squatted down and said slowly:

'Hello. What—is—your—name?'

'I'm Rada,' she answered, looking at me. 'My mum read your book and told me so many stories about you! How you live in a tent, hunt wild animals and so forth. It's really nice to finally meet you.'

My mouth fell open. This four-and-a-half-year-old Bulgarian girl had an extraordinary command of English.

'Sometimes I feel like exploring myself, and I go into the forest,' she continued: 'I really like it, that you just survive in the wild, with your . . . what's the thing you usually use to hunt with?'

'Bow?' I couldn't believe my ears. The English term *'usually use'* I had learned when I was about twenty years old.

I n this village there were five other families from all over the world who had similar views about the education system. Every day, the children played together and along the way they learned each other's language, read words and practised writing—without the use of any official structure. The parents valued natural skills and being outside. I respected their courage to stand against an education system they didn't want for their children.

Rada often came to visit us at our camp. She had selected a flat stone for a chair, which suited her well: it was like a little throne. She had an aura of confidence and good nature, and her facial expressions and gestures were exceptionally advanced, too. The little girl seemed to have an incredible presence about her. After we got to know her, we had the impression that it was Rada who should be called Chunmay—the supreme consciousness—rather than Simon.

We had noticed that Bulgarian people nod when they mean 'No', and shake their head when they indicate 'Yes'. When I asked Rada why, she looked at the ground and pondered for a while. 'I don't really know the answer to that. But I guess those gestures are quite abotray anyway. Abotray?'

'Arbitrary.'

'Yes, arbitrary. Because is there actually a real reason why it should be the other way around?'

We chatted a while longer, then she said she had to go back to the house to see her grandparents who had come to visit. She promised she'd be back.

An hour later, she reappeared out of the thickets. She had just walked a zig-zag path of fifty metres in the pitch dark without a flashlight. The day before, she and I had seen a big snake on that same track.

'Are you not afraid in the dark, Rada?'

'It's only the back yard!' She shrugged, and took a seat on her stone again. 'I have been here a hundred times.'

'What about that snake?'

'I stamp like an elephant. This will make him go away, right?'

Another time I was just busy cracking and eating walnuts, and Rada quietly joined me. A grey cat turned up. It was one of the two cats we had seen a lot around the place. The creature crawled into Peter's lap. When he began stroking it, it purred happily.

'Nice cat,' said Peter. 'Hmm. Very nice indeed. Even tasty perhaps,' he murmured. 'I'd love to eat it. Can I eat your cat?' asked Peter as a joke, and I worried if Rada would appreciate his sense of humour.

'No!' she said, not shocked or surprised. 'No, you can't really.'

'Why not?'

'Because it's not my cat!'

One day we were walking with Rada when she led us off the trail and through the forest. Eventually we came out at a big rock. She took us around the stone and climbed on top of it.

'This is a very special one,' she said, and looked at us expectantly. 'Do you see it?'

'See what?' I asked, but she didn't answer. We couldn't quite understand what she was trying to convey. I wondered what energies or entities we are not able to see anymore—which senses we had lost during adulthood.

She led us back to the path, then we came to the river, where she tried climbing a tree. I lifted her up to the first branch, and noticed she seemed uneasy. This wasn't the usual impatience of most four year olds who want to try everything themselves. It was as though she found it a little annoying to be so small that she needed help. Almost as though she was surprised to be in a child's body.

'*Pas op, pas op!*' she said, before jumping down.

'Can you speak Dutch as well?' I said.

'Not really, but I hear the Dutch kids talking all the time.'

She told me the other words she had learned, and I was astonished by her flawless pronunciation.

We loved our several weeks' stay in the village. The evening before we left, everyone came to say goodbye.

'Well, you have been very nice company,' Rada said on our last morning, when it was just the three of us. 'Thank you so much for your visit. Don't forget the snack my mum made for you.' She moved the Bulgarian pastry closer to us. 'Are you going home today?'

'No, we don't have a home!'

'Oh, yes, I forgot. You are going to explore the world again. But you can also stay at my house.' She lifted her eyebrows and nodded. 'Forever, if you wish. You are welcome here any time you like.'

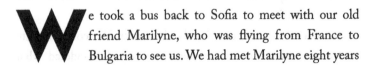e took a bus back to Sofia to meet with our old friend Marilyne, who was flying from France to Bulgaria to see us. We had met Marilyne eight years

earlier when I was working as a physical education teacher in New Zealand, and we had kept in touch ever since. She had hiked a lot in France, Canada and other places, and was keen to see Bulgaria on her month-long holiday. So, instead of travelling onwards to Turkey, we decided to stay in the country and walk the Rhodope mountains with her.

Marilyne is French, about the same age as me and very kind and easy-going. It is almost impossible to imagine her angry. An ecologist, she is extremely knowledgeable and precise about the smallest plant or animal. She is also a brilliant artist, and spends much time drawing and painting. She, Peter and I liked each other very much, and we formed a good team.

None of us had been in Eastern Europe and we could not speak a word of Bulgarian. We had no idea where to go, and everything was new, which was both exciting and a little daunting. We found a very inexact and rough map of the Rhodope region, boarded a bus and left the city behind.

In the lowlands it was hot and dry; the temperature felt about 25° Celsius. From the city of Plovdiv in the south, we went into the hills, and the higher we went, the colder it became. It was now October, and the leaves were already changing colour.

At some ugly, Soviet-looking town, we transferred into a minivan with Bulgarian pop-music playing from the speakers. The sounds and language made me feel as if we were in Central Asia, and I liked it very much. I looked at Marilyne, who grinned back excitedly.

We plodded slowly up the winding roads, alongside deep gorges and steep rocky cliffs. The old minibus stopped for anyone who happened to be walking on the side of the road. We passed old Russian mopeds, horses and donkeys, and every now and then an expensive car overtook us at great speed.

The higher we went, the more rustic the villages became. The mountains had slowed time, and warded off progress and technology; the old people were still living in traditional ways. The houses here were built with large stones, and each dwelling had its own vegetable garden.

By the time we reached the end of the road, there were only two elderly women left with us on the bus. They were dressed in old-fashioned skirts and scarves, and moved with surprising agility. We followed them out and stepped straight into the cold air. We were now at an elevation of over fifteen hundred metres. It felt no warmer than 10° and mist was hanging between forested peaks.

The streets were empty. There were two beautiful old walnut trees surrounding the bus stop. A rooster crowed and smoke was whirling from chimneys, bringing a pleasant smell of wood fire to the village. While we were shouldering our packs, the women gathered their plastic bags full of household articles from the rear of the van. They asked us something in Bulgarian.

'Where will you sleep tonight?' translated the bus driver.

'In the tent,' said Peter.

'The old lady here invites you into her house.'

'Thank you so much. But we are going . . . there.' He pointed at the valley above the village.

'They are going there,' said the driver to the women, and also pointed at the valley.

They looked incredulous and spoke again to the driver.

'Very cold there. You freeze. There are bears. And wolves. Better you come to inside,' he said to us.

'She'll be right,' said Peter in his New Zealand accent.

'She is all right?' asked Marilyne, confused.

'He means that we will be okay,' I explained.

The man translated for the women, and we waved goodbye.

We walked up the road that quickly turned into a dirt track. We set off in a good mood, but I hadn't forgotten the warning. I had no experience with dangerous animals, and felt nervous just hearing the word bear.

'They don't attack people,' said Peter.

'How do you know?' I asked. He had never been in Europe before. He had never had anything to do with bears in his life.

'Oh, they might snatch a lamb,' he said, 'but they don't eat people. Bears have learned that humans are tricky little monkeys, they won't do us any harm. In fact, they will smell us and move away.'

'In Canada I walked on my own for ten days through bear country,' said Marilyne. 'I constantly made noise and rang my bell to ward them off. I was taught to put food in the tree, well away from camp, and eat in a different place from where I slept.'

'That's Canada with grizzlies and all,' said Peter. 'Here the bears are a lot more friendly. I've never heard of any person getting killed by a bear in Eastern Europe.'

A t this time of year, the days were getting noticeably shorter. The late afternoon felt like evening. We walked about five kilometres out of the village and as the sun disappeared behind the mountaintops we came to a river valley. We pitched our tents under a tree, lit a fire, drank from the river and cooked rice with vegetables. We were not terribly far from the last house, but already it felt very wild, and the possibility of bears and wolves lingered.

The moment the sun had fully set, the temperature dropped below zero. We followed up Marilyne's suggestion of hanging all the food in the tree, away from the tents.

'Euh, Peter? Maybe we should not brush our teeth in the camp,' said Marilyne. She had a sweet, soft voice that made me want to agree with everything she said.

'Oh,' said Peter with his mouth full of foam, 'Too late. I have already spat it on the ground. See, here.'

We looked at the white blob of toothpaste in the grass.

'Toothpaste is a very strong smell,' said Marilyne. 'It might attract the bears.'

'If the bear can smell that,' I said, 'it can also smell my breath at night!'

'Well, let's do whatever we can to stop bears coming into the tent,' Marilyne said.

'Should we then *not* brush our teeth?'

'Hmm.' She took the question seriously. 'Rinse your mouth thoroughly maybe? Best to spit the toothpaste out in the creek.'

We sat close around the campfire to keep warm and sipped our tea. Around us, the darkness came with silence. The first stars appeared. When we felt too cold we crawled into our sleeping bags.

A few hours later I woke up for a pee. The air outside was freezing. Back in my sleeping bag I couldn't warm up. I was already wearing all of my clothes and my woollen hat, and decided there was only one way to get my blood flowing again.

'What are you doing?' whispered Peter.

'Push-ups,' I whispered back. 'To get warm!'

We went back to sleep. Sometime later I woke up to a sound in the distance. I lay dead still, all my senses directed to the noise. It was definitely a big animal, but it was impossible to know what. It came closer, and I could hear something stepping on stones. Then we heard a snorting sound and the clatter of several animals.

'Horses!' I whispered to Peter. We zipped the tent open, and looked out to see the sharp silhouettes of five beautiful horses grazing in the riverbed. The plumes of their breath were visible in the pale moonlight. They placed their hooves gracefully between the stones and moved along slowly. It was so still and beautiful.

Their presence made me feel very safe. It felt like the most natural thing in the world to have horses peacefully grazing around our camp at night. They were not afraid of us, and must have belonged to the village people.

The next day, a three-hour walk took us to a village at the end of a dirt road. The place was quiet and only half the houses appeared inhabited. An old woman was splitting wood in the middle of the street, using the type of double-headed curved axe that I had only ever seen in medieval drawings.

Another old lady sat in the sun in front of her house. We greeted her, and when her husband turned up he began talking enthusiastically, using his hands to make himself understood. He asked where we would sleep.

Marilyne took her notebook and drew a tent.

'*Palatka!*' said the woman, delighted to understand it. I found some paper and wrote down my first Bulgarian word phonetically: *palatka*.

Then Marilyne drew a little bear.

'*Mechka*!' The old lady shook her head, pointed at the forest and mimicked a frightful face.

Matchka, I wrote.

'And this?' Marilyne had drawn a little fire.

'*Ogun.*' It sounded like *organ*.

'Fire good?' signalled Marilyne.

They shook their head, meaning yes. Fire was not a problem. So we learned our first Bulgarian words: tent, bear and fire. The rest of the day we repeated the three words out loud.

With help from our map, we followed a dirt road that seemed to run parallel to the border with Greece. It led to an abandoned house, and after that turned into a small walking path. We aimed to ascend five hundred metres to the top of a mountain, follow the range and descend to the other side where, according to the map, we would find a village again. This leg of the journey would take about a week.

We followed the track, but it became increasingly vague. In the end we were merely guessing. When the path was most definitely gone, we sat down. The sun was high up in the sky, and we ate walnuts, some bread and cheese.

'I'm glad you are both very experienced in all this, but do we know where we are?' asked Marilyne tentatively.

'Yes, well, not the exact spot,' said Peter. 'There is no indication of altitude on this map, so I can't see clearly where the pass is. The map is actually not so useful. And the treeline is very high up, so we can't climb above the trees to look out. Orientation is a little bit of a challenge at this point.'

Marilyne switched on her phone. For a few expensive minutes we stared expectantly at the GPS on her screen. It showed a vague map of a big area, but Marilyne could not ascertain where we were. Eventually she gave up, and switched it off.

'It doesn't really matter,' I said. 'We have enough food for a week, we can roam for a long time. Eventually we will come out somewhere. You can live for many days without food. As long as we find some water.'

'That's a good point, where *is* water?' said Peter.

We all fell silent, trying to hear the sound of a creek.

'Well, it can't be far away,' I said. 'This country doesn't strike me as being too dry.'

'Shall we follow the compass? Going south-east?' asked Peter.

I felt a spark of excitement. This was starting to feel like a real expedition.

Peter was leading, Marilyne followed him and I was at the tail end. At first the forest was quite open and not too steep. We could walk at a good pace. But then the vegetation became thicker. We pushed our way through branches, sidled around patches of blackberries and didn't make much progress.

Then Peter walked towards an open clearing. He stopped and looked down. We gathered around him without a word, and saw in the mud a clear footprint. It looked like a gigantic human foot. There was the ball of the foot, five toes and five nails: *a bear*.

The mud was wet, the prints were fresh. I closed my eyes for a second. Here we were, lost in a Bulgarian forest, not a soul to be seen, but bears all around us.

Marilyne fell on her knees: 'Oh, wow! What a fantastic footprint!' she cried. '*Magnifique*! Look at those toes!'

'This is quite a big animal,' said Peter, crouching down too.

While they were inspecting the print, I was looking around for the bear.

'I think maybe at least three hundred kilos!' Marilyne found her camera and took many pictures.

'I am so glad that Bulgarian bears are not dangerous,' I said.

'Yes, well,' Marilyne stood up again. 'I wasn't going to tell this story, because I didn't want to scare you . . . but I have two good friends from Paris. Last year they went to Romania on a holiday. You know, Romania is not that far from here. They went to a campground, but it was quite noisy, so they put their tent something like fifty metres away. When it was dark, a young bear came, clawed the tent open and took the leg of the girl. While she was trying to move away, the bear ripped the man open, from his throat to his stomach.' Marilyne demonstrated the length of the wound on her own body. 'People heard them, some help came and the bear ran away. They both had to go straight to the hospital for surgery because they were severely injured. They were lucky to survive actually.'

'Jesus . . .'

'Yes, it was quite an incomprehensible attack. The bear wasn't after food, but just seemed to be angry. Maybe the fact that they were near a campground had something to do with it. I don't know, but see, these attacks do happen, I mean, these are not stories I heard of, these are my own friends. They now live in an apartment in Paris and are still afraid of the dark. They want to sleep with the lights on all the time. They even need psychological help, like counselling.'

We stared at the prints for a minute, then Marilyne shouldered her pack again.

'Do you want to continue,' asked Peter, 'or shall we turn back to the last village to ask directions? This map is really quite useless.'

'Do you know how to go back?' asked Marilyne.

'Of course. We came this way. We've been following this spur for some time, and we will come out in the valley again if we keep going west.'

Peter led the way back in silence. Our footsteps in the leaves suddenly sounded very loud. I kept peering into the trees to detect movement in the distance, and was startled at every strange sound. After Marilyne's story I felt a lot more insecure in the mountains and wondered how I would like the nights, when fears always seemed to multiply.

By the time we were back at the dirt road it was almost dark, and we stopped to make a camp where we could see some houses in the distance. Assuming that bears would give villages a wide berth, I felt safe and had quite a good night.

Next morning we walked back into the village. The same couple sat at the same house. They were surprised to see us back so soon. The woman rushed inside and brought us a plastic bottle with runny yogurt in it. Peter tried to give her some money, but she wouldn't accept it.

In the village shop we found a man who spoke a few words of English. He drew a map on a piece of paper that showed the quickest way to hike over the mountain range, and we set off on a dirt road. This time we were determined not to stray off the track.

We walked for many hours, and came to the top of the range from where we could look far and wide. We sat down and poured the liquid yogurt into a cup. I took a sip. The taste was so strong my whole face wrinkled up. Marilyne mixed in some vanilla powder she'd brought from France, and it tasted much better. While Peter and I enjoyed the brilliant panorama of forested ranges, Marilyne began searching behind us for more signs of animals.

'Wolf shit!' she yelled. 'Over here! Come and look!'

We gazed at her wolf faeces as she explained in detail why it belonged to a wolf and not a dog. She picked it apart and showed us what it had been eating.

'*Oh là là*, we're in such a wild place!' She looked up at us, her eyes showing wonder and excitement.

F or days we followed the dirt track through the forested mountains along the border with Greece. Sometimes we had a panoramic view of the many high peaks in the seemingly endless ranges. We had only a rough idea of where we were until we spotted an ancient Orthodox monastery in the distance that was marked on our map. It was both strange and wonderful to walk through such wilderness, and the only building we could see across the ranges was an old monastery.

Eventually, we came to a natural grass clearing where a stream had carved a narrow channel. With good drinking water, the place was perfect for a campsite. Marilyne and I pitched our tents side by side while Peter collected firewood.

When the sleeping gear was all organised, we cooked a dinner of fish pasta with plantain, dandelion and yarrow we had found along the way. Afterwards we hung up all our food in the fir trees.

The darkness came quickly and cold air rolled down the mountains.

'There could be wolves here,' said Marilyne as we sat around the fire. 'If they have been on the top, they could be here in this valley. Shall we call them?'

'*Call them?*'

'I have done it in France as part of a research team. We sit in the forest at specific GPS coordinates. Then we call wolves and count the replies. It gives an estimation of existing numbers. It is really good fun.'

I imagined calling out, hearing a reply, and then the wolf coming closer, like a roaring stag coming to the hunter.

'I'm quite happy to know that they exist, but I really don't need to see them right now,' I said, and felt a bit of a wimp next to Marilyne.

'Are you scared?' She laughed. 'Hey, wolves are shy and don't attack people.'

'We thought that about bears too, before you told us that story,' I said.

Eventually we went to bed. We chatted a while through the tent fabric, then wished each other good night. It was silent; the creek made no sound and it was wind-still.

Then, half an hour later, I heard something. It sounded like a big animal that had knocked over something heavy. It certainly wasn't a horse this time. I lifted my head out of the sleeping bag so as to hear more clearly. There were sounds of breaking wood in the forest. They didn't seem too far away.

'Do you hear that?' I whispered.

We kept silent. All of us were listening.

'There is an animal trying to get our food, right now.' Marilyne spoke as though she was witnessing it.

We stared into the darkness.

'Well, what are we going to do about it?' said Peter. 'The next village is three days' walk from here. We cannot afford to lose that food.'

'Don't worry about the food,' I said, 'as long as he doesn't come and eat us!'

'Indeed,' said Marilyne.

'I won't let any bear take our supplies! We've got to protect it!' said Peter. 'Who will come with me?'

I said nothing.

Neither did Marilyne.

'Well, who's coming?' said Peter again. He was getting out of his sleeping bag.

'No, don't go!' I imagined a bear running at us at in the middle of a dark forest, and felt my heart in my throat.

'If you two are too scared, I'll go on my own.' He switched on his solar-panel torch. It had not been charged for a few days and the light was a little bit on the weak side. He picked up his walking stick and a knife.

'Are you sure you want to carry all that?' I asked.

'Well, it would be good if you could hold the flashlight!' he said.

'Have a look first, and if you see something, call out and we will come and help,' I said, knowing that it was a pathetic plan of action.

He grunted some sort of agreement, then he left.

Soon it was completely silent again. I lay down and stared into the darkness. My whole body was tense. I felt such a coward. I was terrified the bear would attack Peter, but I was even more frightened of going out myself.

Somewhere out there, Peter was looking around for a bear, with a stick and a knife.

'I hope he will be all right,' I said softly.

'Hmm,' said Marilyne from the other tent.

Eventually I asked, 'Do you have a headlight?' I considered going out. Then I saw flashes of light on the tent, and the sound of Peter's footsteps.

'Absolutely nothing!' he called from the distance. 'There was nothing! You girls are hearing ghost-bears! The bags of food were untouched!'

'Untouched? We must have heard something else,' said Marilyne meekly.

'Well, it was certainly no bear eating our food!' said Peter as he came into the tent. Then everybody was talking and laughing at the same time. 'Holy moly! I was so scared!'

'Me too!' called Marilyne. 'Peter went to fight the bear! Peter is our 'ero!'

'Yes, our 'ero!' I shouted.

'Good god,' laughed Peter.

Next morning we rolled up our tents and continued the journey.

One afternoon the sun was shining and the red leaves were accompanied by a sweet earthy smell that belonged to the autumn. The peaceful atmosphere wiped away my fear of bears, and I wondered if I would be brave enough to walk by myself.

I told Peter and Marilyne my plans, and increased my pace to get ahead. Following the path for half an hour or so, I kept my eyes open for movement. I went quietly, alert for any swish or crack. Without our chatter, the forest seemed especially silent. My senses were alert—as though I was hunting, but this time I was the prey and the bear was the predator. What would I do if I saw one? Bears could climb trees, and outrun me easily. I would have little choice but to surrender. It was extraordinary to feel so vulnerable.

I kept alert, constantly looking—and spotted movement high up in the tree. It was a huge black chicken. I was surprised to see it so far into the forest, and watched it for some time. Eventually it flew away, and I carried on.

'What? You saw a *black chicken*?' said Marilyne when she and Peter caught up with me. 'That could have been a *Tetrao urogallus*! Western capercaillie—sometimes they call them wood grouse. They are extremely rare. It is amazing you saw one! Where did you see it?'

We walked ten minutes back where I had seen the bird, but there was no sign of it now. Marilyne climbed twenty metres down a steep slope to search the ground beneath the tree for droppings.

'*Oui, oui!* I found some grouse sheet!' She took her time taking pictures before joining us back on the track.

'They are very heavy, so flying is no joke for them. In the winter they need so much energy to keep warm that they cannot afford to fly. If you disturb one and they are forced to fly, it could kill them!'

'Do you think this one died after it flew away?' I asked.

She was reassuring. 'No, only in the snowy winter, when it is below zero.'

After a week in the mountains, we made it to the first village on the other side. As soon as we saw one of the residents, Marilyne threw her pack down and took out her notebook. She drew with surprising speed a picture of the rare wood grouse.

'You know this?' she asked.

The elderly woman shook her head, meaning yes. She put up her thumb and said something that sounded like potatoes, and motioned eating with a spoon.

'She likes to fry the grouse with potatoes,' said Peter dryly.

Marilyne looked at her, searching for words. The woman looked back expectantly, but we could not convey that the wood grouse was on the brink of extinction, and should not be eaten with potatoes.

The next day we came to a village that had an old mosque with a sickle moon on top of its spire. We had walked from the Christian side of Bulgaria into the Muslim part. Long ago the Turks had invaded this part of the country and converted the people to Islam. But there seemed few other differences. There were old houses with beautiful vegetable gardens, some lazy street dogs on the pavement, gypsies with horse carts, chickens loitering in the berm, a boy leading a donkey down the road while cars swirled around them. It was very pretty, the sun was warm, and we felt content. We stopped at a café for a coffee. We bought some bread, eggs and vegetables.

Then we left the village behind and followed a remote four-wheel-drive road. We were surprised to hear a slow vehicle approaching: police driving a Lada Niva.

'What are you doing?' asked an officer in English.

'We are walking,' said Peter.

He shook his head. 'Good. Where will you sleep?'

'We don't know,' I said, a little on my guard. What were the regulations? Should we pretend we were looking for a campground?

The officer smiled. 'First of all, you camp wherever you like, and light a fire wherever you like. Over there is a very sunny spot, but if you walk one hour further you will come across a clearing with water. Camp anywhere.'

This was starting to sound like heaven.

We chatted some more, then he said, 'Maybe you can help us.

We are looking for a boy of twenty who went missing.'

'Since when?' asked Peter.

'Yesterday.'

'Oh! He just drank too much!' I began to laugh, and mimicked drinking from a bottle. 'He's just sleeping it off under a tree!' I don't know what had come over me, but the more I laughed, the less I could stop. The officer looked at me with amusement. 'Don't worry,' I said, leaning on the bonnet, 'you will see that he is just *drunk*!' I didn't notice that the others weren't laughing so much.

When the Lada drove away, Peter looked angrily at me.

'What?'

'Didn't you see the father sitting next to the policeman? You made a mockery out of it all!'

With a shock I remembered the passenger in plain clothes. I thought of my own parents. My father driving around with the police because I was dead and ditched in the forest. What had I done? Poking fun at the situation would have been so hurtful.

'I feel so guilty for laughing.'

'And so *over the top*!' said Peter, to make matters worse. 'It wasn't just a little chuckle.'

We walked on in silence, and I replayed the whole scene over and over in my mind. I felt very miserable.

Two days later, we came to another village and asked after the boy who had gone missing.

'Oh, Aleksander!' said the shop owner with a dismissive gesture. 'They find him next day at trees. Just drunk. He little crazy. He go missing every time.'

My eyes caught Peter's. 'That is good news,' I said with a grin.

For weeks, Marilyne, Peter and I carried on through the Rhodopes. The nights became increasingly cold, but the days remained warm and sunny. It was a beautiful autumn. The forest around us changed from bright yellow into orange and red. We followed little pathways, sometimes dirt roads, sometimes deserted asphalt roads.

In some of the most isolated villages we were met by inhospitable looks—frowning faces and wrinkled noses. That's when I realised that the inhabitants had so little contact with the outside world that they were not aware of their own expressions. Always after the first greeting, they turned most friendly and helpful.

Often we saw bear prints in the mud. They still made me nervous, but without bears and wolves the place would have been barren in some ways. This was their territory and we were merely visitors.

It was not always easy to keep that perspective. One day we climbed a hill through the forest and came out at some pasture. Ahead of us was a flock of sheep—and five dogs that ran towards us, barking viciously. Three of the dogs were enormous.

'I've never seen so many dogs for a flock of just fifty sheep,' said Peter while we moved away from the sheep. 'Those big Anatolian shepherd dogs are for chasing away bears!'

A little further on we found a place to camp among a patch of oaks. It was a conveniently flat spot and the autumn colours were brilliant. It was only after we'd pitched the tents that Marilyne spotted some bear shit. Bears love acorns, we realised too late.

We lit a fire and Peter fried up a bit of meat we had bought from a village shop a couple of days earlier. It was very fatty, and without much thought he poured the fat on the ground.

The darkness grew around us, and nobody was in a hurry to leave the safety of the fire and retreat to the tent.

'That was a bit stupid of me to pour the fat on the ground,' said Peter.

'Yes,' I said.

'Yes,' said Marilyne.

Eventually, we had to face the night. We crawled into our sleeping bags and discovered we were in the most unfortunate place. It was the time of falling acorns, and every time one came down it made the leaves rustle, exactly as though a big animal was taking three steps.

I had never been more afraid in my life. All night long, I expected a bear clawing through the tent at any moment.

After waking up a hundred times, it was an extraordinary relief to find the morning clear and the three of us unharmed. I felt incredibly cheerful—the complete opposite of how I'd felt during the night.

When we arrived at the next village a couple of days later, we heard that around the time we had been in the area a bear had attacked two sheep from that particular mob in that field.

Towards the end of Marilyne's month with us, it became very cold. We had walked through so many beautiful, half-empty villages that we wondered whether we could rent a place for some weeks before Peter's visa expired and we would have to leave the European Union. But how could we possibly make ourselves understood in a place where so few people spoke English? Then one day we came to a village where a small crowd of people were waiting in front of an empty shop for the supply truck from the nearest town. We sat down too.

We waited for an hour or so, until the supplier came roaring around the corner, and everybody sprang into action and unloaded the supplies. When it was our turn to do some shopping, we discovered the man spoke English.

'A place for rent?' he asked, a little surprised. He talked to the people in the shop and pointed at a strong-looking young man with a bald head. 'He has place for rent, but look first. Very primitive.'

Our prospective new landlord, called Dimitri, spoke no English at all, but he had a friend with him who had worked in Germany. So we conversed in German, and discovered it would take only twenty minutes to drive to the cottage in their little four-wheel-drive. Would we mind sitting tight?

Peter was squeezed underneath his pack on his lap. Marilyne sat half on my lap, half on her pack and was literally folded double. I was squashed between her and our packs. With every bump, Marilyne hit her head against the roof. The little vehicle forded creeks, drove over humps, through hollows and stretches of mud, and eventually came to a standstill. When Dimitri at last opened the door, we rolled out.

In front of us was a nice-looking cottage at the top of a tiny, near-derelict mountain village. The panorama over the valley below was astonishing. The place was so quiet we could hear only the sound of flowing water next to the cottage where a pipe provided eternally gushing water. The downstairs area inside had once been an animal shed, which Dimitri had converted into a kind of a living room. There was no tap in the house, but there was electricity for lights and upstairs were two beautiful bedrooms.

There was only one old man remaining in the village—right next to our little cottage, just fifty metres away from us. His name was Zdravko. He had seven sheep, two goats, three dogs, a cow with a calf, a cat and a ruin of a house. From his window he looked straight down into our yard. He greeted us cheerfully and seemed happy with the prospect of company. It was clear from the start that we were going to live with Zdravko.

We learned that our landlord Dimitri was twenty-nine and currently on leave from serving with the army in Afghanistan. He was a sniper and loved guns, which he aptly demonstrated by firing wildly into the forest. This cottage had once belonged to his father, and Zdravko was his uncle. He used this accommodation when he wanted to go hunting. Next week he would fly back to Afghanistan.

We paid one month's rent, wished Dimitri good luck, and the men left us with the key.

T hat night I slept soundly for the first time in a month. Inside our cottage, we were safe from the bears. Next morning, we were sitting on the edge of a stone wall, drinking tea and admiring the view, when Zdravko wandered down the garden path.

'You want to milk the cow?' he signalled. He had no English, and we could speak only a few words of Bulgarian.

Marilyne and I stood up eagerly.

Near Zdravko's house was a shed where the cow and her calf spent the nights. During the day they grazed in nearby clearings while tethered to a long rope.

The stench in the shed was powerful and penetrating. It was very dark, but I could feel my sandals sinking into the wet cow-shit. Zdravko indicated we should wait outside, took a shovel and pushed the manure into one corner. Then he picked up a three-legged stool, swung it underneath him and started milking. We came back in to watch. This was surely an ancient scene. For centuries people had milked cows on mornings like this one, in mountains like this one, and in sheds just like this one. I glanced at Marilyne. She seemed just as excited as I was.

After a demonstration, Zdravko indicated I should try. I sat down and imitated his movements. It was surprisingly difficult to get any milk out at all. I had to squeeze the udder very tightly, and still the effect was miserable. Marilyne did not perform much better. After a few tiring minutes, Zdravko finished with impressive speed and efficiency.

We walked with him back to his house. While we waited underneath the big walnut tree, he disappeared inside, leaving the milk with us. We looked down. The plastic bucket was unbelievably filthy. There was grey and purple mould growing on the inside. He had not cleaned it in a long time.

Marilyne rolled her eyes. 'How could he drink milk that comes out of such a filthy bucket?'

'I guess it's all right if he boils it,' I said. 'Maybe it aids making yogurt?'

Zdravko reappeared with a sieve and another bucket. Both were also covered in grey mould. He poured half of the milk into the other dirty bucket and handed it to us as a gift.

Thank you, we said—one of the few Bulgarian words we knew. *Merci.*

A little later we sat together in the warm autumn sunshine, eating porridge with creamy milk. Zdravko came down with his cup of sweet black Turkish coffee. He sat calmly, smoked his cigarettes and looked at the view. He was dressed in a blue jumper and black pants. When he took his hat off, I saw that his little remaining hair was white. His eyebrows were still dark, he had a friendly smile, and his brown eyes twinkled when he was amused.

Zdravko had two dogs that were allowed to roam freely. One of them was very healthy-looking, but the other one was so thin it seemed nothing but a skeleton. We called him Skelet and tried to feed him a little extra. A third dog that looked a bit like a small wolf was tied up all the time. Later we understood that if he was let loose, he would hunt the sheep.

There were only a few days left now until Marilyne had to go home. The three of us helped milk the cow, shovelled shit into wheelbarrows, drank a lot of milk, tried Zdravko's yogurt, cracked walnuts, and Marilyne made a beautiful aqua painting of the cow with the materials she had brought with her.

Then Marilyne's holiday was over and she had to go back to work in France.

Zdravko had tears in his eyes when he said goodbye. He had fallen head over heels in love with her. He hugged her and said something while clutching her painting on his chest. Marilyne smiled kindly, and said, '*Merci. Merci beaucoup.*'

O ur life now became very quiet. Every morning, I woke up early. While Peter was sleeping in or reading a book, I wandered over to Zdravko with my pen and notebook.

He had a four-bedroom house, but the second floor was damaged by a leaking roof, so he used just one small room downstairs. There was a bed, a chair and a table with an old television set on it.

Every morning he would open his door with a smile and ask how I was. '*Kaaksi?*'

'*Dobre, dobre.*' Good, I would say, and you?

'Yes, good. Coffee?'

'Yes, please.'

I'd sit on his bed, and he'd disappear into his half-fallen-down kitchen that had one electric plate to cook on. While he produced a tiny cup of sweet Turkish coffee, I'd look at the old photographs of his sister and brother on the wall, and the big Coca-Cola calendar that was two years out of date. When he reappeared, he'd grab a chair that I could use as a coffee table.

I would quietly sip my coffee as he toasted a slice of white bread on his electric heater. For some reason he did not use the firebox in the corner of his room. The electric heater was at least thirty years old, and the thick cord was so damaged in one place that I was surprised it still worked. Zdravko managed to increase the heat by connecting two wires, using conducting tape to protect his fingers. Upon connection, sparks would fly off, and the whole thing looked horribly dangerous to me.

Learning how to say *What is this?* allowed me to discover all the names of things around me. Every morning Zdravko taught me more words, and every evening I would study them until I knew them by heart. Slowly, over the following weeks I learned how to converse.

'What's the name of your cat?' I asked.

'*Kotka*,' he answered.

'Just cat?'

'Yes,' he said. 'Just cat.'

Peter and I always named any animal we saw more than once. Hares that lived around the camp were called Harry; friendly birds, squirrels, even spiders and insects that had found their way into our tent quickly received names. To have a cat without a name was incomprehensible to me. It was as if Zdravko did not want to get attached to anything.

What fascinated me was that Zdravko put up with almost unbearable circumstances. We once had a massive thunderstorm. The wind broke the window in his living room. Instead of finding another piece of glass—he had plenty of spare materials—he pinned the curtain in front of the hole with his pocketknife. He received a pension and had plenty of money to renovate parts of his house, but he chose not to do anything. Every year something else broke, and every year he adjusted better to the bitter-cold winter in the mountains. He was not proud of being tough, nor was he ashamed. He just didn't care. Crazy as it seems, I thought there was a kind of strength in this detachment to the physical world and his ability to endure tough conditions.

I learned most Bulgarian words from Zdravko, but I also had another teacher in the valley. If we walked an hour down a steep slope covered in pine trees, we came out in a village with a shop and a small library. Silvia, the librarian, spoke a little English, and was happy for me to use her computer to access the internet. Every time we needed groceries, I visited the library to check my email, after which we sat down with a cup of tea and I practised my Bulgarian and she practised her English.

In this way my Bulgarian was improving fast. I learned to count to hundred, all the colours, types of weather, and everything that I could point at. Then one morning I had coffee with Zdravko and he pointed at himself and then at me.

'We?' I asked. Thinking he was teaching me pronouns, I wrote the word down.

'Yes.' He smiled. Then he clumsily put his arms around me and tried to kiss me.

'No, no, no,' I said, embarrassed, moving him away.

'Zdravko loves Merriam,' he said.

He was like a seven-year-old boy. It was irritating and a bit comical, but not for a second was I scared.

We were silent for a moment, watched the television, then I finished my coffee and said goodbye.

I remembered what my sister had told me when she was nineteen and I eighteen. 'Men will always give it a try ... and mind my words, mostly twice!' So early the next morning, I hiked down the mountain to find Silvia. We chatted about this and that, and I asked how to say 'No touching'. She didn't ask me why I wanted to learn those words.

Next morning, the whole scene with Zdravko repeated itself, but this time I could say, *Ne me pipai*. His first reaction was surprise, then he burst into laughter. It was such genuine joy, I couldn't help laughing too. But a minute later he grew more serious. He stared at the television while I saw him thinking that he was my language teacher, yet I'd learned these words from someone else. I had no way of saying that there was no need to worry, I had not told anyone about what had happened, but in any case he never tried anything again.

For a month the three of us lived harmoniously in that deserted and ruined village in the high mountains of Bulgaria. In the early mornings I drank coffee with Zdravko. In the afternoon, Peter and I collected firewood for the winter, and on good days went for long trips through the mountains. We stopped in natural clearings, enjoyed the views and soaked up the last of the warm sunlight. We came across mushroom hunters who taught us what we could eat. Gradually, we were starting to learn more about the Rhodopes and their inhabitants.

One day, we met an old woman in a nearby village, who asked where we were from and what we were doing. I said that we were renting Dimitri's house, the one next to Zdravko, and we pointed over the hill.

'Ah! How is Zdravko?' she asked.

'Very good.' I shook my head to say yes.

'You want to buy?' she asked.

'Buy what?'

She pointed at a house fifty metres from where we were standing. The roof had collapsed, and only three walls were left. It was an absolute ruin, but maybe you could recycle the stones to build something better.

'Ask how much,' said Peter to me.

'*Kolko struva?*' I asked.

'Five thousand euro,' she said.

'No thank you,' said Peter.

I nodded, and said, '*Ne merci.*'

But with her suggestion, an idea sprang up. There were so many houses that would fall down in the next decade. The locals might be happy to see some younger people moving in. When we heard that you could buy a house with a decent roof for ten or twenty thousand euro, our interest grew.

Suddenly, our day walks had a new dimension. It was a very different feeling to walk through a landscape that would soon turn into a distant memory than to stroll through villages that could become part of our future. We imagined living in this cottage or that village, renovating this house or that shed. With every offer colourful visions took hold in our brain, and the Rhodope mountains slowly became part of us.

T he librarian, Silvia, told me a little bit of the history of our area. About 3000 BC the whole region west of the Black Sea was part of Thracia. It was home to an ancient civilisation first mentioned in *The Iliad*, where Thracians were described as allies of the Trojans in their war with the Greeks. Even now, people still found hoards of Thracian treasures.

Relatively recently, Ottoman Turkey had invaded this part of Bulgaria with much violence. Its people, who disliked conflict, had moved further and further into the mountains. They survived by cooperation. 'That's why,' she said with a laugh, 'the people who live in the mountains are more friendly and social than the ones in the lowlands.'

One sunny day, Peter and I followed the road further up into the mountains. We came to an isolated village called Miliva. It had a small shop, and the people greeted us kindly. From there a dirt track led out into the forest. We knew that only a short distance away were Thracian ruins.

We came to a clearing and sat down in the long grass. The view down the valley was astonishing. Apart from Miliva, three kilometres away, there was no sign of habitation. We could see many spurs coming down into the valley, and in the far distance some mist drifting between the tops. Then we spotted old trees surrounding a little grassy plateau. Curious, we wandered on down. There was a large beech tree at each of the four corners. I felt a peculiar energy in the middle of this flat square, and said to Peter that this could have been some sort of holy place. Of course, we will never know, but we sat down under one of the old trees, imagining Thracian worship and rituals performed in this very spot.

We were about to turn back when Peter's eyes fell on a little walking trail that went down the spur past some apple and pear trees. We followed it for fifty metres until, to our surprise, we came to a cottage. It was a basic square building, about seven by seven metres, with an iron sheet as a door and big windows on the side. By standing on our toes, we were able to peer in. There was a wooden floor, a bed, a table and a little cabinet. It looked just adorable. While Peter walked around the building, I sat down on the steps, and saw myself sitting in exactly this spot in the future.

On the way back we asked some people in Miliva about the cottage, but we had trouble making ourselves understood. We tried for weeks, but failed. In the end, we gave up and tried to forget about it.

Slowly, the red autumn colours began to turn dark, then brown. First a little breeze turned up, then the wind followed. Big storms came over the mountains and down the valleys, and all the brown leaves were flying like hundreds of butterflies in the air. When all the dried-up flowers, leaves and dead branches had found their place on earth, the world became dark and sombre. Without foliage, the bones of the mountains became obvious, revealing rocks, spurs and narrow gullies. The hills and peaks suddenly looked small and naked. The sky was big and wide and grey. Then the first snow arrived, and the world became still and white. A thick layer covered the roof, the long brown grass and even the smallest branches of the barren trees. People moved inside their houses and closed their doors.

We too moved inside and sat next to the fire. Our landlord Dimitri had renovated the ground floor into a narrow, elongated sort of living room. He had put an open fire at the far end, brought in a long table and chairs, and some old-fashioned cabinets, and there were pictures of wolves and bears on the walls. With one small window, the place resembled a cave. We often sat very close to the fire with all our clothes on to stay warm, with the door open to get some fresh air and reduce the smoke.

The bedroom upstairs was very light, with white-painted walls and a good bed. On snowy days, when it was about −10°C, we lay in bed to keep warm. With the white mountains around us, our room was brightly lit up, and Peter called these retreats 'hospital days'. It was the time for deep rest. While the trees outside were growing their roots, we were also calmly strengthening our foundations by doing nothing but lying in bed and enjoying the timeless silence.

When the wind came from the north, it brought cold dry snow from Russia. Small streams turned into ice; waterfalls froze solid. One day I walked outside, took a chair to sit in the sun and exclaimed that it was a hot day. Peter took a thermometer and recorded 3°C. On those warm days, we went for a walk in the snow. I found an old pair of shoes in a box—four sizes too big— and Peter discovered a pair of gumboots. He had never lived much in the snow and thought it was marvellous. We walked through the forest and, without being able to see a path, went anywhere we wanted. It was beautiful and still, and there were many animal prints. Since all bears were hibernating, we saw none of their prints.

Towards the end of December, we were starting to think of what to do next. It was again via the internet that a new door opened.

In the small and warm library in the valley, I received an email from a Turkish woman who had read my book. She had just resigned from her job as a city guide because she wanted to live closer to nature. In Peru she had done a lot of hiking, and now she asked if we were interested in walking the Lycian Way together. She said the south of Turkey had a mild winter, and it was the only time it was not too busy with other walkers. She invited us to her aunt's apartment in Istanbul, then suggested we travel together to the start of the five-hundred-kilometre walk in Fethiye. This was a very attractive offer—all the more so because it revived our original plan to go as far as Turkey. By the time Peter's visa was about to expire, we were ready to take a bus to Istanbul.

Although we had not at first been impressed with Bulgaria, during the three months that followed we had grown to love it dearly—especially the Rhodope mountains with their endless forests, distinct seasons, the bears and wolves, the lack of rules and fences, the small villages with friendly inhabitants and their practical way of living. We loved the Rhodopes so much that we decided we would come back in the spring to look for a house. We would never buy a home to live in forever, we said, but a holiday house sounded wonderful. Would it not be great to have a little cottage here, somewhere hidden in the forest?

On our last morning we said goodbye to Zdravko, and tears welled in his eyes. We hugged him and wished him well. I looked at the broken windows of his house and wondered if he was going to survive the winter.

'We'll return in spring!' I said, and glanced at the picture of him and Marilyne that I had printed out. He had put it on his table near the television.

We walked with our packs and sticks down the snowy mountains in our sandals. We hitchhiked to the nearest town, caught a minibus to Plovdiv, and boarded a big bus that went towards Istanbul. We were going from a village of one person to a city of eighteen million.

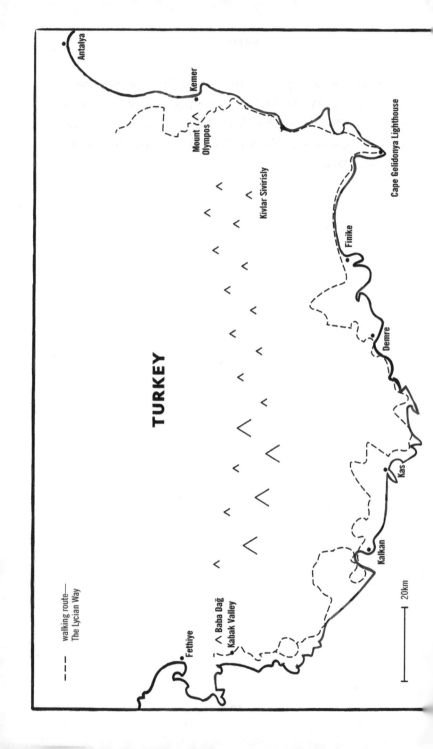

TURKEY

Antalya

Kemer

Mount
Olympos

Cape Gelidonya Lighthouse

Kıvlar Sivirisly

Finike

Demre

Kaş

Kalkan

Fethiye

Baba Dağ
Kabak Valley

walking route
The Lycian Way

20km

CHAPTER 5

TURKEY
THE LYCIAN WAY
IN WINTER

The bus went only as far as the border town of Svilengrad. While other passengers were met by family and friends, we stepped into the freezing darkness and wondered what to do. Snow was drifting down as we gazed at incomprehensible Cyrillic writing on signs and buildings. Had we been in the forest, we would have pitched the tent with our flashlight, gathered some wood and cooked some food on a fire, before crawling into our warm sleeping bags. But here, among buildings and roads, we felt lost.

Thankfully, a stranger took pity on us and asked in Bulgarian if we needed help. I explained that we intended to go to Istanbul. Sheltering us under his big umbrella, he accompanied us into town. He pointed at the office where we could book a bus for the next day, then guided us to a hotel, which was closed, but a number was pasted on the door. Our man had a cellphone and rang the owner, who turned up a minute later. We said a grateful goodbye to our friendly stranger, and went inside.

We wanted to let Yasemin know that we were delayed and would arrive the next morning instead. The hotel owner let me call, but I got only an answer-phone response: 'You have reached the voicemail of 905347223499.' I left a message, then I realised with a shock that I had no proof that this Turkish woman actually existed. It could all have been a scam. Anyone could fabricate emails and send fake pictures. What had we got ourselves into? The worry remained, but I decided to focus on the present. After all, we could have a hot shower for the first time in three months. There was a soft bed with clean white sheets. We could watch television, and boil water in an electric jug. Everything was convenient, except that the double bed was rather small. If Peter turned over, I would wake up. So I slept on the floor on my mat in my sleeping bag.

At nine o'clock next morning we walked through a thick layer of fresh snow to the booking office, where we were told that the bus would not come into town but would stop at a petrol station on the highway. We could take a taxi to get there.

We arrived an hour too early and waited in the icy wind under the big roof. When it stopped snowing for a minute, I walked around the petrol station to look for a toilet. I was shocked to find myself on the edge of a slum. With bits of plastic and iron, people had created makeshift huts. There was slushy snow and mud everywhere, rubbish, old tyres, lumps of scrap metal, kids with few clothes. People lit fires to keep warm and cook. Who lived here? I wondered. Where did they get their wood from? I had never seen such atrocious living conditions in Europe. And in winter too.

Back at the petrol station, a truck driver offered us a coffee.

'Where are you going?' he asked in Bulgarian.

'Istanbul.'

'Istanbul?'

'Yes.'

'The bus comes from that way.' He pointed west. 'And goes that way—' pointing east. 'You have to wait on the other side of the highway. If the bus driver doesn't see you, he will drive right past.'

I looked at the busy four-lane highway and told Peter what the man had said. 'But I'll go and wait for the bus,' I said when I saw his pale face. 'When it comes, you run across. No need for two of us standing in the snow.'

Fifteen minutes before the bus was due, I watched for a break in the traffic and ran with my pack across the highway. I climbed over the low fence, waited for some trucks and ran the second half to the small strip of pavement where the bus would pull up.

The weather was coming from the west, so I faced east. I left my pack on my back for extra warmth. Every few seconds I looked over my shoulder into the snow to see if a bus was coming. Then the wind picked up, and it began to feel like a snowstorm. I remembered the wild horses we had seen in New Zealand in the rain: they would just stand with their backs into the wind and wait patiently.

The land was flat and without trees. Right beside me was a huge, deserted Soviet-style factory. Every window was broken, and the building was surrounded by a barbed-wire fence. It was the most ugly of all human environments. To stand quietly on the side of the highway near a town called Svilengrad, in a snow storm, with trucks thundering past and this hideous-looking old factory so near, was almost surreal and therefore fascinating. It felt like being on the outskirts of some deserted city in the old USSR.

The bus was only fifteen minutes late, but it felt as if I had been waiting for hours. When it finally arrived we were welcomed aboard like heroes. The five people in the bus, all Turks, had seen me waving in the snow and then Peter running across the highway. The men lifted our big packs into the cargo room, the women sat us down with hot coffee and chocolates. They shook their heads and rolled their eyes. 'Unbelievable that you were waiting in the snow storm!' I nodded, grinned proudly, and learned my first Turkish word: *Hoşgeldiniz*. Welcome.

The moment we crossed the border into Turkey we saw more traffic, better roads, a lot of agriculture and bigger towns. Kilometres before we entered the first suburbs of Istanbul, high-rise apartment buildings popped up on the horizon. The city was vast. As we drove closer, it started to feel frightening. But we were glad we'd made it—even if we hadn't walked.

Inside the city was a mixture of beautiful, well-kept old buildings and others that looked mouldy, broken down and rusted out. We saw big trees growing among the apartments, and I realised that living things were growing and rejuvenating every day. And at the same pace, man-made structures were being degenerated by sun, rain, wind and rust. What an incredible power the living force is, I thought.

Eventually we arrived at an enormous bus station where hundreds of people were milling around. I wondered how Yasemin would find us. I had her number on a piece of paper, so asked a friendly-looking man if I could use his phone.

'Is she Turkish?' he asked while putting out his cigarette. 'Let me ring her for you.' He typed in the number, explained our location swiftly to Yasemin, and a minute later she appeared from around the corner. Her long curly hair flowed behind her when she ran towards us. 'Sorry you got my voicemail last night, you must have wondered whether I actually existed!' was the first thing she said, and we burst into laughter.

She was of slight build and had sparkly brown eyes and a warm smile. She spoke excellent English. 'Let's go to my aunt's home,' she said, and conducted us towards the metro. We shuffled into the full compartment. From there we caught two buses, then walked the last kilometre through little lanes until we came to a new apartment building that seemed to have been subject to machine-gun fire. Bullet holes marked the entire exterior.

'Hail,' said Yasemin with a laugh. 'We had a terrible storm a few months ago. Look at the other buildings—the whole street looks like a war zone!'

Yasemin's aunt was away for a week. We settled in, then in the evening set out to explore.

We had been warned for nearly a year about dangerous Istanbul, but it felt safer than Paris. People seemed happy to see foreigners who had not been scared off by reports of bomb attacks and other bad press. We ate local food, wandered through ancient covered markets, had tea with carpet sellers and listened to wonderful street musicians. We returned around one o'clock in the morning, and Yasemin offered us a cup of tea before bed.

I said, 'Sure', thinking it would take two minutes to boil the kettle and within ten minutes we'd be asleep. But this was not the case in Turkey. Yasemin had a special Turkish kettle, which boiled black tea for a long time. Only after an astonishing hour was the tea allowed to be poured. She filled the cups halfway and filled the rest with boiling water.

While waiting for the tea, she smoked a cigarette and told us that she was forty years old, had no children and liked travelling the world. A little later she said that she did in fact have a daughter, but by the time the baby was two years old, she knew that motherhood was not for her. 'It's a long and complicated story,' she said, 'but I divorced my husband and let's say that I didn't make it very difficult for him to keep the baby. It was a horrible time, though. Having children here in Turkey is about the most important thing a woman can do, so there is a lot of misunderstanding and judgement if a mother walks away from her child. Istanbul attracts all walks of life, and I don't notice the judgement too much here, but in the countryside it is more obvious.'

She told us that she had worked for twenty years as a city guide but was ready to move away from the crowd and go to the beaches in the south, where the climate is better and the natural world closer at hand.

After our cup of tea we went to bed and a few hours later I woke up with the call of the muezzin. One of the three thousand mosques in Istanbul happened to be right next to our apartment.

We had good fun in Istanbul. We laughed a lot and felt very relaxed around Yasemin, whom we nicknamed Turkish Delight. She had a wonderful sense of humour, but was also full of radical and harrowing stories. When we walked through the streets, she told us how she had joined the protests in 2016 when the government had decided to cut down trees in a central park to make space for more buildings. Things escalated and in the end there was an attempted coup d'état against President Erdoğan. It was a scary time, said Yasemin, but exciting to be part of a revolution that was something bigger than everyday life.

We drank coffee in little cafés when it was raining, and walked through markets when it was dry. It was midwinter and Christmas time in the west; in Islamic Turkey you would never have guessed. For me, Christmas was a distant memory. During all those years in the wilderness, we had lived by the sun and moon, and particular dates and holidays had seemed rather irrelevant. I had good memories of Christmas in my childhood, with real candles in the pine tree in the living room, but they were so specific in time and place that I hardly ever thought of them.

The Blue Mosque was the most wonderful religious building I had ever been in. Apart from its exquisite architecture, there was something in there that created a profound calmness within. I had experienced this feeling with certain mountains or old trees, but it was the first time I felt a sense of holiness in a building.

Yasemin said she was still eager to hike the Lycian Way, the 540-kilometre trail between Fethiye and Antalya. It follows the coastline and sometimes goes up into the rugged back-country, and normally takes about a month to complete.

On Christmas Day we took a domestic flight to the south. We went from cold, wet weather to dry, warm sunshine. Yasemin's friend Akif picked us up from the airport and took us to his house in Marmaris. Akif looked very Greek with his black curly hair and fine features. It was delightful to be in the Mediterranean. I felt very cheerful and remembered again how important it is for general happiness to live in warm dry climates.

We spent a few days with Akif and his wife. In the afternoons we wandered to the boulevard, where a gentle breeze brought the salty smell of the sea. In the evenings we sat around the table, ate wonderful meals and drank Turkish *raki*, fragrant with aniseed.

'Raki is not *just* alcohol,' said Akif while rolling a cigarette. 'It gives us the ability to think poetically, to philosophise, to ponder about reality. It's truly remarkable how we become different people when drinking raki.'

He poured me a small glass, then added some water, and the clear liquid became instantly cloudy. I was astonished.

Akif was also an early riser, and while he smoked his first cigarette in the back yard, I joined him with a Turkish coffee.

'I used to feel the call of the mountains,' he said. 'When I heard it, I would jump on my motorbike and ride into the forest. Sometimes it would even be in the middle of the night. I'd get out of bed, and ride until I reached the top of the mountain. I'd stand and look up at the stars and breathe the fresh air. In silence. It was wonderful.'

He picked a mandarin from the tree right beside us, and I did the same.

'But I haven't had a call from the wild for a long time. I wonder why.' He sounded puzzled, rather than sad. 'Meeting you and Peter reminds me of these experiences. I should look for wild places again before it is too late.'

And while everyone was still sleeping, we rode on his motorbike on little pathways along the coast and into the mountains. It was exhilarating to go so fast, feel the wind and be so vulnerable on a bike.

Akif was a professional DJ and he didn't work in the winter. He considered walking the Lycian Way with us, but he was afraid he was not fit enough. Peter said he shouldn't worry; the first week would be hard, but after that he would get fit by walking. But he wouldn't come. So, on 28 December, we did our final shopping and Akif took us to the start of the trail. We were sorry to say goodbye.

Yasemin had a guidebook and a map, there were some signposts along the way, and we felt very confident with a Turkish speaker who could ask the way. The place was stunning, the weather was perfect, and all of us felt cheerful and optimistic. We walked up a steep rocky track covered with white stones, below us the beautiful turquoise sea. After ten minutes Yasemin began to fall behind. We slowed down, waited for her and encouraged her on.

After three hours we arrived at the spot where the guidebook recommended setting up camp. It was a small grass clearing on the top of a hill.

'If the wind picks up, we'd be better off underneath the trees,' said Peter. 'Back there.'

'But it's crystal clear!' said Yasemin. 'Not a sigh of wind! Look at this place, it is stunning!'

We had a fantastic panorama over the calm Mediterranean, with

Greek islands in the distance. Down below we could see beaches with golden sand, and in the distance the mountain Baba Dağ.

Peter grudgingly agreed, and I pitched the tent in the open, while he collected firewood. I was dead tired after a week of late nights, and a minute after sunset—about six o 'clock—I said goodnight, plonked into the tent and fell asleep within seconds.

Yasemin, however, was used to staying up late. When I briefly woke some hours later, I saw the light of her cell phone through the tent fabric. Just after midnight a strong breeze blew up, and rapidly turned into a ferocious windstorm. The tent shook with every gust. Then it began to rain heavily.

At dawn, which was about seven or eight, the sky was blue and I felt a whole lot better. I lit a fire with the dry wood Peter had collected, and began to prepare breakfast. Peter was soon at my side, but Yasemin was nowhere to be seen. It took some time for her to answer our calls. Eventually she crawled out of her tent.

'I didn't sleep much,' she declared. 'Feels like I've been awake all night.'

I felt sorry for her, made a seat on a rock with my jumper and offered some breakfast. She sat down and stared at her hiking boots. The rain had turned the red sand into a very sticky kind of mud that stuck to their soles.

She looked up at me, and then at Peter. 'Shall we have a rest day?'

'A rest day? But Yasemin, we only walked three hours yesterday!'

'Well, we are not in a hurry, are we?'

'Oh, no hurry at all,' said Peter sympathetically, 'but let's have a rest when it rains. Since it's winter, we could expect quite a few bad days. We should make the most of the good weather.'

'I'm so tired,' she said.

Peter smiled. 'Yes, me too. The first days are the worst, but it's better after a week.'

'Also,' I said, 'if we stay here we'll run out of drinking water by afternoon. We need to walk on to the next tap or fountain before we can rest.'

We discussed how we could lighten Yasemin's pack and I offered to carry her food. She handed me about two or three kilos, and I thoroughly regretted not checking her pack before departure. I was now carrying all the supplies for all three of us.

The winter days were so short, we had to be as efficient as possible in the morning with lighting a fire, cooking, taking the tents down and packing our bags. Yasemin, however, had not much experience with winter trekking and needed some help. But it was another good day for walking, and we set off again in a good mood.

We followed the coastal track, and climbed up and down rocky slopes, past beautiful olive groves, white rocks and old exotic-looking trees. In the late afternoon, just when dark clouds drifted over our heads, we walked into a charming little village. It looked medieval, with big olive trees, stone walls and ancient houses. A sign read 'Guesthouse', but the place seemed closed for winter.

As the first drops of rain began to fall, Yasemin knocked on the door and asked if we could shelter. We sat on top of a wooden platform underneath a big corrugated-iron roof, and waited for the rain to stop. When it worsened, Yasemin asked the woman whether it was possible to stay the night.

'Of course! You can sleep in the house if you like!' she said.

We were happy to sleep outside and rolled out our mats and sleeping bags on top of the platform. Yasemin liked a little more privacy and pitched her tent under a roof in the yard.

The woman came out again to say that dinner was ready.

Delighted, we shuffled into her tiny kitchen. There was a firebox for warmth, and the room was furnished with beautiful mats and pillows. There was no table or chairs, so we sat on the ground while our host and her sister served a delicious soup. Yasemin explained that it was *tarhana*, a traditional winter soup. The base was made from plain yogurt, flour and chopped-up vegetables that had been left to ferment for some days. After the soup, we ate from one big metal plate. There was plenty of bread, feta and olives to go with it. It was delicious.

After the meal, Peter retreated to his sleeping bag to study the map in the last light, while Yasemin and I drank small glasses of black tea prepared just the way Yasemin liked it. We chatted with the two sisters, one of whom had given birth to eleven children, the other eight. I had many questions about their way of life, and Yasemin translated. Then one of them asked who that man was.

'That's Peter,' said Yasemin. 'Miriam's husband.'

When the woman replied, Yasemin roared with laughter. 'She says Peter is a grandfather!'

I joined the laughter, but didn't think it was all that funny. I felt quite hurt. They were all talking at once, but when it became quiet again I said, 'Well, he is my husband.'

Yasemin didn't translate.

I wanted to say that even though he might look like a grandfather with grey hair and a grey beard, I loved him. We didn't share the same age, but we did share the same interest in life. But I didn't say anything.

A little later I thanked the women for the meal and walked out into the rain. The temperature had dropped significantly and everything felt damp.

I crawled into my sleeping bag. Just when I was about to tell

Peter about the conversation, the mosque next door called '*Allahu Akbar*'. Then I heard thunder and, shortly after, a massive lightning storm passed overhead. It was too noisy to talk, so I listened to the rain drumming on the roof and wondered why I felt hurt.

I was sad that they had ridiculed our relationship; they had mocked something beautiful. I felt like a kid who wanted to show the others a flower, but instead of seeing its beauty they stepped on it—not by accident but just for a laugh. Then I thought of Yasemin's story of walking away from her baby girl and the condemnation that had come with it. Maybe she had laughed with the women because normally she was the victim of judgement—and for the first time I could understand how painful it was to be in that position.

I n the morning we woke to the sound of the mosque call. A little later a rooster crowed, and another one answered somewhere else in the village.

'Those roosters have probably never seen each other,' said Peter while packing his bag. 'One only knows that the other exists by their call.'

While we had breakfast inside, the warm sun dried our sleeping bags. We paid the landlady, said a grateful goodbye and packed the last of our gear. By the time we were ready to go, however, it was raining heavily again. We waited under the shelter in the hope it would clear, but it continued pitilessly. Yasemin talked to our host, but the old lady did not encourage us to stay another night.

When we set off between showers, Yasemin was rather angry with her. 'The bitch,' she grunted.

'Bitch?' I had been about to say how lucky we had been.

'Argh! She sees us packing, sees the rain, she could easily invite us for another night!'

I pulled my hood over my head and pondered the best approach in a walking life. Mostly we didn't need help from others—that's why we were set up to be independent. If help did come unexpectedly, we felt lucky. For Yasemin, hardship was merely suffering. When I thought about how Peter and I had overcome this, I realised it was our idea of freedom. When things were rough, we adjusted to increasingly primitive circumstances. We believed that living with the bare minimum and no attachment to luxury was a form of freedom. The less we needed, the more free we felt. If we did not think that way, would we still live the life we did?

We continued up a trail towards the tops, with me in front and Yasemin and Peter following. Just as we were walking over a big rock face, lightning struck—followed by incredibly loud thunder. I ran to a nearby tree. I knew you're not supposed to do this but it felt safer than standing in the rain on an open rock-face.

'Where was the last marker?' asked Peter when he came up.

'Don't know, but this is obviously the track.' I pointed above us.

Peter consulted the map.

'Ah, that's what I thought,' he said. 'The track doesn't go over the mountain but goes down into the next valley. We must have missed the turnoff.'

We scrambled back down the bare rock face as lightning flashed around us. There was a clump of pine trees to shelter under at the bottom, where it was surprisingly dry.

'Exciting, isn't it?' I shouted over the top of the thunder.

'No, I've had enough,' said Yasemin, mopping her face. 'I am going to look for a hotel tonight.'

W hen the storm passed, we continued the trail that led into the Kabak valley. There were plenty of hotels and guesthouses, but nearly all of them were closed for winter. Yasemin called numbers on her phone. Eventually she was lucky, and we walked her to a hotel. She said the price was astronomical but that she couldn't care less.

We promised to meet again in the morning, and climbed down a very steep track to the beach. We found a little flat spot looking out over the sea. The water was very clean, and there was not even much rubbish on the beach. To the north was the mountain Baba Dağ, now covered in snow. We pitched the tent, lit a fire and cooked our food.

Next morning I climbed back up the cliff to see Yasemin. To my surprise she was dressed in a totally different outfit, one more suitable for going out to restaurants than a day's hiking. Apparently, she had carried all that on her back.

'How are you feeling?' I said, joining her at the table where she was just finishing her breakfast of toast and omelette.

She grinned. 'A lot better after a hot shower and a good sleep. I'll certainly have a rest day here.' She took her packet of tobacco from the table and leisurely rolled herself a smoke.

It was 31 December, and I asked if she wanted to celebrate New Year's Eve. She said she was happy just to relax at her hotel.

While the rest of the world partied, Peter and I sat on a cliff, looking out over the calm waters. The colours of the sea were changing to green, blue and turquoise with the setting sun.

'Another year has passed,' said Peter. 'I wonder what the new year will bring.'

'Nothing but good things!' I said confidently. My cool hand slipped into his warm one.

'Let's hope you're right,' he said.

'What, do you think something bad will happen?' I looked at him in surprise.

'Something will change, I think. If we're resistant to change, we might call it bad. But change is inevitable: in the end we exchange life for death. That's our last change. Would you call something so inevitable bad?'

'Yes, if you die, that is very, very bad for me, my sweetheart.' I kissed the back of his hand, looked out over the sea, and pointed at some migrating birds high in the sky.

Next morning, we met Yasemin at her hotel, wished her Happy New Year and set off with renewed enthusiasm. The sun had come out and it was hot and dry. We walked up a big canyon, where a small path was carved out through the rocks. Drooping Turkish pines grew on the sides, and many birds enjoyed the sanctuary. We'd been climbing for only half an hour when Yasemin said, quite out of the blue, 'I'm dying for a cold soda right now.'

I wasn't sure what to say to that, for we were not walking towards cold sodas, and we wouldn't see a shop for a couple of days. Nor was I sure whether a person who was dying for this sort of a thing on the third walking day would be very eager to struggle onwards for another five hundred kilometres.

That night we found a lovely camp spot in an ancient olive grove overlooking the distant sea. We pitched the tent underneath the biggest olive tree we had ever seen. It was probably more than a thousand years old. People had adorned the tree with flowers and trinkets, and held up the branches with v-sticks.

We sat around the fire and had a good evening of storytelling. Yasemin was slowly adjusting to the hardship of walking with a pack, the weather had been great that day, and I thought everybody was feeling positive until Peter asked, 'You're not going to give up yet are you, Turkish Delight? The first week is the most difficult. You have to push through those initial days!'

'Yes, I am,' she said, matter-of-factly. 'It's too hard, I can't enjoy it very much. When we come to a village with a road tomorrow, I will catch a bus back to Fethiye.'

We were sad to see her go, because we were only just getting to know each other. We also felt more vulnerable without her. Yasemin had translated everything for us, and it had made the going rather easy. We hugged goodbye and walked away feeling a bit deflated.

From the village we followed the track that sidled back to the coast. We had a good view over the route ahead: we were going to walk past many secret little beaches and coves beside an endless turquoise sea, stretching into unknown territories. In such a stunning landscape I started to feel excited again. Now it was just Peter and me, and we were about to discover new frontiers in the east—like true explorers.

'All that lies ahead of us is waiting to be discovered,' I said with a grin, while marching down the track towards the sea.

The Lycian Way is an ancient Greek pathway, with Greek and Roman ruins all along it. We were walking through history. The bigger sites had become tourist attractions, but I loved it best when we accidentally stumbled across ancient pillars, burial stones and other evidence of people who'd lived in the same place so long ago.

Once I went looking for drinking water, and climbed a thickly forested hill. I kept pushing onwards, and in the end crawled like a goat underneath the prickly bushes to get to the other side. I suddenly found myself among the walls of a huge amphitheatre. Because it was so unexpected, it took my breath away.

Every dawn, the wind carried *Allahu Akbar* to our camp in the uninhabited hills. It always reminded me of our visit to the Blue Mosque in Istanbul, where we had felt a presence of something holy. Walking the Lycian Way allowed us to touch the colourful fabric of Turkish society.

One day we followed an ancient Greek aqueduct for a few kilometres. It had been carved out of rock more than two thousand years ago and, if repaired, would still have functioned today.

We found a grassy area nearby and pitched the tent close to the path. We lit a fire, cooked our food and went to bed. It was already very dark when we suddenly heard voices.

For a while we listened carefully, and could make out three men only about fifty metres from our tent. What were they doing? There were no houses anywhere near us, so they couldn't have been local villagers.

'Where's the knife?' whispered Peter.

My heart was beating hard when I slowly, noiselessly zipped open the top of my pack to find our hunter's knife in its lightweight cover. The total length was about twenty centimetres, and to a non-hunter the thing looked quite frightening.

'Put it here.' Peter patted between our pillows. He was half laying on his stomach, ready to stand at any time.

The men were talking among themselves. How many were there? I wondered. I detected a fourth voice. Their tone was serious, subdued even. What were they doing there if not planning something?

'Smugglers?' whispered Peter.

Below us, perhaps one hour's walk away from where we were camping, was a remote beach. Maybe they had moored a small boat there, and were bringing goods up to the road. From the movies I knew that smugglers hate eye-witnesses . . . I started to feel nervous. I rolled to my stomach, ready to get up. My ears strained to grasp every little sound. Would I be able to hear one of them walking through the long grass? I wasn't sure. My headlight was in the side pocket of the tent, but where was my Swiss pocketknife? After some rummaging I found it and held it tight in my hand. If they were coming our way to attack us, we would not go down easy! We would fight. Yes, I'd fight them to death. Unless they had guns, we could defend ourselves! Men were easy compared to bears. Maybe they were after money? I moved slowly to my pack to check where all our valuables were stored.

'Shh,' whispered Peter. 'Keep down.'

I lay down again. Maybe it was better to keep all that hidden in the packs anyway.

Then we heard shouts from below. More people seemed to be coming up the track. Everyone was talking amiably. The newcomers joined with the first group, and they moved on. The whole scene had nothing to do with us.

'Thank god for that!' I fell down on my pillow and noticed how tense my body had been.

Peter switched his solar light on.

'Weren't you scared?' I said in a slightly louder voice than I intended.

'I was, yes,' he said while putting the knife back in the pack. 'It's just a bit of plastic between them and us.'

We knew we were vulnerable inside a tent on public land. We didn't know who was out there; anything and anyone could come at any time. But I'd rather sleep in a tent, where I can hear the creek flowing, the call of the owl and the first songs at dawn, than be locked safely behind walls.

T he track took us over steep hills, rocky coastline, little roads and sandy beaches, and over the weeks we felt fit and strong again. One day we woke up with an icy wind rolling down the valley. When we looked up we saw fresh snow on the mountains. We broke up camp and walked past a small harbour where herons flew around empty boats and a lonely dog sat around deserted restaurants.

We walked into Demre for supplies. It is a busy coastal town where, we learned, the original Santa Claus—Saint Nicolas— came from. I'd thought he came from Spain, Peter thought from Finland; we had no idea that the real saint came from Turkey. We visited his ancient church and saw images of him on his donkey, giving presents to the poor. We realised that so many of our stories, including Greek legends and culture, comes from the land around the Lycian Way.

While Peter went to the vegetable market, I looked around for an internet café. On the way, I saw a little shop selling umbrellas. I bought two, one with pink flowers for me and a blue one for Peter. As I stashed the umbrellas away, I saw an old man dressed in traditional clothes sitting on a wooden bench. He sat quite upright, as though he was waiting for something. He was still but didn't seem at ease. When our eyes met, something happened. For a moment I was able to look at the world through his eyes and I felt he was completely lost in this modern place. All that he knew and loved had been torn down by machines. The original pathways had been obliterated and replaced by a grid-patterned road system. Sometimes he was angry about it all, but since he could do nothing about the massive movement towards progress he felt mostly helpless. The merging of minds was only a split second, but the image was strong, and for a moment I understood him.

I greeted him when I passed by, and looked up at the unattractive new apartment buildings, inhaled the fumes, and wondered what this place had looked like when the man was a boy. It would have been a fishing village, with donkeys in the streets and children playing. The houses would have looked out over the mountains and the fields, while a little wind brought fresh air from the sea. The town had grown so rapidly that it had left the old people behind. They sat dazed on the side of noisy roads wondering what had happened.

Eventually I found an internet café. On the walls were a dozen flat screens. Each big screen had a small couch in front of it where teenage boys were playing war games. A lot of them were sneezing and coughing while shooting their digital guns. Luckily for me, there were also a couple of normal computers where I could check my email.

'Because of the recent successes of your book *Woman in the Wilderness*,' I read, 'you are invited to the Byron Writers Festival.'

This, I read, was a prestigious Australian event that provided an opportunity to speak in front of large audiences during an interview on a stage, or in a panel with other authors. The festival would pay for the talks and cover the flight: either a return trip for me, or two single tickets for Peter and me. The festival was in the first week of August, a bit over six months from now.

I looked at the screen in shock, half excitement, half in disbelief. Would it mean we could go to Australia?

'That's marvellous!' said Peter when I found him in the market. 'But are you sure you want to go to Australia? You've been telling me for ten years that we will die of thirst in an Australian desert!' He handed me a bunch of carrots to put in my pack.

'Well,' I said when everything was stowed away. 'You hear stories of people with cars that break down who die of dehydration within hours. If we are going to drive through, maybe we should learn something about mechanics. We know New Zealand like the back of our hand but nothing about Australia. Ignorant, ill-prepared people like us die over there.'

'Yeah, we'll learn,' said Peter. He then pulled my arm and said, 'Hey, look what I found, camel sausages!' He pointed at a nearby stall with a picture of a camel. 'You want to try?'

The market still had an atmosphere of old times. I felt as if I was back in India, with lots of people, narrow pathways, and an abundance of vegetables and unfamiliar fruit like pomegranates, which grew so easily in this climate.

After thinking about it for a few days, we decided to regard the opportunity to go to Australia as an open door. It was indeed a very easy and affordable way to move back to the southern hemisphere. We would attend the festival, then quietly glide into the outback. We had no idea where we would go or how to go about it, but we trusted something would come up in the next six months.

A couple of days after my visit to the internet café, I came down with a bad cold and severe diarrhoea. I had so little energy that my mind felt lethargic and dazed. From my bed, all I could do was gaze at the world around me and in this slow state of mind it appeared extraordinarily beautiful. Our campsite was a grassy place surrounded by high rock walls. It was like a big natural amphitheatre. The morning light shone on the cliffs, turning the white rocks to blazing orange. Little new flowers were growing in the old cracks and grooves. Birds were chattering in the bushes, and everything seemed at peace.

During the evening I became sicker. That night my cough was so violent, it hurt my lungs. I felt utterly miserable for waking up Peter all the time. Then the fevers started, and I sweated so profusely that my sleeping bag became soaking wet. When I zipped it open, my temperature dropped and I shivered from the cold.

I was so weak I felt myself changing into another person: to my surprise I was concerned with things I had never considered before. When I wanted to wash the sweat off my body, I was reluctant to be naked among the short shrubs. There was nobody around, but I felt too exposed. When I poured the well-water over my back, it felt so horribly cold that I almost cried. Another torment was the small prickly bushes that scratched my legs painfully wherever I walked. The worst thing was the dirt. Everything felt so filthy all of a sudden. My greatest wish was to get everything clean. For the first time in my life I longed for a room and a bed with clean sheets and a soft pillow.

My only comfort was Georgie, a dog that had followed us from the last village. In the beginning we encouraged her to turn around, but she kept following us faithfully. She had walked with us up the stony track, over rocks, and through the forest.

Suddenly we were a little team of three, and I had enjoyed her company very much. Then I got sick, we had stopped walking and Georgie stayed with us. At night she slept near the tent, and in the morning we gave her something to eat. She left us on the third day when she spotted people in the distance and followed them back to the village.

After some days resting, I recovered from my illness. My desire for a house disappeared like snow in the sun, and when my energy returned so did my happiness. The two seemed totally interlinked.

Before we continued our journey, I went back to the nearest village for more supplies. In the middle of a busy street with lots of foot traffic I felt a wet nose against my hand. I looked down, and there she was: Georgie! I was so touched and so happy to see her that I knelt down and hugged her. I had heard of people getting attached to dogs, but I had never experienced it myself until now. Georgie was the sweetest dog, who belonged to nobody but herself. She accompanied me to the supermarket, but when I came out she was gone again.

A few days later it was 22 January, the very day I had met Peter twelve years earlier. It was in a local restaurant in southern India. I had taken a seat at his table and we played a game of chess. I had been travelling on my own for five months, and he had roamed India already for five years.

'If you're willing to live very, very basic,' he said, 'you can live without working.' It sounded logical enough, but until I met Peter I had always presumed a house and job were essential. I didn't think having a home and doing interesting work was a bad thing, but having options sounded fascinating.

TOP The beautiful and imposing Neuschwanstein Castle in the Ammergau Alps, Germany.
WIKIMEDIA

MIDDLE Setting off into the Rhodope mountains, Bulgaria.
MARILYNE FOUQUART

BELOW Camping under the oaks in autumn, Bulgaria.
MARILYNE FOUQUART

TOP **For every meal we light a fire, and everything we own smells of smoke.** *MARILYNE FOUQUART*

BOTTOM **Marilyne and Zdravko, Bulgaria.**

Rada on the banks of the Yantra River, North Bulgaria. *GALYA*

TOP Winter in the Rhodope mountains, Bulgaria. *F. FLOK*

BOTTOM Walking the Lycian Way along the coast of Turkey—our first night with Yasemin and a few hours before the storm hit. *YASEMIN*

TOP Walking the Lycian Way through a canyon with drooping Turkish pines on New Year's Day.

YASEMIN

BOTTOM Our cottage in Bulgaria, altitude 1200 metres.

TOP A local beekeeper on a horse explains that his hives
have been destroyed by a bear, Bulgaria.

BOTTOM Godley River in the Southern Alps of New Zealand, where
we climbed high mountain ranges without a trail. *TAMAR VALKENIER*

**Female expedition with
Tamar in the Southern Alps
of New Zealand.**
SAMIAN 'EN MARGE DU MONDE'

TOP Catching a hare for dinner in the Wilberforce River, New Zealand.

TAMAR VALKENIER

BOTTOM Sunrise viewed from our house in Mārahau, New Zealand.

JF ROBERT

'Yeah.' He shrugged laconically. 'Why not do something different, you know, if you can? If you have responsibilities towards family, or you don't have a penny in the bank, or are held down by bad health, well, fair enough, then it's best to create some security. But if you are blessed with health, courage and savings, I'd say, let's live an adventure!' His eyes were bright with excitement. 'Hey, why not? I'm not talking about a holiday. I was thinking of a wholly different way of living.'

I never stopped smiling that night. I realised that this man meant serious adventure.

We had been planning to celebrate our twelfth anniversary in some way, but unfortunately Peter was now sick. The night had been rough, with a hailstorm passing over, and we had not slept very well. We were camping underneath a big carob tree. There was not a blade of grass to be seen; the earth was covered in a layer of depressing red mud.

Peter came out of the tent and sat down on a log, while holding his umbrella. He began eating his breakfast of four chapatis I'd painstakingly made in the rain.

'Could you put that big plate out to collect water?' I asked, for we had not much to drink.

Peter looked at me in disbelief. 'In these horrific conditions you worry about collecting water?'

'Yes, we don't have much!' I said grumpily. I stood up, walked angrily through the rain to where he sat, picked up the plate and put it under the tent flap.

'You may as well collect some in the frypan then!' he said, and tossed the pan with three chapatis right in the rain.

'Do you know how much effort went into that?' I growled. I sounded a little more aggressive than I intended.

'I'm not hungry.' Peter went back into the tent and left his tea sitting in the rain.

'I'm going to eat it then!' I shouted after him. I wasn't going to waste precious food.

The rain was trying, the mud irritating, it was cold, Peter was sick, and we had an argument. Instead of a festive day it was our worst anniversary in twelve years.

I sighed when I looked at my feet. They were covered in brown stains. I had not been able to wash them for days. At night I wore special mud-socks to keep my sleeping bag clean. I put some more wood on the fire and thought of the day I'd met Peter in India, and his stories about the Himalayas. In the previous year he had slipped off an icy mountain and had miraculously survived. The moment of near-death had been mystical, he said. During those precarious minutes of climbing back to a safe foothold, not a shimmer of thought had disturbed the sense of absolute stillness and purity in his mind. He said those few minutes that had felt like an eternity had transformed his entire life—his personality, his thinking, his mind, his existence. There were two parts to his life: before Kugti Pass, and after.

The night after our first meeting, I went back to my guesthouse. Next morning I packed my bags and walked to Peter's hut. When I stepped inside, I heard a clear voice in my head: 'If you go with him—then you will see him die.' I saw a flash of sorrow and grief in the future, considered the matter and decided consciously: yes, I will be with him, even though I will see him die.

We climbed many passes together, but he never fell off. A year later, he contracted two strains of malaria in Papua New Guinea, but he didn't die. I had the impression death was always near him, as if it was hovering over his shoulder, almost like a companion—

to make his life intense, to remind him constantly to never waste a moment on a thing that he deemed a senseless obligation, or a compromise to his sanity.

For an hour I thought about the past years while eating carob pods under my umbrella. When at last the sun came out, I collected more wood and made two fresh chapatis. This time I covered them with cheese, tomatoes and salami.

'Good morning, Peter!' I said. 'Look what I made this time!'

He zipped open the tent, and his face lit up when he saw his pizza.

We walked over the beach past Fineke, and saw nothing but plastic tunnel houses, just like in the west of the Netherlands. This area provided most of Turkey's greenhouse vegetables. After buying some fresh tomatoes, capsicum and courgettes, we followed the track towards the lighthouse.

The narrow road ended at a beautiful little cove, where a whole family were having their Sunday picnic. The cove seemed small, but there was a sign saying that it once had been a popular Greek harbour. It was amazing to think that as much as three thousand years ago people sat at exactly at this spot. The rocks and clear sea would have looked much the same as now. And in another few thousand years, perhaps it would still look the same.

The family invited us to sit down and share their meal of chicken and tomato salad—and ouzo. We wanted to contribute our vegetables or feta and olives but they would not accept it. We could speak only a few words of Turkish, but still they wanted us to join them. The Turkish people in general were incredibly hospitable and welcoming. We always felt very touched by their kindness.

We followed the track up into the dry pine forest. The route went to the lighthouse at the tip of the peninsula, but halfway along we saw a secret little trail going into the forest. It meandered through a bed of ivy, past scrub and through the trees. We followed it for a long time and in the end came out at three big pine trees with a grassy flat underneath. We were perched on the cliff, and below us was a deserted bay with clear turquoise water. Big waves were breaking onto the rocks. There was one rocky island nearby on which some gannets were spying for fish. We were facing the mainland, looking out over snow-capped mountains in the distance.

'They call New Zealand the most beautiful country in the world,' said Peter, looking across the blue Mediterranean, 'but this is absolutely stunning. Beautiful places are everywhere really.'

We stayed the night. Next morning I returned to the picnic area where there was a tap for drinking water. I filled up all our bottles and walked back to camp. We sat for four days around the fire, looking out over our incredible view, and ate a lot of fresh bread and vegetables. It was, by far, the most spectacular campsite of our journey.

We had been on the Lycian Way for six weeks when we came across a large area in the forest ploughed over by wild boar. Since most Muslims don't eat pork, wild boar are very numerous. Among all the pig-rooting, we stopped for a short rest. Peter put his pack on a big rock, I put mine on the ground. While he took out his water bottle for a drink, I found us something to eat. When we had rested enough, I shouldered my bag and took up my walking sticks. But Peter did not shoulder his pack. He stayed simply looking at it, and I understood at once that he was loathing its weight. The one backpack that carried all he owned. He was tired of it, totally done with it. Not only for that afternoon, or this week, or the Lycian Way, but for the rest of his life.

This is it, I realised when I saw his face. These were the last days of long-walking. He had walked five thousand kilometres in the last three years, and he had come to the end of a walking life. The days of traversing steep mountains, looking for camp spots and firewood, with little water and basic food, were over.

'You've had enough, Peter?' I said softly.

'Yes,' he said, leaning on the rock with both hands.

'Are you done with long-walking?' I asked.

'Yes.'

He turned around and looked in my eyes. He did not need to explain what he felt. I saw sadness of not being able to walk with a pack anymore. I saw exhaustion. I saw someone who had met his physical limits and faced having no choice but to listen to his body.

'I'm sorry, Miriam. I can't keep this up anymore.'

'You, my sweetheart, have done exceedingly well,' I said. 'There is not a person in the world who has more respect for you than me.'

'If we do more walking, we need a donkey or a horse. I cannot walk with a pack anymore.'

I took two bottles of water from his pack and fitted them into mine. I lifted his pack from the rock, so that he could shoulder it more easily, and handed him his walking poles.

I indicated he should go first so that he could set the pace.

We agreed to walk to Mount Olympos only a couple more days away. I felt sad that the long-walking was over. We could organise a donkey to walk through Dagestan, or Georgia, but there were many regulations to follow and you had to provide food for the animal. Nothing was as simple as walking with our tent on our back through the country, sneaking into the forest at night, setting up a small camp that nobody saw.

It was hard not to have the security of a home, a place for Peter to rest, but I loved this simple life where everything was precious. We carried all we owned on our back and we could not even afford losing a spoon, for a spoon is priceless. One sweet orange is a treasure. A flat camping spot with firewood is worth gold and one sunny afternoon is a gift from the gods.

I knew I would miss the indescribable intensity of this way of life.

CHAPTER 6

BULGARIA
THE RETURN

Most of the guesthouses on the coast were closed for winter, but we persuaded a friendly owner to open one of his basic cabins. We spent a beautiful month under Mount Olympos until our visa expired, then headed back to Zdravko's village in Bulgaria.

After three months in Turkey, we had forgotten how run-down

Bulgaria could look at first glance. Even the people seemed strange and distant—until I remembered some of my Bulgarian words. Then their faces would light up.

The lowlands showed signs of spring, but the further our minibus from Plovdiv drove into the mountains, the more we moved back in time. Eventually we were back in winter. The air was humid and cold, the forest dark and sombre. Some shady places had not seen the sun all winter, and there was still snow on the ground.

It was late afternoon when we arrived back in our village with the tiny library. Silvia was so genuinely happy to see us back. After a cup of tea and an exchange of news, Peter and I started walking up towards our old cottage. The trees looked barren and forlorn, and the road was wet and muddy. The higher we climbed, the colder it became. Many storms and floods had ruined the track—a four-wheel-drive would have had difficulty reaching the cottage now.

We climbed up the spur and heard barking.

'Skelet!'

A little later the thin dog turned up, wagging his tail, excited to see us again. The three of us walked the last kilometre to the village. We reached the cottage, found the key and let ourselves in. Everything was the way we left it.

Nobody had walked on the grass track between Zdravko's house and ours, and the place looked forlorn. There were no signs of life from our old neighbour, so I went over and knocked on the door.

There was no response. No shuffling, no creaking door, no '*Kaaksi?*'

I climbed over some broken roof tiles to get to the dirty window, and peered through. Zdravko was lying in his bed. I knocked on the window.

'Zdravko!'

He looked up, and I waved.

'Zdravko! *Kaaksi*!?' I shouted.

He slowly got up. He opened the door and greeted me with his familiar grin.

'Merriam!' He hugged me and asked how we were and where we had been.

'Everything good! We walk Turkey! Walk five hundred kilometres!'

He was astonished. Evidently he had no idea that we done four-and-a-half thousand in the years before that.

'How are you?' I asked again.

He looked tired and seemed to have lost weight.

'Yes, good,' he said, and shook his head. '*Rosdenden* today.'

Rosdenden? It took a while before I remembered what it meant. 'Ah! You . . . birthday today! Happy birthday! Years?'

'Seventy-two. Come in, come in!'

All the leaks in the house had worsened over winter. A storm had broken some windows upstairs; rain had come in on the second floor and leaked into his living room. Water had dripped right onto his pillow. Instead of fixing the window or ceiling, he had simply moved his bed a little to the side.

'You stay here?' he asked hopefully, pointing at Dimitri's cottage.

'*Da, da*, Dimitri say we stay, until we buy house.'

'You will buy a house? Buy that!' He pointed at the ruined houses in the distance.

'No, no, that's broken,' I said.

In simple Bulgarian he explained that he had been very sick— he kept tapping on his heart. He had spent some time in hospital. Someone in the village down the valley had taken care of the cow and calf. Somebody else was going to buy his sheep later.

'You happy or sad cow is gone?' I asked.

He shrugged his shoulders. 'Is okay,' he said.

On one of these cold days before the spring arrived, I set off in the early morning to find a dentist in Smolyan, some eighty kilometres east. All I knew was the word for dentist: *zubolekar*. The road to the city was more or less straightforward; there was only one winding road across the range.

After an hour's walk down the mountain, I put up my thumb and a black Mercedes van stopped. It was an expensive-looking vehicle compared to the half-broken-down cars that normally rattled by.

'Smolyan?' I said when I opened the door.

He was not going all the way to Smolyan, he said, but to some other village along the way.

'A little way is good.' I climbed in.

'But if I make some phone call . . . maybe Smolyan. My name is Boris.'

He was a big man with a big ox-like face and flabby lips. He spoke not a word of English, and we conversed in Bulgarian.

'Would you like a cup of coffee?' he asked. 'I just had one.' He had one sip left in the plastic cup that was sitting in the holder. He picked it up, swirled it around and said, 'Would you like the last bit?'

Huh? This was the queerest question I had ever heard. 'No, thank you.'

I asked where he lived and whether he had a family—the usual pleasantries. He looked at me as he talked, which made me nervous on a winding road with traffic coming towards us. There was something else about him that made me feel uncomfortable: he was acting so cheerfully.

'Water,' he said as he pulled over next to a spring. It was quite common to fill up your own bottles at sources in the mountains.

He got out, and for some reason, I found the sound of the sliding door most unnerving. What was he doing there? I spied on him through the rear-vision mirror, but a minute later he was back with a bottle of fresh spring water. He handed me a bottle too, but I politely declined. I shouldn't be so paranoid, I told myself. He was just a very friendly man with some odd mannerisms.

He drove on, but every minute with him made me more wary. After some time I suddenly knew it. I sensed fear. I think humans can—like all animals—smell fear. It's the first survival instinct we were born with. But why was the man so nervous? Was he scheming something?

'Okay,' said Boris. 'Here I make phone call, my friend will come here, then you go to Smolyan ...'

I was confused. 'Your *friend* goes to Smolyan?'

'No, yes, my friend goes Monday, Wednesday and Saturday.'

He pulled the van to the side of the road and made a call, which made me very nervous—they could well be making a plan of attack now.

'Your friend goes to Smolyan?' I asked again after he put down the phone.

'Yes, friend. I go and have coffee over there. Do you want coffee? Only two minutes. No problem?'

'No problem,' I said softly. I had no idea what was going on.

We carried on, and I made sure to take in every detail. I felt like a detective looking for signs. What did he look like? Boris had plenty of hair; it was grey and cut short. His hands looked big and clumsy, but showed no sign of calluses or dirt. He hadn't done much gardening or work with his hands. He favoured his left hand for driving. The little finger of his right hand never seemed to come straight. Perhaps a calcified tendon. What company was he working for? I searched around for any name or logo but couldn't detect anything. Would there be any weapons in the car? It was impossible to see in the car's side pockets. His jeans fitted too tight to have space for a knife.

A few minutes later he pulled over at a roadside café. 'Very good coffee here. Favourite.'

I took my bag, opened the door and observed the central locking system. Even if it was locked, it seemed I could manually open it. I made sure I was slightly behind him when I glanced back over my shoulder. Black Mercedes van, registration plate KL9661TR. KL for Kuala Lumpur, 96 was the age of my grandfather when he died, 61 was the number of the house I grew up in, TR for Totally Ridiculous situation. Following him into the shop, I noted the way he looked, walked, smelled and communicated to others.

He ordered two coffees and we sat down.

Use all your skills now, I told myself. With intuition I could prepare myself; being surprised was a deadly mistake. I had observed him closely enough to describe him clearly if I had to report him to the police. With my strength I could fight. I glanced at him. His size could be a little overpowering, but if anything happened I could run. I looked around: the forest would provide cover. You could hear the road in the narrow valley for miles, so there was no chance of getting lost.

'This Mercedes: transport?' I asked.

He started talking, but I couldn't understand a word. I could walk away now, I thought, and hitchhike on. There were plenty of cars on the road. But for what reason, really? The man had done nothing wrong—he had been kind and even given me coffee!

Then, without making a phone call, or meeting anybody, Boris stood up again. A little confused, I followed him back to his van.

'Smolyan,' he said before he turned the engine on.

I pointed ahead of us. 'Smolyan, dentist.'

See, the man was friendly. He will now go to Smolyan. It was just a misunderstanding.

We drove up a mountain, and the quiet road became more and more narrow. As we zig-zagged slowly up into a thick forest, I could feel a tension building up, and shifted uncomfortably in my seat. After about fifteen minutes, he said something and pointed to the right. I picked up the word *pochivka*.

'What?' I stammered.

'*Pochivka?*' His small blue eyes looked treacherous. I sensed something malignant crouching beneath the surface.

He steered off onto a dirt track and drove for another hundred metres until we could go no further. He switched off the engine and turned on his seat, so his shoulders were square to mine.

'You, sex? Here in the van?' He pointed behind us. 'I have a bed.'

My heart was racing as I stared out of the window in front of me.

'No,' I said shakily. 'I hitchhiking to Smolyan.' I pointed north. I wondered if I had the courage to fight him.

He said something more.

'No,' I repeated. I was terrified—until I glanced at him and realised that he would not turn violent. 'I'm hitchhiking.' My voice didn't sound afraid anymore, just annoyed.

To my great relief, he turned the engine on and drove back to the road. There was an icy silence that I didn't intend to break.

'Come on, talk to me a bit,' he said eventually. He waved with his right hand. 'Talk about your job.'

'Okay,' I said. 'I wrote book about life in New Zealand. My husband and I lived in the wilderness. My job was hunting. Before I had bow, now I have gun.' I acted it out. 'Bang.'

'What do you hunt?'

'Goat, deer, rabbit . . . and humans,' I added for good measure.

He smiled and was quiet for a while. Ten minutes later he asked whether I wanted to have sex.

I sighed. 'No.'

Five minutes later the same question came. Then his phone rang, and he pulled over onto a small bay.

This was my stroke of luck. The moment he stopped, I grabbed my bag and jumped out.

With deep gulps I breathed the fresh forest air. I was once again among the living!

But Boris must have thought I had changed my mind. He hurriedly broke off his phone conversation and, with an electrified look on his face, indicated he would open up the doors of the van for us.

'No! I go Smolyan!' I walked as far away from the vehicle as possible and put my thumb in the air, even though there was nobody on the forest road.

Once he understood that I was not coming back, he began to yell. He stood in front of his van, and kept on shouting and waving in an exaggerated, panicky sort of a way. I looked at him and saw how angry he was.

Then something happened. It was as if I had suddenly stepped into his head and saw his own memory. The scene was projected as if I was watching a movie. During those few seconds I saw him standing in his own kitchen, with his wife at the table. He was shouting at her, while she stared passively in front of her. The fact that she would not utter a word made him so exasperated, he threw a chair on the ground. He felt utterly frustrated with his life. Why would she not talk? Why did he feel so utterly lonely in his relationship? Why could he not have some love or affection, for once—before his life was over?

Then Boris stopped shouting. The fury was gone and his mouth became slack, his cheeks flabby. His whole face suddenly reflected defeat.

While my thumb was still out, a battered Citroën came racing around the corner and screeched to a halt. Two young guys sat in the front. I got myself settled in the back, and the car took off. I looked over my shoulder to see whether Boris would follow, but he never came. He never had any intention to go to Smolyan.

I leaned back, and smiled a great, victorious smile of pure content. I breathed in slowly, and a warm glow settled in my stomach. It was, I realised, the first time in my life I had escaped a really precarious situation. I had done it. I had saved myself: I had jumped out of the vehicle. The feeling of bliss lasted all morning.

The guys dropped me in the city. I walked the busy streets, and came to a tall and stately mansion with a big picture of a tooth in the window. At the end of the garden path was a wooden door, but I was uncertain which of its four bells I should ring. I tried one, and a minute later a woman hung out of a window on the second floor.

'*Zubolekar?*' I asked.

'Yes! One minute!' The window closed again. I looked at the house a bit more closely. The paint was peeling from the window frames. The white facades were cracked and blotchy from neglect. If the owner of the house is that poor, I thought, he obviously had very few customers. Maybe he used to be good at his job, but then became an alcoholic, or maybe just too old . . . The longer I stood there, the less I wanted his rusty instruments in my mouth.

I made my escape. I ran down the path, through the forlorn garden, through the little iron gate and back into the street. With no destination in mind, I ran up the road, until I heard somebody calling behind me.

'*Zdravei!*' The woman, in an old-fashioned dress, stood in the middle of the road and waved.

A little sheepishly I walked back down.

'Would the dentist be able to see me?' I asked in English.

'Yes. I *am* the dentist,' she said, also in English.

Feeling even more foolish, I decided to not insult her any further and followed her meekly into the practice. There was no sign of any other patients.

While she put on her gown, I took a seat in the yellow-walled waiting room. I'd have been happier if the room was painted bright white, I thought—then stopped myself. The colour of the walls said nothing about the quality of the dentist.

She came back, and I took my place in the chair. It didn't go back very far, so I sat almost upright, but that didn't matter to her. She located the hole in my tooth with a little hammer and a metal pin. She then mixed a powder into a paste on her side table. When I asked what that was, she told me it was the filling material. I raised my eyebrows. Never in my life had I seen such archaic methods.

'Do you have anaesthetics?'

She looked at me in surprise. 'Of course.'

I leaned back again.

She injected the anaesthetic and filled the cavity. Twenty minutes later it was all done.

We talked for half an hour about life in Bulgaria. The bill was a fraction of any dentist's bill I had paid before.

'Come back, any time,' she said.

I laughed. Any time, I thought.

I felt happy to have accomplished the dental appointment, for every little thing with a foreign language and an incomprehensible script was a challenge. As I walked back towards the edge of town, I saw a library. I checked my email and found a message from Western Australia.

Hi Miriam and Peter,
We read your book—fantastic! Feels like you are an extension of ourselves! We love you two! I myself am also originally from Holland. Met my Aussie hubby in 1999 in Darwin. I was 19, he was 40. We have been travelling around Australia for the last 17 years—always sleeping in our swag. We settled in Western Australia for a fair few years and we bought a bit of land to keep our sheep, pigs, horses and a few chickens on. There's no dwelling on it either—as we prefer to camp all the time, and live in nature and smell the smoke from the campfire. We try to live totally self-sustainable. We would love to meet like-minded people. To have you around our campfire would be a dream! Hoping to hear back from you when you get a chance.
Kindest regards, Kate and Kevin

I brought back the good news to Peter. This was the opportunity we had been hoping for. We had our flight tickets to Australia in August but no plans yet for after the writers' festival. To stay with people who had horses was another piece of luck. Since Peter did not want to walk with a pack any more, we were now thinking of travelling with a packhorse or donkey. The opportunity to learn about horsemanship seemed perfect timing. I was very enthusiastic, and over the following weeks I asked Kate many questions about their lives and the care of horses.

Over the months, they told us that they thought people should be living in clans or tribes, rather than isolated in couples. They had driven eight times around Australia, found the most beautiful place and settled near Grayburn, two hours out of Perth. Our trip to Australia sounded more intriguing by the minute and we looked forward meeting them.

Winter was still present in the Bulgarian mountains, but after a couple of weeks we could feel spring pushing its way through.

In December we had more or less forgotten about bears. They were hibernating and we had seen no sign of them. Now we saw fresh footprints in the snow. I could just imagine how hungry a two-hundred-kilo bear would be after a winter of hibernation. Instantly the forest felt very wild again.

Then, from one day to another, the clouds disappeared, snow melted and all living things began to grow. Leaves unfolded, flowers popped open, new sprouts appeared, and we discovered we were surrounded by cherry trees, each with hundreds of bright white blossoms. The whole village was covered in flowers, with a carpet of petals on the ground. It was the most beautiful spring I had ever seen. In a matter of days, the whole world around us had changed from dark grey and brown to bright green leaves and countless flowers. The people in the valley came out of their houses and began their spring cleaning. Zdravko's sheep and goats gave birth to a new generation. We realised that we could travel by sitting still in this country. With the deciduous mountain forests, the world around us would change with every season.

While the spring unfolded, we walked over countless forest tracks, looking for a house to buy. We imagined owning a cottage, and were full of ideas about how to renovate it: which colours to paint the house, and what to plant in the garden. The problem, we very quickly learned, was not the supply of empty houses, nor the willingness to sell them, but the lack of ownership papers. The houses had been built a long time ago, passed on from one generation to the next, and if there were ever papers they were now long lost.

By walking for weeks on end, however, we created a small list of houses for sale with ownership documents. We also discovered that every village was different, depending on the lie of the land. Some were built in a narrow valley, and all the houses were cold and damp, others were on a ridge and exposed to the wind. The best villages faced south, where all the houses were bathed in warm afternoon sunshine.

One day Silvia, the librarian, told me there was a house for sale in the middle of Miliva, a village at the end of a road, far away from others, high up in the mountains. We decided to have a look.

The village was about one hour's walk away from our rented cottage. Behind the village shop was a pathway that came out at a cluster of three houses built only metres apart.

'*Zdravete*!' I called, to see if someone was home.

A small, thin man came around the corner.

'What you need?' he asked, frowning.

'We look for house to buy,' I said, and named the owner.

His face cleared instantly. He pointed at the house that was right next to his own. He was not the owner, he said, but the door was open. His name was Davin. He shook our hands vigorously. He showed us around. We liked the house, but not the fact that it was built so close to other buildings.

After the tour, he introduced us to his wife, Emma. We drank a little of his homemade wine, shared some snacks under his grapevine, and soon his son Anchov, who lived in the third house, joined us. Nobody spoke any English, but the family's hospitality was heartwarming.

'We will become neighbours!' said Davin with great enthusiasm. His eyes were bright and little sparks of excitement were dancing in their centres. Davin weighed not much more than fifty kilos, but he was strong and sprightly. Each day he walked fifteen kilometres in the hills to find mushrooms. Back home, he would sit down with his wife to cut the fungi in pieces, dry them in the sun, and sell them for relatively good money to people who trucked the produce to Italy.

After our first visit, we came back regularly. Sometimes we had a cup of tea, sometimes we enjoyed a plate of the famous local butter beans. One day I drew Davin a map of the place we had seen and fallen in love with in the autumn. It was only three kilometres or so from Miliva.

'You know this cottage?' I asked him.

'Yes, I lived there, before marriage,' he said. 'Old shepherd's cottage. I herded sheep a long time ago. No electricity there. Nice place, in forest. But be careful, bears live there.'

'You know owner?' I asked.

He nodded. 'Don't know.'

'Ask if he knows any other houses around here,' said Peter.

Davin seemed to know a great deal about the area. Over the weeks, he found out which houses were for sale. Many of them were in the middle of villages.

Then one day we expressed again our wish to find the owner of the cottage we loved.

'Oh yes, I find! Owner is Milko! *Haide!*' he said, and stood up at once.

We followed our friend up the road to a house. Davin rang the bell and an old woman opened the door. They exchanged some pleasantries, but when Davin asked after Milko she merely pointed at the mountains.

Eventually Milko arrived with his horse and buggy. He had gone into the hills to find firewood. While Davin explained our interest in his cottage, Milko slowly stroked the neck of his horse. He looked about eighty, and still as strong as an ox. His face was broad and his hands were big. His eyes were steady and calm. He was dressed in traditional tweed clothing, and everything about him was proper and decent.

'You want to buy?' Milko looked at Peter.

I shook my head. '*Da, da.*'

'Sure?' He frowned slightly. 'There is no running water, no electricity, very far from village.'

'No problem,' I said. 'We like.'

Milko had held a high position during the Communist era, and still had the air of an army commander. But our little friend Davin was not to be undermined, and chatted with him like an equal, hopping from one foot to another.

When it was silent for a moment I asked the most important question, a line I knew by heart, because it was the only thing that counted: 'Do you have the ownership papers for the house?'

'Ownership papers?' He looked at me and then at Peter.

'*Da*?' I shook my head.

'Of course,' he said sternly, as though it was normal that every Bulgarian had documents for his house.

I looked at Peter, a small smile became a grin, and we laughed. I wanted to hug the man out of sheer delight but I nodded solemnly and said, '*Dobre*.'

There was a little window of opportunity for us. A beautiful little window of opportunity. Every time I looked at Peter, he smiled.

It took at least one month to jump all the hoops to buy the cottage we loved. With my European Union passport, I could purchase the property in my name. I was eager to learn the whole process. Peter had bought and sold houses in the past, and was glad to stay out of it.

We first had to register ourselves at the district council, based in Smolyan. I hitched several times to the city. Each time I was told I had to fill out another form or document. We also had to prove where we were living with a signature from our landlord. Given that Dimitri was a sniper in Afghanistan, getting a signed document from him was rather difficult. So we asked Zdravko if we could pretend we were living in his house. This wasn't as easy as it sounded either, as the mayor decided he needed to see Zdravko in person—and I knew our friend would never feel like walking all the way down the valley to sign a piece of paper.

'Zdravko very, very sick. Hospital. Winter,' I told him.

Eventually he relented and allowed me to collect Zdravko's

signature. When I thanked him with a sugary cake, I felt as if I had bribed him.

After registration, I was allowed to open a bank account. But the bankers spoke only Bulgarian and Russian, and their questions were incomprehensible, until I gave them Silvia's phone number and she was able to translate.

'We go Australia in August, maybe next year, we will not return. Problem I not pay house tax?' I told the clerk at the council building one day.

'You pay interest on your tax,' he said.

'How much for this house?'

He searched on his computer for a long time before he said, 'The property tax is one *leva* a year.'

This equated to fifty euro cents a year.

At last, one sunny afternoon in May, we sat around the notary's big ebony table to sign the final papers. To write my full name in Cyrillic felt awkward. I had to copy strange symbols from an example, not recognising one letter of my own name.

Eventually, I received all the right documents and Milko received the money. It was a tiny amount, compared to phenomenally high house prices in New Zealand, but for Milko it was enough to pay for his wife's medical bills. All of us were happy, and I was as proud as a rooster. I had single-handedly mastered buying real estate in Bulgaria. I had jumped through all the incomprehensible hoops in a foreign language and now, at thirty-four, I owned a property debt-free. That it was only an old shepherd's cottage in which even the locals were unwilling to live made no difference to me.

The day after the settlement, we packed our bags and said goodbye to Zdravko. It took us an hour to walk up the mountain and into Miliva, where we ran into Davin, just back from the forest with a big bag of mushrooms.

'Welcome, welcome, welcome!' he said when we told him of our purchase. 'You are now officially part of Miliva!' He gave us a heartfelt hug—his head resting on Peter's chest for a second—as though it was an official inauguration. Then he bounced up again and applauded with such joy that even his wife Emma, who was standing in the doorway, smiled. His son brought a tray with *chushka biurek*, a delicious traditional Bulgarian dish of stuffed peppers, served with tomato salad.

'Rakia time!' said Davin after everyone had eaten. He disappeared to a shed in the garden and came back with a bottle of schnapps. 'I make!'

Davin poured everyone a small glass.

'*Nazdrave!*' we laughed. Cheers!

'For good house!' said Davin.

'For good house,' we repeated after him, and I took a sip. The strong alcohol produced a strange feeling from my throat to my stomach. I tried to explain the sensation of burning alcohol in Bulgarian, much to the delight of the others.

After the celebration, we shouldered our packs again and continued the last hour of our journey.

After Miliva, the road became a dirt track. We halted at the big cherry tree and ate all the ripe fruit we could reach. Then we continued towards the terraced fields. A horse was grazing lush clover on a lead, and behind the plum trees a couple of women were raking the cut grass for animal fodder in preparation for the harsh winter. Then we entered the forest, where it felt instantly cooler. Sunlight played with dark shadows, little creeks came darting through the gully, and every hundred metres we stopped to eat blueberries. The track sidled around a deep forested ravine, and eventually we came out in a clearing. We walked through fields of flowers while gazing at the valley below. We were now at more than twelve hundred metres' altitude and the endless dusky ranges stretched ahead of us. Finally, we arrived at our holy Thracian place—the patch of grass between the old big trees—that had attracted us to our cottage in the first place.

We slowed down to take in every flower, every scent and every butterfly. Because, just fifty metres from there, hidden among the fruit trees, was our beautiful home. Our cottage with a terracotta roof.

I took a big breath while Peter turned the key. The iron door sagged on its hinges and scraped over the cement floor. We stepped into the little entrance room where there was a cabinet to store food. The room to the left had a cement floor, and one wall was partially crumbled. The window was covered by planks because most of the panes had been broken by wind. The room on the right was bathed in sunlight. It had a firebox and a beautiful wooden floor with very wide planks. There was one big window. Its wooden windowsill was big enough to sit on. This was a place I had dreamed of as a child.

I opened the window and breathed the fresh mountain air. The hillside above us was a cascade of yellow flowers, and in the distance was nothing but forest. The air was pure, the sky had a deep blue colour. And apart from the birds, it was totally silent. No machines, no airplanes, no noise. We had reached the end of the world, where everything lived in peace.

Peter lit the fire in the firebox, and we made a cup of tea. Then we walked through the two rooms for the fifth time, admiring the space as if it were a palace. Peter pointed out possible renovations;

I thought of the colours: green for the doors, yellow for chairs, turquoise for the window frames. For the first time in my life I was allowed to bring some permanent colour into a house, because it was ours.

In the morning I woke with a warm glow in my tummy. This is a place I love, a place to call my home, I thought. Something I had never valued at all—yet now that I had experienced it, I was surprised by how wonderful it felt.

The next day we began cleaning the whole house thoroughly. There were tables, chairs and cabinets. There was one wooden bed with slats, the other one needed planks and fixing. In the following days some tradesmen turned up to repair the wall and window. A little later, I walked with an empty pack three kilometres back to Miliva and hitchhiked down the mountain to buy tools, paint and fabrics in yellow and orange. Within a week we had made our house as cosy as it could be.

So we lived quietly in our house on the side of the mountain. Each morning we collected water in buckets from the pipe thirty metres away from the cottage. Since we had no kitchen, we lit the fire outside the door, boiled some coffee in the billy-pot and looked at the view.

Below us was forest, and on the edge of the clearings roamed roe-deer—the same little barking deer that we had encountered so often in France. Many birds nested in the forest, and there were dragonflies on the puddles, butterflies in the fields, small fish in the creeks and frogs in the wetlands. The place was full of life. We spent most afternoons eating out: we picked kilos of cherries and plums as well as raspberries, wild strawberries, blueberries and blackberries.

One day a man passed by on his horse. He looked distressed, and it took us a while before we understood that he was a beekeeper whose hives had been destroyed the night before by a bear. He explained that the bear population had increased since the fall of the Soviet Union. The fence on the border with Greece had fallen down, and in the last ten years, quite a number of bears had roamed in to this area. A little later we met with a local hunter who had put up a motion camera near a feeding trough a hundred metres from our house. The camera had caught three different bears. Since we did not have a bathroom, we had to dig a hole in the forest every time we needed to go to the toilet. To walk out into the forest, sometimes at night, and look around for a bear before squatting down was unnerving, to say the least.

There were always little chores to do around the house. Gathering wood from the forest, washing and cleaning, collecting buckets of water. Peter planted some pumpkin seeds in a sunny spot without any fertiliser. We would not be staying long enough to eat the vegetables, but we were curious to see how rich the soil was. The seed became a little plant, the plant grew and grew, and soon we had a small garden with one plant. A few months later Davin would harvest a good crop. This was very promising for the future, for we planned to come back the following spring and plant a whole garden.

Every few days we walked back to Miliva. We introduced ourselves to the shopkeeper, and soon the whole village knew about us. At ten in the morning and four in the afternoon, the shop would open and all the old people would gather. They bought one cigarette, or a cup of coffee, or a packet of biscuits. We could not get milk, yogurt or eggs in the shop, so we bought these from old women in the village. On Fridays we saw the imam entering the mosque. These people were Muslim, but none of them struck us as particularly religious. They didn't eat pork but did drink alcohol. No woman wore a burka and I never heard anyone say '*Inshallah*'. However, Muslim hospitality was very tangible.

There was one sad aspect to the village. The headstones in the cemetery next to the mosque were the only recent additions. The people were old. There were no young people and no children. In the end the cemetery would be full and the houses would be empty.

It was a painful reality, of which the old people were very much aware. In some villages we felt some despair. In others, like Miliva, they seemed to have some hope that young people would return from the cities. Peter and I moving in, perhaps, showed that not everything would be falling apart over the years to come.

I was very happy living in our little cottage, but three months earlier, after Peter had declared he'd had enough of hiking with a pack, I had been sad that our walking life was over. On our last day on the Lycian Way I'd had an idea: even if Peter wouldn't walk anymore, it didn't mean I had to stop too. I decided I should join a true *expedition*. The word alone filled me with excitement.

'Why join someone else's expedition?' Peter said one morning. 'Most expeditions are immensely complicated. It requires huge logistics, planning, high costs, sponsors and obligations, a team of people and therefore politics . . . This summer we will be Down Under anyway. Why not organise your own expedition in New Zealand and keep it simple?'

'Organise my own?'

'You've learned enough in the last ten years to lead others into the New Zealand wilderness, haven't you?' he said with a smile.

Later that day, the whole plan came to me: I would put a clip on the internet, asking for the five strongest, bravest and wildest women on this planet to come with me on a three-month expedition into the wilderness of New Zealand's Southern Alps. We would set off in summer, and survive almost entirely off hunting, fishing and gathering. Apart from on popular walking tracks, I had seen so few women in the wilderness that putting together a women's team was an exhilarating prospect.

After I uploaded my expedition request on YouTube, I received many messages. Among all the applicants, Tamar Valkenier caught my attention. Three years ago she had resigned from her job and cycled from The Netherlands to Istanbul, bought her own horses and camels in Mongolia, and trekked sixteen hundred kilometres through the Altai Mountains.

We exchanged many enthusiastic emails. One day she wrote that she was rock climbing in Greece and could hitchhike to Bulgaria to see us for a few days. We made arrangements to meet at midday a week later in the village down the valley. We had to guess the time, and she was already there when Peter and I arrived.

She laughed and waved when she saw us. She had blonde hair reaching her shoulders, her back was straight and her shoulders relaxed. We had a coffee and talked about our lives—where we'd come from and where we planned to go. She told us she had worked as an investigative psychologist with the Dutch National Police. It was an interesting and challenging job, she said, but she had given it up to try something completely new. She wanted to see the world and travel slowly.

After the coffee, she swung her pack on her back and we started the two-hour hike back to our cottage. Tamar was dressed in black shorts and elegant sandals, which looked like flip-flops but were stronger than they looked, for she had walked the Altai Mountains in them. The same could be said about her stick-thin legs. Although she walked with quite a heavy backpack, the steepness of the terrain did not affect her. She stopped every now and then to look at the view or at certain plants. She wasn't racing to prove that she was fit.

I also noticed that she did many things the same way as me. It was almost like meeting a twin. For example, when we left the asphalt road to turn into a forest track, I said, 'Asphalt is only good for one thing . . .' I lifted my toes, leaving my heel on the ground. Tamar knew immediately what I meant: 'Indeed! Scraping the callus off your feet!' she exclaimed. If you walk every day in sandals, you develop a layer of callus on your heels. In dry air, this will eventually crack, causing excruciating pain.

There were blueberries along the way, and we spent a long time picking and eating them. When a shower of rain passed over, we sheltered under a tree and saw several yellow and black salamanders crawling up the road. They walked slowly and awkwardly. Not quite a frog, nor a lizard. They were rare in other parts of the world, but common in the Rhodope mountains. Tamar was delighted and let the salamander walk on her hand.

She loved our newly bought cottage and was especially pleased with the wild vegetables. She picked a whole variety and cut them up for dinner. The usual afternoon thunderstorm arrived. While the rain was drumming on the roof, we exchanged stories. I sat on the bed, Peter on a chair and Tamar on the windowsill. She looked as if she had always sat there, and seemed very at home. Later we lit the firebox and Tamar made a delicious dinner for us in a matter of minutes with edible plants, some left-over rice and a few peanuts. Before being an investigative psychologist, Tamar had been a Michelin-star chef.

Although she had travelled so much and—we discovered—slept so little, she appeared calm, enthusiastic and content. Nothing appeared to be a problem for her. We were both so happy to meet each other. We were of the same calibre, and mutual respect wiped out any possible competition and envy. 'Life and the world are too beautiful to miss out on,' she said with one of her surprised laughs. She felt like a very kind, considerate and understanding friend, as well as a strong and competent adventurer. Within the first few minutes of meeting her, I had known she would be an excellent expedition member.

After three wonderful days we said goodbye, and promised to see each other in New Zealand six months later. Coincidentally, Tamar had already planned to explore New Zealand long before hearing about the expedition. She had her tickets, and was flying out in November.

T owards the end of July, we stored our belongings in boxes and locked our house. I was not very sad to leave, because we knew we would return and I was excited about Australia.

We shouldered our packs and walked for the last time to Miliva. On the way we looked at the quince trees, and the apples, pears and walnuts that would be ready in future months.

'We're going at the wrong time,' said Peter. 'Look, it's still summer here and it's too early to leave. Timing's not right.'

I sighed. 'Yes, I have heard you saying this a hundred and thirty-seven times. We booked the tickets, your Bulgarian visa is running out, we can't stay. We are going through an open door.' I lifted my arms and said, 'Peter! We have to embrace insecurity and step into the unknown!'

He didn't look at me. 'I don't want to go,' he said, and shook his head.

'That is number one hundred and thirty-eight! Stop worrying, Australia will be a great adventure.'

We had coffee and biscuits at Davin's house, and gave him the key, for he would look after the cottage until we returned. We wished him well for the autumn and winter, and said we would be back in May next year, nine months from now. We promised to bring him seeds of special New Zealand vegetables. Davin had never heard of kamokamo, or even swedes and apple cucumbers, but was keen to try to grow them.

Davin wished us a good journey. His small but strong arms clutched my shoulders, and his body was still for a moment. Then he pulled himself back and nodded gravely.

'Bye bye,' he said. I saw tears in his eyes. 'I love you both.'

'*Da*,' said Peter, and shook his head, meaning yes. He too had tears in his eyes.

Then Emma and Anchov hugged us, and when we all walked to the shop, the storekeeper had opened up, and her brother was there to say farewell, and there was the man with dementia too, and the lady from the chickens, and the man from the horse, and the bee-man, and the man with one leg, and the woman with the cow, and the old lady who sold yogurt, and the old deaf lady, and Milko. Good old Milko, still going strong. He came to say goodbye while his horse waited in the street.

Four months later, in the winter, Davin died of cancer. We were intensely sad and shocked when we received the message from Davin's grandson. Our friend had always looked so healthy and vibrant—we didn't know whether he knew he was sick when we last saw him.

Upon reflection, we had noticed that Davin had been particularly open-hearted and loving. Maybe he knew his life was drawing to an end. Perhaps that's why he had tried to love every day, and everybody in his life, very much.

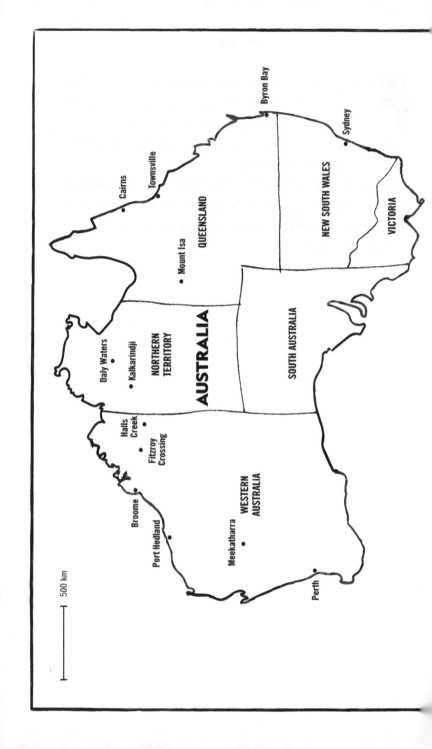

CHAPTER 7

AUSTRALIA
UNEXPECTED
MADNESS

After nineteen hours in the plane, we stayed a night in Sydney before flying a couple of hours north to Byron Bay, where we were met by people from the festival. We were guided to a taxi and taken to our incredibly luxurious accommodation. Suddenly, we were in the land of riches, being treated like a king and a queen.

We laughed and fell into our soft bed, threw our clothes on the soft carpet and walked into the hot shower. We washed our smoky clothes in the basin, and made ourselves a cup of English tea while eating our welcome gift: a jar of chocolate-coated macadamia nuts.

Next morning, we went for a walk around the block and we could talk to anyone we wanted. It was wonderfully easy to be in an English-speaking country. The town was beautiful, with big old banyan trees full of fruit bats on the side of the road. Compared to Bulgaria, the people looked rich and satisfied, and it suddenly occurred to me that affluence could possibly create a false sense of security.

I had five different public-speaking events, all held on the festival grounds, which was a grassy area near a stunning beach. The weather was warm, but the grounds were shaded by trees and the author events were held in vast tents. The atmosphere was relaxed and welcoming.

I spoke to large audiences about the book, and our experiences and insights in the wild. To my surprise I was not very nervous. Years ago I would have been so anxious in the days leading up to such an event, but now I realised there was no real danger. There were no bears, no lightning storm; I did not need to cross a flooded river and I was not about to fall into a crevasse. I was safe, so there was no need to be afraid. Over the years in the wilderness, my irrational fears seemed to have diminished. Without fear of failure, the events were very enjoyable.

We listened to other speakers and went to all the parties. At night I didn't sleep because of jet lag, and at the end of the week I was very tired. But I didn't mind—it was one of the most exciting weeks of my life.

And then it was over. Our next stop was Perth, six hours' flight away.

Stepping out of the plane, we were met by a cold southerly wind. It was still winter here.

Kate welcomed us at the exit with much enthusiasm. She was pretty, with long, dark, silky hair and a slim figure, and wore an elegant shirt and skirt. When I gave her a hug I smelled nice essential oils. She pointed to a ute that was parked right in front of the airport hall. A man sat casually on the back, his feet dangling over the edge. He was in his late fifties, barefoot, wearing old jeans and a merino shirt with stripes and a couple of holes.

'And you must be Kevin!' I said.

I stretched out a hand, but he was quick to jump down for a hug before loading our packs into the pick-up. Once on the road, we talked about our experiences in Bulgaria, the festival in Byron Bay, and their impression of Perth.

'Is Kate your real name?' I asked after a while, for it didn't sound Dutch. She had an almost flawless Australian accent.

'No, no, I left Holland behind, no one knows my Dutch name here and I never speak Dutch.' She shrugged. 'I regard Australia as my home.'

'We really loved your book,' said Kevin. 'We read it twice. The second time, Kate read it to me while driving on those long stretches of road in the north.'

Kate looked over her shoulder to face us and said, 'We have driven eight times around Australia, and now we've settled in the best place we could afford. Our land might not be as pretty as the forested mountains in Europe, but it is a special spot. We created a pond and have a lot of fish now. It's wonderful having all our own animals.'

Kevin talked about their pigs, chickens, ducks and peacocks, and the mobs of sheep that were grazing pasture elsewhere. He said they wanted a really good and healthy life for their animals—and at the end they ate them.

As we approached the highway, Kate said to Kevin, 'Better slow down around here, honey. Last time we got a speeding ticket here.'

'Oh. God, yes. The cop was a real bastard. I had to really calm myself down, otherwise I would have given him a hiding. I didn't want to tell him my address. Our official address is a caravan close to Perth, but we actually live in a place near Grayburn about two hours from here. No one knows where we live. I want to keep it that way, because I reckon the cops are looking for me.'

'Oh, why is that?' I asked casually.

'Nothing too serious, just a couple of stolen gates and stuff. But still, better to lay low.'

'How is Okey Dokey?' I asked, to change the subject. Kate and I had been emailing each other for months, and I knew all about their animals. Okey Dokey was their donkey. I also asked about horse trekking.

'I haven't done much trekking, but we can start now!' she said.

I was surprised by this, for I had understood she had experience.

We talked then about the possibility of hunting wild meat, and Peter asked whether Kevin had a firearms licence.

'I'd love to be able to hunt, but I can't stand the whole process of getting a licence. I'm not good with forms and exams, and I'm sure to fail when I'm surrounded by a bunch of people. I can't stand crowds.'

'Kevin doesn't see many people,' said Kate. 'While I go into the shops, he waits in the car park.'

'That's right,' said Kevin. 'I also can't stand the vibe in the supermarket. They're the symbol of fucked-up corporate bullshit. They're busy destroying the world for the sake of a buck.'

I looked at Kevin through the rear-vision mirror. He had thin lips, and his mouth was a stretched-out letter M. He wasn't bad-looking but he didn't smile very much. Hardly ever, I noticed. He had short, curly hair, slightly grey. His sleeves were up, and I could see his muscled arms and strong hands.

'After reading your book,' said Kate, 'we thought of attracting like-minded people to create a community. Not really a community, more like a tribe. Any change in the world must come from people working together, right?' She looked at Kevin.

'Yeah, we need people like the four of us,' he said, 'who can live basic, who are not planet destroyers. Every one of us can contribute a skill. I'll do the flock of sheep, providing home-kill. Kate can look after the other animals.'

He seemed to be waiting for our contribution, so I said quickly, 'I can get an Australian firearms licence and go hunting!'

'Yes, I'll dig a garden, I'm good with growing vegetables,' said Peter.

I asked Kate how often she drove to town, since Kevin didn't do shopping.

'Oh, I don't drive, never got my driving licence,' she said.

No licence? In this vast country, where everything is done by car, not being able to drive seemed an incredible dependence.

I looked out the window. We had travelled through a large eucalyptus forest; now the trees became smaller and sparser, and the road became quieter.

'We have been longing to live with others for some time, but it's hard to find like-minded friends,' said Kate. 'People think we're crazy when we say that chainsaws, tillage machines and chemicals are banned from our patch of nature. We do not see our neighbours and don't know any locals. This is what we want,' she said, 'because we have nothing in common.'

'The other thing that other people don't understand,' said Kevin, 'is our loving but polygamous relationship. We don't treat each other as possessions and we don't like to keep secrets from true friends.'

It suddenly dawned on me that we had little idea of where we were going. The only thing I knew was that we were driving two hours in an eastern direction. We were now in the wheat belt and all around us were green fields. There were hardly any trees to be seen. A couple of roads for machinery went through but there were few other signs of habitation.

'We hate the wheat production with a passion,' said Kevin. 'The chemical spray they use is outrageous. They are poisoning us. People should boycott this evil shit.'

'Wheat is also really bad for your body,' added Kate. 'It's like sugar. It's poison. A few years ago we completely changed to a keto diet. We cut out all carbs, and only eat meat and vegetables, and we feel a lot healthier! It's a growing movement; eventually people will come to their senses and will experience it for themselves.'

It began to drizzle and Kevin turned on the windscreen wipers. The left wiper squeaked with every movement. I closed my window to stop the wind and rain coming in.

Eventually Kevin stopped so that we could get our first glimpse of their land. I was curious, because this would be our home for the months to come.

In front of us was a natural depression, a sort of a dip that could be called a small valley. There was a stream and a pond in the middle, and about one hectare of trees surrounding it. The rest of the panorama was of fields of wheat, as far as the eye could see. It didn't look too appealing, but perhaps their camp was settled in a beautiful place.

Kate opened the farm gate and we drove into the young eucalyptus forest. We came to a storage tank with a corrugated-iron roof over the top.

'We collect rain from this roof for drinking water,' said Kate. 'It goes in the tank and we fill our jerrycans. Our camp is about one kilometre from here.'

'You collect *rain* water?' asked Peter. 'Does the wheat spray not reach that roof with the wind drift?'

'Yes, sometimes,' said Kevin. 'That's why we hate the wheat belt. It's poisoning all this land.'

Kevin drove the last kilometre slowly. We were on a narrow track with a film of water covering grey mud. He pulled up outside their tent.

I stepped out of the car, careful not to slip in my sandals. It was drizzling, and the air felt very cold and humid. I put my woollen hat and raincoat on, and glanced at their square canvas tent. It looked old and the bottom part was mouldy. Everything was brown, grey and ashen. The muddy camp was next to a swamp, and in winter the whole place looked cold and miserable. That they had travelled eight times around Australia and decided this was the best place they could find was almost unbelievable.

I felt depressed. We had flown six hours to get here from Byron Bay and the place reminded me of that gypsy or refugee camp I had seen in Svilengrad on the border with Turkey. It wasn't snowing here, but it had a similar horrible, desolate feeling to it.

'Come have a look inside our tent!' said Kate cheerfully.

I followed her in hesitantly. The vestibule contained a table with food boxes and a fridge. Behind a canvas door was their bedroom, but it was so dark in there, I saw little beside a bed and a cabinet.

Kevin brought in some supplies from the ute and said, 'Now, for the first days, you can pitch your tent over there—' he pointed at an open spot near the creek— 'and maybe after a week, we can sort of move into the tent together.'

Into the tent *together*? I didn't like the fact that he seemed to direct everything, and felt a slight panic coming up.

Kate showed us around their camp. 'We cook on the fire,' she said. 'And the compost toilet is here.'

'Where?' asked Peter, looking for a little building in the distance. 'Here!'

Three metres from their tent was a big drum with a lid.

I laughed and said, 'Are you just shitting right here?'

Kate laughed too. 'Yes, it's conveniently close to the tent when it rains. If you open the lid you'll see a toilet seat. But you can move it!' she added. 'Move it to wherever you want! Or just find a little place in the forest.'

We go as far away as we can,' said Peter when we were alone.

We found a flat spot under a tree to pitch our tent about fifty metres away, and put our packs on top of a fallen log to keep the bottoms free of mud. We were in the middle of a vast agricultural area. This dip was a catchment for all the spray in the surrounding land. The water in the creek and pond would be chemically polluted and very unhealthy. I wondered whether it was safe to wash in it. When a big truck drove past, we realised the road was very close by. Then we smelt the fertiliser coming from the truck. This spot was one of the most toxic places we had ever thought to stay. It was certainly not suitable for living long term. We were puzzled by why Kate and Kevin had come to live here, since they seemed so concerned about their health.

Our mood brightened a little when we saw the four horses in the distance, grazing on the other side of the swamp. They looked strong and gracious. For months I had looked forward to learning about horses, and hoped we could go riding the next morning.

Back in their camp, Kate and Kevin were busy with daily chores and feeding all their animals before dark. I wanted to give a helping hand, but the path that led to the pigsty and the other enclosures was so muddy it required gumboots. So I cleaned the kitchen instead. This was a wooden structure made from poles, and a makeshift table with two water tanks. The sink was dirty with black autumn leaves. Overhead was a roof made from plaited twigs and branches. In the summer this possibly gave a little shade, but in the winter a decent plastic tarp would have been more practical.

Kate had already prepared a beautiful meal of their own home-kill mutton with vegetables. When she returned from her chores, she heated it up and we sat down to eat. During dinner the conversation went back to food and the allergies and illnesses that Kate believed had been cured by her carbohydrate-free diet.

We tentatively raised the issue of how we were going to live together, since Peter and I were still quite fond of our bread, chapatis and pancakes. 'Maybe we should cook separate meals,' I suggested. 'So that everybody is happy.'

They took it the right way and agreed to the plan.

'Yes, one problem solved!' concluded Kevin cheerfully. 'But what I wanted to say is that we really loved your book, and especially the part about open relationships.'

After the comment about sleeping together in the canvas tent, I became a little disquieted. Why exactly had they invited us?

Next morning, I woke up early, zipped the tent open and walked to the stream. I looked at the green wheat fields and experienced a feeling of utter isolation. We had spent seven years in the wilderness in New Zealand, choosing the most remote places in the mountains to live. Sometimes we had been four days' walk from the nearest dirt road and not once had I felt lonely. Nor had I ever felt it in Europe.

Yet now it felt as if the world was going on without us, and we had been cast off into the wastelands. We were stuck in the wheat belt, which stretched for hundreds of kilometres around us. We had no means of communication, and nobody knew where we were.

We helped with killing a sheep that morning. Kevin had eight mobs grazing different pastures all over the region. Wool and mutton were their source of income. He had driven some fifty kilometres in the early morning, killed a ewe and brought the dead animal back.

I helped to skin it. The many knives in his workplace were all razor sharp, and the job was easy. We had a delicious brunch from the offal. After the meal the conversation went back to food. They told us about the incredible ways the body changes when you are on a keto diet, and how you get slowly sick if you eat wheat and other sugars like fruit. We said we'd been eating wild fruit all day long in Bulgaria, and we were feeling quite healthy.

'Oh, no, no, I really think it's as bad as sugar,' said Kate, shaking her head.

In the afternoon, while Peter was reading a book in the tent, I walked over to their camp and poked up the fire to get some warmth. Even with all my clothes on, I was freezing. I was busy breaking up wood when Kevin came over, and again brought up the topic of open relationships.

'We are going to organise a Free Love Festival this summer,' he said.

'Oh?' I replied, wondering what this would entail and how he would stand the crowds of people.

He explained the details of location and advertising while I was busy hanging a billy over the fire for some tea. At the end of his speech he said, 'I just really love hugging.'

I straightened myself and said with a laugh, 'Really? I *hate* hugging.'

It was such a ridiculous statement that anyone would take it as a joke. But he didn't laugh, and over the course of the afternoon I saw his personality change from overly cheerful and full of good ideas to one that was more moody and tense.

I had the impression this was not going the way he had planned.

On the third day Kevin needed some tools in town, an hour away by car. It was our first opportunity to do some grocery shopping, so we went along too. While they waited for us in the car in the car park, we ran through the supermarket. Accustomed as we were to Bulgarian prices, we were dumbstruck by the cost of food. We quickly selected the cheapest vegetables, and basic products like flour, rice and lentils. While waiting in the queue at the counter we spent five minutes discussing whether we really needed that jar of Vegemite, and still the bill was nauseating.

Back at camp, Kate helped us with unpacking, and her eyes fell on a dozen eggs.

'Those are cage eggs,' she said.

'I just grabbed the first ones I saw,' stumbled Peter.

'And they were the cheapest,' I said, feeling very ashamed. 'I guess we were just so shocked by the prices. We will get used to it though. Next time we'll buy free range again.'

'We buy everything organic,' said Kate. 'We believe that you're voting with your dollar; the consumer can make a difference.'

'In Bulgaria we just bought the eggs next door, where the chickens were,' said Peter. 'We bought the milk and yogurt from the lady with the cow. All of it was organic, local and cost little. We just have to adjust a bit here.'

Kevin arrived. The conversation went to organic food versus non-organic, vegans, paleo diet, keto diet, bad sugars in fruit, and Kate came back to the evil eggs again. Kevin shook his head and looked dark. His chest became more puffed up, his voice became argumentative, and Kate went more quiet. The tension was building.

When Kevin mentioned again the terrible wheat industry, Peter said that if he was really concerned about the planet he should also think about his use of petrol; whole wars were being fought over oil. And what about his money in the bank? His bank possibly invested his money in the armament industry. Many people in the Congo would have died for the rare earth elements in his cellphone and computer. 'I mean to say,' said Peter, 'every consumer is guilty in one way or another. I believe the key is to consume as little as possible. The real changes will have to come at a legislative level.'

It became a heated argument, until it was dark and we went to bed.

We talked for a long time. This was not going to work. But what should we do? We didn't know where we were exactly, or in which direction we should go. Eventually, we decided to go north to escape the wet winter weather. Driving was not our preferred method of travelling, but we had few options in a land with so little water. So we'd have to buy a second-hand car. We had savings for unexpected expenses, but generally survived—without having a regular job—by keeping a close eye on day-to-day spending.

Worried how we would organise a sudden road trip, we fell into a fitful sleep.

During the night all the horses had moved across the creek towards our tent. Two of them were standing solemnly next to the entrance when we woke up. We talked to them and patted their beautiful hides before we nervously walked over to Kate and Kevin.

Peter carried an armful of firewood, and I had a small bag of flour and an egg. While they were preparing their own food, I made up the batter and baked pancakes over the fire. As we silently worked on our chores the tension built up and Kevin began to talk. His tone was aggressive. He continued yesterday's conversation about organic food, bad human health, animal welfare, evil consumers, and even said that vegans were destroying the world. When I questioned how that could be the case, he became so angry that I dropped the matter.

As Peter was about to eat the last pancake, Kevin seemed to explode. 'If you cannot even see that wheat is so goddamn evil, what are you? Fucking blind? Or fucking stupid? Look all around you and see what it does!'

My heart missed a beat, and I felt a rush of adrenaline. I kept my head down, and started to gather our belongings.

'We are not blind or stupid,' said Peter. 'Calm down.'

'Calm down?' he shouted. 'Eh? Why the hell should I listen to your advice? Who are you to tell me to fucking calm down!' He was almost panting. Then he went on in a low voice. 'Listen, mate,' he said threateningly. 'We cannot live with people who are supporting the wheat industry. With buying those cage eggs you're voting for poor animals having horrible lives. We *love* our animals! We *care* for them! We don't even want to give your non-organic lentils to our pigs!' His anger took hold of him again and he shouted, while articulating his words carefully: 'It is all fucking poison, the planet is getting sicker and sicker, and you're supporting it! You better get the fuck out of here. You hear!'

I saw Kate's face. She was as white as a sheet.

'Do you fucking hear me?' shouted Kevin.

I saw the terror in her eyes and knew this wasn't the first time Kevin had been angry like this.

Peter lifted his hands, and said to Kate, 'Do something!'

But she had learned over the years what worked best, and she disappeared into the tent without a word.

We backed away from their camp, but Kevin was barring our way. He stood swaying on the balls of his feet, as if he was getting ready for a fight.

'You better be careful,' said Peter. 'There are two of us.'

'There are two of us too!' he yelled back, but we knew that Kate was not coming out of that tent again.

I looked at Kevin with big eyes. It was pure fear but, interpreting it as a possible threat, he shouted, 'Don't look at me like that!'

I was shocked. His screaming words felt like a physical assault. I glanced around for a weapon of some sort, then realised that we should avoid confrontation at any cost, because Kevin was wild. Furiously wild. In his rage he seemed to acquire almost super-human powers. If I took up a weapon, he would reach for his butchering knives, which were all razor sharp, and we would have no chance.

'Okay,' I said in a calm voice. 'We are leaving. We are going to break up camp. Pack our bags now. There is no problem.'

'Yeah, get the fuck out of here!' he said. 'We can't live with you! You're the same as all the other bloody hypocrites and planet destroyers!'

Peter and I moved towards our tent with Kevin on our heels. My heart was beating in my throat while Kevin kept shouting how evil we were. His normal voice had changed into a strangely loud booming tone, like that of a worked-up preacher in a church. It was frightening and surreal.

'You're preaching to the wrong congregation!' shouted Peter, which made everything worse. Kevin never stopped screaming after that.

'We need to get rid of you!' he yelled as he circled our tent while we rapidly packed our bags. 'I would do the planet a favour by chopping your fucking heads off! And burying you in the swamp!'

I looked up in disbelief. My hands were shaking uncontrollably.

'Nobody would ever know it! I would even enjoy doing it! *I would fucking enjoy it!* You hear it? Save the planet from you fucking idiots!'

We were in a very dangerous situation. One wrong word and Kevin's fury could ignite and he would attack us. The man was absolutely mad. If he killed us, my parents would not even start searching for another two months.

While I rolled up the mats, I saw Peter moving towards some branches next to our tent. He selected a hard piece of wood and positioned it carefully against the tree.

'What are you doing?' I hissed.

'I'm getting ready to defend,' murmured Peter. He turned his back towards Kevin, and put the hunting knife in his shoulder bag.

Adrenaline was still racing through my body, and my heart was pounding as we kept packing as fast as possible. Problem was we had just bought a week's food. After a dreadful half an hour of listening to his threats, we miraculously managed to fit everything in. Our packs felt like a crippling thirty kilos as we began to stagger like tortoises over the muddy track, while Kevin followed us. I felt very vulnerable: one little push and I would fall over.

I kept looking out of the corner of my eye to see where he was. Like a barking guard dog, he followed us to the end of his driveway. When we came to the gate and the edge of his property, he stayed behind. For fifty metres we could hear him shouting behind us.

'Is he still there?' asked Peter when we couldn't hear him any more.

I looked over my shoulder. 'Yes, he's still there.'

Only when I checked for the third time did I see he was gone.

I relaxed then, and sudden tears welled up, blurring my vision. The pack was so heavy, my legs were shaking. We went over a little hill, and when we were out of sight of his driveway I sat down with terror and exhaustion.

'We will walk to the first house,' said Peter, 'explain what happened, and ask where the nearest police station is. I think the police should know about Kevin.'

'Yeah, we need to talk about Kevin,' I said with a wry smile.

We walked down the asphalt road toward Grayburn. From memory Kate had said it was nothing more than a junction with a petrol station about ten kilometres away. The walk took us in a big arc around their property, and we kept looking to our right for any sign of Kevin.

At last we came to a house, where a man was just getting ready to go to work. Still distressed, we told him what had happened.

'He lives just there,' said Peter, pointing at the neighbouring land.

'Somebody is *living* there?' He was astonished. 'In a tent?'

'Yes, in a swamp,' I said.

He asked some more questions about the neighbour he never knew existed, before he put our packs in the boot. 'I'll drop you at Grayburn,' he said. 'From there you can hitch to the police office in Tavelton.'

We had barely driven a hundred metres when somebody jumped out of the bushes as we flashed by. I looked over my shoulder and saw Kevin standing still in the middle of the road. He was the picture of aggression. He had run across his land, and out to the public road. I shuddered to think what might have happened had we not been in a car. It was like something out of a horror movie. I was certain that we had just escaped an attack.

y legs were still shaking when we stepped out in Grayburn. I kept looking behind to see if Kevin was coming after us in his ute.

We decided to hitchhike to a bigger town, buy a car in a sales yard and drive north—away from Kevin, away from the wheat belt, away from the cold weather and all the horrible things that had happened in just four days.

A father and son from Perth picked us up. They had just been on a hunting trip. They listened with appalled fascination to our story of how Kevin had wanted to kill us and bury us in the swamp to save the planet.

'There are a lot of nutters in the outback,' said the father. 'Have you seen the movie *Wolf Creek*? That massacre was based on a true story. Things like that do happen here.'

They drove us into town to check out the car yards, but it was Sunday and they were all closed—as was the police station. The son, Mark, suggested we stay the night with him and his family back in Perth, and we took up the offer gratefully. We had enough food to cook a meal for all of us, and at nine o'clock I crawled into bed.

Still shaken from the scariest day of my life, I suddenly longed to become invisible, to become a completely normal citizen with a day job and a steady income, insurance, a standard house in the suburbs, a clean kitchen, a washing machine and a nondescript car parked in the garage. The feeling was profound, but shortlived. The next morning my fear had ebbed away and I felt myself again.

We visited a car yard, saw a Toyota Camry V6 for $2500, and bought it. We considered buying a more expensive four-wheel-drive vehicle so that we could go into the desert, but decided we'd stick to the safe asphalt road. It was not very adventurous, but with thousands of others on the same highway we reasoned it was safe.

The moment we had wheels, we went to the police. We sat down with an officer and told him the entire story. He asked whether we wished to lay charges: threatening to kill was a chargeable offence, he told us. All we wanted was to support Kate, we said. If Kevin ever turned his anger on her, she could go to the police and find supporting evidence.

'I would strongly advise he be declined any future firearms licence should he apply,' said Peter. 'If he'd had a gun he may well have killed us.'

We told the officer that we would return as witnesses should there be any future incident. We also told him Kevin had said the police were looking for him.

The officer checked the database. 'He is not on the Wanted list,' he said. 'He sounds like a very paranoid, crazy man.'

CHAPTER 8

AUSTRALIA
'LIFE IS A
JOURNEY
THROUGH
THE DESERT'

Next morning we said a heartfelt thank you to Mark, the nicest Australian we had met. With a fresh supply of food, water containers, a shovel, bucket and tools, and a map of Western Australia, we drove north towards the sun and warmth, space and the wilderness.

We passed through the wheat belt again and shivered at the

memory of what had happened only two days earlier. For the following weeks and months, the images of the madman would circulate in my mind, making me feel sick in the pit of my stomach.

The first day we drove eight hours towards Meekatharra, taking the inland route to avoid too much traffic and tourists. It felt great: we were on the move, but the vehicle was doing all the work. Every hour we warmed up a little more, and in the afternoon we could finally take our jumpers off.

The land was vast, covered in low-growing bush. The trees were so widely spaced we could see the ground beneath them. It was the time of wild flowers for which Western Australia is so famous, and we spotted here and there small purple and pink desert flowers.

We were following a straight line on the map and any junction was a big event. In the late afternoon we spotted a dirt road on our left. Too late—we raced past at a hundred kilometres an hour. After a kilometre we finally came to a standstill. We turned around and drove back.

'Cattle station—no thoroughfare', we read on a sign. Given the station was probably ten thousand hectares, we cautiously continued. After a couple of kilometres there was a small track into the bushes. When we drove in, we saw that we had not been the first ones to do so. We stopped when the track petered out, unloaded the boot, pitched the tent and gathered branches. All the wood was bone dry, and starting a fire was a delight. The evening temperature was wonderful. I took a deep breath, and felt a soft breeze touching my skin. I smelled the dry air and felt immensely relieved to be back in the warmth and the safety of the wilderness. Nobody around, no madness, no death threats, no danger, just silence.

After fifteen minutes the flies found us. They were small, quite ordinary-looking and rather sluggish. They went for our faces, and especially the moist corners of our eyes. More and more of them came, but at least they didn't sting. We discovered that if we stood in the smoke, the flies stayed away.

When the sun lost its heat, Peter went for a walk to explore the land. I did the same on his return. I had to orientate myself in a new way. I had to find landmarks, and remember everything in the right order. I saw a termite hill—a tower about one-and-a-half metres high. When I looked closer, I noticed the mud was densely packed and had little holes in it—an amazing construction. There was an extensive system of tunnels and chambers inside that functioned as a ventilation system to keep the nest cool. I spotted kangaroo prints in some dried-up mud, and followed them for a while until they disappeared. I saw a white rock, a hump and a dead tree. I looked back the way I had come and saw no sign of our camp, not even smoke. I had not walked more than a hundred metres, and began to feel nervous. I was so used to spurs and ridges, valleys and streams, and didn't trust myself not to get lost within minutes in the Australian outback.

I tracked my own footprints back to camp, but I knew it would take me a long time to learn to navigate in this type of landscape.

Next morning I woke up at dawn. The air was beautifully cool, so I got up and followed the dirt road to a sandy clearing. The sky slowly became yellow, and I felt a sense of immense space. To my delight I saw a kangaroo on the edge of the clearing. It looked at me quietly, timidly. When I kept still for some time, it stepped forward, a little awkwardly, and nibbled some grass. When I came a few steps closer, it took off—first calmly, then a little faster. Soon it was bouncing with unbelievable speed across the horizon. The tail was moving up and down, balancing the animal to marvellous perfection as it jumped maybe three metres at a time. The kangaroo merged with the desert and moved like a wave. It was quite unlike anything I'd seen before.

We had planned to rest a day, but when the sun came up the flies arrived and at ten o'clock it was scorching hot. Apart from a little hill in the distance, the land was dead flat. The shrubs with their few thin leaves didn't offer much protection from the sun. There was no real dark shadow to be found. And so, when we were slowly coming to a boiling point, we escaped. We packed up, wound down all the car windows and hit the road.

We drove and drove and drove while the sun flared down on our black car. For days we kept on driving over the parched earth. Hot air blew through the open windows and the dust settled slowly on every surface. We were the smallest ones on the road—the others were all campervans, big trucks or road trains. Often we could hear the road trains at night because it was hard to get away from the highway. At about fifty metres on each side was a fence to prevent cattle from straying to their death—and us from exploring the desert. Sometimes our only option was the free roadside campsites where there was a toilet but no drinking water. We filled our containers with chlorine-tasting water at petrol stations. I was surprised that freedom camping was problematic but lighting a fire was no issue at all; we never saw a sign to say there was a fire ban.

The spectacular places were locked up in national parks. You had to pay to get in and share the space with hundreds of other tourists, most of them the Grey Nomads who lived permanently in their trucks and RVs, moving around the country with the seasons. Mostly we kept on driving, in the hope of finding something better.

For days we kept heading north. Each evening we pitched the tent, lit a fire, cooked food and enjoyed the sunset. Each morning we packed up and drove on, burning up petrol and money. We stared at the flat shrubland that never seemed to change from behind the windscreen. And I grew more and more bored and unhappy. Driving would be a great solution if I ended up in a wheelchair. But I had plenty of energy and felt trapped in a car. I became irritated, Peter became grumpy, and we fought over the slightest things.

As we arrived in the small but busy town of Broome, we drove over something sharp and had a puncture. We went straight into a garage to fix it. While Peter waited with the car, I looked for a library to check my email. There were many applications for the New Zealand expedition. The aim was to survive off the land, but so far none of the two hundred women who had expressed interest was very experienced with hunting or fishing. Most wrote that they were quick learners, but I remembered how long it took for me to master the skills. I forwarded some of the applications to Tamar to see what she thought of our potential new expedition members, but I decided that if I could not find any other experienced hunter we would go with just the two of us. I could provide enough meat for two but not for five women.

Tamar wrote long and enthusiastic emails about our upcoming expedition and more ideas for future trips: finding reindeer herders in Mongolia, for example, or learning about hunting with falcons in Georgia. While I walked back to Peter, I thought of the marvellous, exciting life Tamar had, travelling alone with total freedom at her fingertips. Could I do that one day?

That night I suggested it to Peter.

'Yes,' he replied, 'it's great to go on solo trips, but you can do it when you're older. Look at me—I only started long-walking in my sixties! You and I can still do many adventures in the near future. Why not make the most of being together? I have a feeling I won't be around for too long.'

'Oh, oh, oh,' I sighed unsympathetically and cast my eyes to the heavens. 'Always so dra-ma-tic! What's wrong?'

'Nothing. I don't know. Just a feeling,' he said.

We drove for hundreds of kilometres through a scorched and often barren landscape. We argued or we were silent. While staring at the straight road ahead, I dreamed of the upcoming trip in the Southern Alps. Mountains, clear rivers, glaciers, big forests were waiting for me on the South Island.

My thirty-fifth birthday was coming up in the next week and I was suddenly aware of getting older. In five years I would be forty. I should make the most of this good age while I was stronger and fitter than ever. I thought of the Andes in South America, Afghanistan and Russia, and a feeling of restlessness came over me. I felt I was wasting precious time and money driving through a monotonous hot desert covered in termite hills.

We stopped for lunch at a roadside parking lot. When I began gathering wood to light a fire for a cup of tea, a friendly neighbour offered to boil us some water on the gas. While drinking tea, we chatted in the air-conditioned kitchen of their campervan. The couple had been on the road for years. They had driven up the whole east coast, they said, and were now going down the west coast. They wanted to visit the grandchildren in Perth.

Back on the road, I felt irritated with stories about grandchildren.

'Look at all those old people, I'm so fed up with them!' I said.

'Unfortunately that is my generation. You must think of me as old!' said Peter unhappily.

'They are not like you, don't worry,' I said. But he had a point. He was part of that generation.

'Why are you so irritated with them?' he asked after a while.

'Don't know,' I said. 'I just am.'

In the quiet hour that followed, I thought about all the Grey Nomads in the sunset of their lives. It confronted me with my fear of aging. One day I would be old and weak. One day I would have no opportunities to walk the world anymore. One day I would be sick with cancer or some other horrible illness, and then I would die. But before that time I would have to face all this with Peter. At sixty-four he was getting older, looking older, feeling older, and while I was looking after him he would rob me of all the opportunities I had in the future. Had I made a foolish choice to go with him twelve years ago? Should I escape now? Avoid the arrival of old age while I still could?

I thought it through for about a week. My birthday came and went, and some days later Peter asked where the big knife was. I said I didn't know. He said I had used it last. I said he used it last; it was in the box in the boot next to the tins and he should stop blaming me for losing things.

He silently picked up the knife and I became aware of how angrily I'd spoken. I saw my own behaviour as in a mirror, and knew I was actively destroying our relationship. I realised that arguments never just happen. There is always some choice involved. Behaviour might grow into a habit, and then the habit is hard to break, but somewhere in the beginning there was a choice.

I was shocked to see what I had been doing, for I never wanted to lose Peter. I loved him dearly; he was the most important person in my life. Sooner or later I had to face aging. Either with him or without him. I remembered the ancient saying, *Death is the greatest teacher*. I would embrace my fate and take death as my teacher.

That night, when we were sitting around our little fire, I said to Peter that I was sorry. I said the source of our arguments was my fear of aging—or, rather, him aging. It was a painful topic. It was something that had loomed over us since the day we met. He said he didn't want to trap me and that I was free to go. Anytime, I could go. He was so glad I had been with him this long already.

I said I didn't want to leave him, and when I said that, I cried.

I said I would be there for him. And hopefully there would be somebody there for me, when I was old.

With all these conversations about aging and death, a sense of foreboding about Peter's health kept creeping into the back of my mind. Something was coming. It felt like a subtle eerie silence before an earthquake.

One day we saw a lake on the side of the highway, with some campervans parked nearby. It was a free campsite on a cattle farm. We drove as far as possible into the bush and erected our camp under three old boab trees. The boabs were shaped like bottles with their fat trunks and thin branches. In the red twilight, their bark looked almost like copper. When I knocked on a trunk, it sounded like the tree could store water inside. Peculiarly enough, I had the feeling that one boab tree liked the company of other boabs. As if they were sad to be too far apart from each other.

This spot was comparatively free of annoying insects, and we stayed for a week. We ran out of water after a few days, but some other travellers kindly filled up our containers from their big tank.

Each sunrise, I walked to the lake to watch a hundred pink parrots in the trees. The sight was breathtaking. The galahs flew in, screeched, circled around and went back to the trees. The individual was completely part of the group. They talked to each other, felt secure with each other and unlike humans, would never consider being alone.

Each afternoon, I washed clothes in the lake that was home to four crocodiles. It was fascinating to watch them appear: first a nose would slowly come out of the water, then the crocodile would open its mouth, showing all its teeth. Maybe it was cooling off but it looked as if it was grinning. A strange grin. After observing them for some time, I decided they were harmless.

One afternoon Peter wanted to show me a big boab he'd seen in the distance and I casually followed him through the bushes. I had a stick, and hit the ground with every step to ward off snakes, which I suspected might be around during the day. Once we had found the tree, Peter suggested walking a bit further.

'What if we get lost?' I said.

'Lost? That would mean we were finally far enough away from the highway. Listen.'

I turned around, and when I cupped my hands behind my ears I could hear the occasional road-train. 'Long live your elephant ears,' I said.

'It's usually a curse, but in the Australian outback it's handy.'

Our feet crushed the tattered leaves and scraggly golden grass, and the sound of it was strangely loud. After a few minutes we felt as if we had left the human world behind, and the further we went, the more I felt myself relaxing. We were floating into the wonders of nature. It was as if I could smell, hear and feel everything for the first time. Slowly, we grew used to the flora and fauna, the lay of the land and the heat. This was not a spectacularly stunning landscape, but it had its own beauty.

The boab trees stuck out high above the rest of the small shrubs and long grass. We walked from one to another. Peter picked up the big seedpods and knocked them together, making a rhythmic sound. Somehow, it made sense to ask help from the trees to find our way back. After a couple of hours we arrived back at the camp without any trouble. Peter put the pods under our tree, as if it was a present from the other trees.

At Halls Creek, we stopped to do some shopping. We still had plenty of tinned food and other basics in the car, but we were looking for some fresh fruit and vegetables. When Peter disappeared into the supermarket, I saw a small medical centre. On instinct, I went in and inquired about entitlements to treatment, should we need it. The receptionist told me there was a reciprocal agreement between Australia and New Zealand and hospitals were free for New Zealanders.

'Why, dear? Is there a medical emergency?' she asked.

'Uh,' I said, a little bit startled. 'No, actually not at all, no.'

'Well, that's good then. Safe travels!'

We filled up our water containers at the petrol station and camped a few kilometres out of town, near a place called Sawpit

Gorge. The road was rocky and covered with about five centimetres of dust; our car would not make it to the gorge. We pulled over to the side, pitched the tent in the dust, and lit a fire with dusty branches. I walked around barefoot, covering my legs in a whitish film of dust.

We talked about the next morning. Either we would take a shortcut through the desert over a four-wheel-drive road or we would just follow the highway north. Peter was keen to take the adventurous route, but I had a sinister feeling about going unprepared into the desert. Still undecided, I walked around the corner to see the gorge. It was a stunning cliff with a pool. Lush vegetation grew around the water's edge and attracted many birds. The cliff amplified the birdsong.

Two men were drinking beer in camp chairs next to a Toyota Landcruiser. We started chatting and I told them about our plan of crossing the desert—or, rather, Peter's plan of crossing the desert.

'You're saying you don't have a four-wheel-drive?'

'Just a town car, a Toyota Camry,' I said. 'We're parked around the corner.'

'Do you have two spare tyres?'

'Only one,' I said.

'Should have at least two, mate. How much fuel do you carry?'

'We have sixty or so in the tank and twenty in a container.'

'How much water?'

'Oh, plenty. Fifty litres,' I said.

'That will last you twenty-four hours in the stinking hot desert. Do you have communication devices, emergency beacon, GPS and stuff?'

'None of that.'

'Not a phone either?'

'No,' I said. 'I wouldn't have thought that there would be reception anyway.'

'No, but do you have tools? If you break down, would you or your hubby know how to fix shit?'

'No,' I answered, and I started to feel very foolish.

'Don't go, mate. You're not prepared.'

'That's what I said to Peter, but he insists.'

'Well, he won't go without you? Surely?'

'I guess not,' I said. I thanked the men for their good advice and returned to our camp where Peter was breaking up branches for the fire. I told him about the men.

'If you don't want to go, we'll return to the highway,' Peter said. 'No problem. Just go back to the road. Nice and safe.'

'I know a solution!' I said. 'We'll let these guys know when and where we are going. We'll write down their number, and we'll ask someone at the other end to use their phone. We let those men know we made it. If they don't hear from us at a certain date, they'll know we are still out there, and they can ring the police. I just have to write down our passport numbers . . .'

'No, no, no. I don't want to involve strangers and make it all so complicated. We'd be better not to go.'

'Well, it's my life too!' I said, and straightened my back.

'Either take the risk,' he said, 'or we go back to the highway.'

'We might die if we go into the desert so ill prepared,' I said. 'Many do.'

'We might die,' he said, 'of boredom. On the highway.'

And I laughed.

We discussed risk management. If we had one puncture we could change the tyre. With a second puncture, we would dig a hole underneath the car with our shovel and hide in the shade.

When another vehicle passed, I would get a ride to town for help or a new tyre, while Peter would wait with the car. If we had a major problem, we would pack our bags and hitchhike out, leaving the vehicle behind.

'If we ever run out of water, don't forget the window-wiper container in the car,' I said.

'Yuck,' said Peter.

'Well, it's water,' I said. 'You just need a straw.'

The next morning we were still undecided. We packed and climbed into the car. After five kilometres we came to the junction.

'Left or right?' asked Peter.

'Right,' I said.

He looked at me and smiled. 'Sure?'

'Yes.'

'There we go!' he said, and turned the wheel into the dirt road that led into the outback.

For the first time I felt excited. We were stepping into the unknown. Now that we had left comfort and security behind, my brain and senses were activated again. Everything we did do or didn't do was important. We had to cooperate, we had to be a team, we had to be alert and careful. We were now responsible for our own lives. We felt empowered, alive and connected.

I was in charge of map reading. It was important to know exactly where we were, because there were water reservoirs along the way. Whenever I saw a signpost, I wrote down our kilometres on our odometer. If we broke down, I knew how far I had to walk back to get water.

Peter drove slowly, sometimes just thirty kilometres an hour, over the dusty and badly corrugated road. Our whole car vibrated, and it was very noisy. When I looked over my shoulder I saw the dust being lifted into the air, boiling like a cloud behind us.

The landscape was more varied than what we had seen from the highway. There were a few hills, trees, sometimes a small cliff. When we saw ahead of us a scrawny eucalyptus, casting a little bit of speckled shade, we stopped for lunch. The moment we stood still, the heat was unbearable. There was not a sigh of wind, and every living creature was hiding from the fierce sun, waiting for the evening. Peter found some dead wood and lit a small fire to boil tea. I opened the boot to get the ingredients for making chapatis, and saw that all the food, bags and equipment were covered in red dust. I wiped my sweaty forehead and the paper was red-brown. I blew my nose and the tissue was red. It was so hot that even in a bikini top and shorts I was baking.

We ate quickly. When the flies became impossible we extinguished the fire with some precious water and a lot of sand, and jumped back in the car. Moving was better than standing still.

In the late afternoon we saw a side track. We drove until the end and parked, elated that we had made it so far without incident. We were on top of a little hill and could look far and wide. Within two minutes a new kind of insect turned up. Sweat-bees. I wiped my skin with a cloth, but they kept coming. Hundreds of little bees crawling on my back, legs and arms—a sensation so creepy it gave me goose pimples. After a while the feeling became so extremely irritating I thought I'd go mad.

We pitched the tent in a frenzy and sat inside. It soon became as hot as an oven. So we walked up and down, slamming a T-shirt onto our backs to keep the insects off. Standing still was not an option.

We took out our big container to drink some water—and now dozens of thirsty honeybees turned up. They were much bigger than sweat bees, and they could sting. Soon a whole swarm danced around the blue container. Peter was flicking his T-shirt in front of my face so that I could drink. It was insufferable—until the magic hour came.

When the big red sun sank into the orange horizon, the insects disappeared, and I could open my eyes and relax again. We went to the top of the cliff and watched the whole world becoming quiet. All the colours softened. There was red in the grassy plains, the cliffs became pink and the bushes turned golden. A cool breeze came from the west, and everything started to breathe. We stared in wonder at the horizon. The earth was magnificently big, the sky was enormous, and everything on the land right now was in perfect balance. There was peace. Everything stood still to rest, to love, to be connected. We had driven thousands of kilometres to feel this one magic moment.

Then the last of the sun disappeared and the first stars were visible. Slowly the bright Milky Way appeared above us. The stars were crystal clear. We felt as if we were alone in the whole wide world. As if our consciousness could soar freely on the wind, like an eagle above the vast plains.

We had only one night in the outback, because the next afternoon we arrived in Kalkarindji, an isolated Aboriginal community. We felt proud that our little car had made it, but nobody acknowledged our arrival. The Australian Aboriginal people who sat around the petrol station had seen plenty of white folk coming through. They had no interest in talking to us. Teenagers with iPhones were staring at a world they would probably never experience. They were disconnected from the desert and very far away from the modern world. It was a sad sight. I wanted to ask the girls about their life in Kalkarindji, what they were thinking and dreaming of, what was happening with their people. I wanted to talk, but for once I was lost for words.

We went into the cold, air-conditioned shop where a head of broccoli was eight dollars. There were kangaroo tails with the skin still on, wrapped in Gladwrap, but $15 a tail was a bit much for us. We put our empty basket where we had found it and walked back into the blinding light and 40-degree dry heat.

After five weeks and nearly five thousand kilometres, we drove into the copper-mining town of Mount Isa. We went into a second-hand shop where Peter bought a grey T-shirt that said 'Life is a journey through the desert'. The printed picture was precisely the desert we had seen. Dried-up mud and a few spindly trees.

We drove on for another sixty kilometres to a dam where freedom camping was allowed. We pitched the tent next to a beautiful pond. It was like a sweet garden with large pelicans floating on the water. In the evening we saw some small kangaroos that had grown used to campers. Apart from some mosquitoes, there were, for some reason, no annoying insects, and so we stayed a little longer at this pleasant place.

We had only one set of neighbours, a friendly couple who offered us a beer and a seat. They had lived for eleven years in Mount Isa, where they owned a pub. At times they could taste sulphur in their mouths, they said. Copper accumulation created aggression, they said, for they had experienced it in themselves.

We chatted about crocodiles in the lake, and the man showed us a picture he'd taken on his phone only the night before, of a tiger snake right next to the caravan. He said the snakes could be very deadly and were fairly common around that area.

'Better be careful walking around at night,' he said. 'Shine your light, don't run, walk slowly, use a stick to let them know you're coming, as they are hunting at night.'

'Hunting at night?' I said, and realised how lucky I had been walking around in the dark without a light. We had been in danger and not even aware of it.

After our beers we went to our tent, using a flashlight. I remember feeling quite cheerful and optimistic—but this was the last carefree evening for a long time.

CHAPTER 9

AUSTRALIA
H FOR HOSPITAL

P eter fell sick with diarrhoea the next day. Having experienced it a hundred times in India, he was not concerned. He blamed the Chinese takeaway in town, or washing his face with dirty water, and he rested in the shade. It was about 35°. In the middle of the day, even under the trees, the heat was hardly bearable. We still had about forty litres of lukewarm water in our containers, and Peter seemed to drink plenty, though every day he lost a bit more appetite, and after three days stopped eating altogether. According to the car radio, the humidity was only about eight per cent, which meant that we were also losing moisture just by breathing. I encouraged him to drink, offered some re-hydration sachets that we always carried with us, and was confident he would soon recover.

I became worried only when Peter told me he fell unconscious every time he went to the toilet. There was no actual toilet: even at night he had to walk with a spade into the bushes some fifty metres away, dig a hole, do his business, clean up and cover the hole. This was an exhausting chore for him now that he had trouble walking. It was quite miraculous that he had not hurt himself falling unconscious onto the rocks.

After five days I tried to persuade him to go to the hospital. He was now suffering from fever and severe stomach pain, dizziness and fainting. At last he agreed and said, 'Maybe tomorrow I will hear that I have something serious.'

When the sun went down and the temperature dropped, he crawled with difficulty out of the tent to sit with me. We grew quiet when sparks of gold streamed through the branches. A red glow fell through the trees as a pelican floated silently by. He opened his big beak and scooped litres of water.

After Peter went back to the tent, I stayed looking at the pond, its surface soft and smooth, reflecting a silky glow. I gazed around and stored the scenery carefully in my mind, for I had the feeling that I would never see it again.

The following morning I packed up and drove Peter sixty kilometres back to Mount Isa Hospital. He sat with a water bottle on his lap and sipped it occasionally.

He was not able to walk from the car to the emergency room, so I ran inside to collect a wheelchair. The receptionist motioned Peter straight in. After hearing two words of the story, the doctor put him on a drip and began heart monitoring to see why Peter was losing consciousness.

That evening he was placed in a single room on the third floor, where I could sleep next to him on an unfolding chair-bed. A window looked out over an air-conditioning unit and a ten-centimetre strip of blue sky. At seven o'clock it was dark, and we lay listening to the strange background hum. It sounded as if we were in an airplane, flying into a different world. There was a ticking clock, too, and every two seconds there was a soft rattle, like a baby woodpecker. Strange sounds after the screeching galahs, the distant call of the dingoes and the thump of hopping kangaroos we had grown used to.

Peter's lead physician turned up the next morning. He was very knowledgeable, friendly and respectful, and was most concerned about the diarrhoea. He recommended taking antibiotics. When one didn't work, he switched to the next one. But nothing proved to be effective. Meantime, Peter was getting sicker and sicker. He suffered from terrible pain in his lower bowels. He was passing a thick yellow fluid. He needed help with wiping his ass. Every time he got up from the bed to urinate he would faint for thirty seconds. I stayed at his side and caught him in my arms. The doctors were worried about the fainting and put Peter through an MRI scanner, but they could not find anything wrong with his brain.

After a couple of days, the physician concluded that Peter was suffering from severe dehydration caused by diarrhoea and extremely low humidity in the unrelenting heat. The next step was to test the state of his kidneys. He told us that many indigenous people and stockmen in the outback suffered kidney failure as a result of dehydration. He ordered a scan, using a contrast dye to enhance the results—and saw that Peter's kidneys were indeed failing. Sudden damage to the kidneys is called acute kidney injury, the doctor told us. The damage was done in a matter of days, and it would take a month or more to recover.

Peter was still on a drip, but now his kidneys could not process all the fluids. His body began to absorb all the water and he started to swell up like a balloon. His chest was pumped up, his stomach became big as if he was ten kilos heavier, and even his eyelids puffed up. The internal fluid pressed on all his organs, causing constant horrible pain. They gave him strong painkillers to get through the day.

They tested his levels of creatinine, a waste product made by the muscles and removed from the blood by the kidneys. If the creatinine level in the urine is high, it's a sign the kidneys are not working. On arrival Peter's creatinine was measured at 120. Three days later it was 450; four days later it was 750. The doctor started to panic, for Peter was deteriorating with unbelievable speed in front of his eyes, and he decided to ring the renal specialists in Townsville for advice. Shortly afterwards, Peter was wheeled off to the Intensive Care Unit.

'He is critically ill with kidney failure,' the doctor told me, 'and there is a possibility of total organ failure.'

Total organ failure sounded deadly, and I was troubled beyond words. A dark cloud was hanging over my head and tears were never far away. I was not thinking of the future; I was thinking only whether he would survive the day.

was not allowed to sleep near Peter in the ICU, so in the evening I drove to a campsite and pitched the tent on the yellow grass. I felt very lonely. I had a sudden sense of what life would be like without him, and that made me even more sad. It was a sleepless and anxious night.

At dawn I rolled up the tent and drove back to the hospital. In the car park was a frangipani tree. Its smell was so soft and sweet that I collected a handful of petals for Peter.

It was ten o'clock before I was allowed to get into Intensive Care. Tears brimmed in my eyes when I saw him. He had a kind of clothes-peg on his finger to measure his heartbeat. His stomach was so swollen he now had trouble breathing. They had inserted a tube into his nose to supply oxygen, but his nose and throat bled as a result, and dried blood stuck to his skin. A catheter to aid urination pulled him to one side of the bed. There were screens everywhere, and in the office a nurse kept watch of his data on a computer. If any apparatus beeped, someone was at his bed in a second.

'Hello, my sweetheart,' I whispered softly. 'I have some flowers for you. Smell them?' I held the petals over his nose. It was something from the natural world for him.

'Nice,' he said. His eyes were dull, his tongue was thick and his speech was slurred. He had barely enough energy to talk, let alone smell my flowers.

With all the chilled water dripping into him, Peter felt cold all the time. Only five days ago he had suffered from the heat in the desert—just outside the door—and now he was shivering. But the worst thing for him was the noise. His room had a wooden door with a spring that made the door slam back with a loud bang. Peter's big sensitive elephant ears, made to save us in the desert, were an absolute curse in the hospital. Every time the door closed it sounded like a gunshot, and every time it broke my heart to see the effect on him. I went to the nurses, explained he had sensitive ears, and kindly asked them to close the door quietly.

With a tube in his nose, a drip in his arm, pegs on his fingers and stickers on his chest, it was hard to believe that it was Peter who lay there. Peter, who had been squatting happily around the fire ten days ago, was now fighting for his life.

At 5 p.m. the visiting hours were over, but nobody sent me away on my second night in ICU. I wasn't sure if that was a good or a bad thing. At six o'clock the doctor came in to say that he was trying to organise an airlift to Townsville Hospital. At seven o'clock it grew dark. I put Peter's hospital towels on the ground for a mat and my book as a pillow. Now that it was too dark in the room to read, I just listened to Peter's laboured breathing. When I heard him sigh, I sat right up to look at him. When nothing happened, I lay down on my towel again. The ground was cold. I was exhausted.

Alarms went off next door. Somebody called out, a woman was crying, nurses were running up and down. Any moment Peter could deteriorate, too, and his machines would start to beep. I waited. Expecting an alarm anytime.

At nine o'clock the doctor came in again to say that a plane was available and Peter would be flown to Townsville, almost a thousand kilometres to the east.

'Assistants will come to take you there in an hour,' he said. He looked at me. 'Please wait for me in the visitors' area. I won't be long.'

'Is Peter's condition life-threatening?' I asked him as soon as he joined me there.

'Look.' He averted his brown eyes. 'I wouldn't fly him to

Townsville if he wasn't in a critical condition, but he will be in good hands there. There's a renal unit with renowned specialists.' The two-hour flight would be hard on Peter's body, he told me, warning me that his condition could have deteriorated when I saw him again. 'Be prepared for the worst,' he said.

I nodded. How do you prepare for the worst? I thought. By planning what to do in case he dies?

Then the doctor spent twenty minutes of his precious time explaining in great detail how to drive ten hours, on a straight road, to Townsville.

'Once you're in the city,' he said, standing up to go, 'it's easy. Just follow the H for hospital.'

'H for hospital,' I repeated. 'Thank you.'

The doctor went home and I was shaken to the core. With a heavy heart I made my way back to the office just outside Peter's room.

'Have you contacted his family, his siblings?' the head nurse asked kindly.

To tell them he is dying? I thought, and tears welled up in my eyes.

'No, we don't have a telephone,' I said.

'Do you want to ring them?' She handed me a phone.

'I don't know their numbers,' I said, 'only email. Would it be possible to use the computer for a minute?'

The moment I was in her seat I felt a complete transformation: I was instantly rational, logical and calm. I opened my inbox, speed-typed one email to many recipients and sent it. While I was there, I quickly checked other mail. When I signed off after five minutes,

I reflected on this sudden cool frame of mind. I found it somewhat disturbing that I could switch so easily from one to the other. Was this the effect of the computer? Or was I unconsciously choosing a coping mechanism? Which state of mind was real? If they are both real, do I have an ability to choose? If not, why was I subject to it, and who was the ruler?

I didn't have the clarity to ponder the answers, because the moment I walked out of the office I saw Peter through the window and I was an emotional wreck again.

A t 11 p.m. a nurse came into the room to give Peter an extra-big dose of fentanyl for the painful two-hour flight to Townsville. The Flying Doctor assistants came with a stretcher. It took four people to lift him off the bed. He was wheeled with a lot of noise through the halls and I ran along behind them. We went through long corridors, around corners, through big doors, and suddenly we were outside in the dark. The air was warm and soft, and a faint smell of frangipani floated by.

'Do you smell the frangipani, sweetheart?' I said.

Peter looked up in utter misery and whispered, 'Yes.'

'Would you like to say your last goodbye?' the nurse asked.

Last goodbye? Surely not. Surely it was not a last goodbye. But if it was, then I should say it.

I leaned over, and tried to hug his shoulder without putting any pressure on his body. I kissed Peter on his forehead. He looked confused and in pain.

'I don't know if I will make it, Miriam,' he said.

'You will,' I whispered. 'Because I love you so much.'

'If you love someone very much, sometimes you have to let him go.'

I felt dazed, kissed him again. What did he mean, let him go?

'Death is only bad if you're healthy . . . Right now,' he sighed, 'death would be a blessing. It wouldn't matter, Miriam, it wouldn't matter.'

'It matters to me, my sweetheart,' I whispered, and I cried silently when they rolled him into the ambulance that would take him to the plane. When it drove away, I stood helplessly alone in the dark night, clutching Peter's colourful shoulder bag with our passports and money.

Then I walked to the car that was the last one left in the car park. I drove to the same campsite and pitched the tent in the moonlight. On the other side of the fence a small kangaroo was eating grass. We looked at each other for a while until I crawled into the tent. I lay down, feeling sick with worry. Half an hour later I heard Peter's plane leaving.

'Please, please, please make it to Townsville,' I cried.

I set off at seven in the morning with not a cloud in the sky. For the first hour I drove straight into the rising sun. Around Mount Isa were some hills, beautiful forest, and here and there a rock or cliff, but after that the land became flat and featureless.

During that ten-hour drive I sometimes felt calm, sometimes sad and sometimes I imagined the worst. I imagined Peter was already dead and they couldn't ring me. I thought of the funeral. Who should I contact first? Did he want to be cremated or buried? How would I even organise a funeral? Where should I put the ashes? My heart felt torn open by a claw of a tiger when I thought of living the rest of my life without Peter. At one point I feared that his body wanted to give up. I felt that he wanted to leave life.

'No! My sweetheart, hang in there! For god's sake, hang in there!' I howled.

When I had no tears left, I grew calm again. I stopped at lunchtime, walked to the boot to find some crackers to eat and nearly burned my bare feet on the black asphalt. Then I followed the long straight road again. The surface was shimmering. I could hardly keep my eyes open, and sat sleepily behind the steering wheel, driving hundreds of kilometres to the east, until I saw the H for hospital.

I drove into the city around six o'clock, straight into the setting sun. I had to merge left and right on the busy highway, and eventually found a car park at the hospital. I grabbed Peter's shoulder bag and ran through the big doors, frantically looking for the information desk.

'I'm here for my husband Peter Raine, who's just been admitted from Mount Isa; he should be in the renal unit.' I spoke extra-fast, so she'd know I was in a tremendous hurry. I had driven ten hours to get here faster. I had prepared myself for the worst: he could have died already. Clutching the map, I ran up the stairs, flew around the corner and raced through the corridors until I found him.

He was alive. He lay in a bed behind three blue curtains, and he smiled. He looked better than I expected. There was only a drip. He could talk, he could turn around without help, even stand up for a pee.

He said he'd had so much pain during the flight that he'd prayed for the plane to crash. 'Which would have been very bad for the pilot,' he said, 'but if I had had a euthanasia button, I would have pressed it then.'

At 8 p.m. a nurse told me to leave, as visiting hours were over. 'Where are you sleeping?' she asked kindly.

I said I didn't know. I had hoped I could sleep next to Peter, but there were three other people on the same ward.

'We have a social worker who helps patients' relatives. You can find her tomorrow at this floor and this room.' She pointed on my hospital map. 'Where will you go tonight?' she asked.

'Maybe in the car? In the car park?'

'Well, let's hope they'll find you accommodation tomorrow. What's your cellphone number?'

'We don't have a phone,' I said.

She frowned. 'But how can we contact you? If something happens to Peter?'

I stared for a moment at the desk and the flowers in a vase. It was the first time in my life I'd not felt proud to say that we lived without owning a cellphone or computer. It suddenly just felt stupid.

'I am here,' I said in a weak voice. 'I will be here all day, every day, until the day he gets discharged.'

Next morning I visited the social worker.

'Take a seat, my dear. How are you?' she asked, and I began to cry.

We talked through accommodation options, and discussed campsites, hostels and hotels. The nearest campsite was an hour away; the cheapest hostel was forty dollars a night and a twenty-minute drive.

'He might be here for weeks!' I said, and started crying again.

Within five days I had changed from a happy and optimistic person into an emotional wreck. I was exhausted and cried at the slightest thing. I felt so vulnerable that I grew afraid of bad news. I became more introverted and tried to avoid talking to strangers, for fear of meeting a grumpy person. One friendly gesture from any kind person, however, did a world of wonders. I had never understood the emotional strain of having a loved one so ill until I experienced it myself. Not long ago I longed to face the heart of the thunderstorm on top of the mountains; now I felt as weak as a kitten, begging for a kind word. It was a fascinating transformation.

Staying in a guesthouse was an option, but I wanted to be close to Peter. Sleeping in the car was by far the most convenient solution. The biggest downfall was that I had to hide from the security guards, who I figured would not allow me to sleep in the car park. But over the days I got into a routine. Every night after I left Peter I walked casually to the car, stepped into the driver's seat and closed the door as if I was going to drive away. Then I locked all the doors and crawled to the back seat. I had taped up the windows with cardboard to stop the car heating up and anyone looking in. All night, I lay down with my knees pulled up. It was so hot in there I started sweating immediately, but if I opened the windows too much it might alert the guards, so I practised slowing down my breathing to lower my temperature. Going to the toilet was problematic. It was almost an acrobatic act to pee in a bucket in a car—but I managed.

I didn't know how long Peter would be in the hospital—a week? A month?—but I had to be resourceful, find solutions for everything and develop a system to survive. When I got out of the car in the morning, my knees hurt from not being able to straighten them for hours on end. But all things considered, I had surprisingly good nights there.

I was never lonely, because Peter was only a hundred metres away. I was also close to wild kangaroos. I found this out one night when I felt I was suffocating, and opened the back door just a fraction. I turned my head to breathe fresh air, and just one metre away was a little kangaroo eating grass, looking at me.

I was always the first visitor in and the last one out. All day I sat on a chair next to Peter's bed. For weeks, we lived in three square metres behind the three blue curtains. I discovered which nurses were friendly, and my favourite one told me where I could collect boiling water. I bought teabags and a packet of coffee and had plenty of hot drinks. Peter had very little appetite and could not finish his meals. So I ate his leftovers, and bought fresh fruit in the shop. Only one nurse knew I was sleeping in the car. When she was on duty, I waited for a quiet moment and asked if I could take a quick shower. And every second morning, I locked myself in one of the toilets at the hospital entrance. In my bag were two or three dirty garments, which I quickly washed in the basin. I hung them over the seats in the car, and they were dry by the time I returned in the evening.

While Peter was sleeping I read a stack of books. I collected them from different wards or from other patients' families, and traded these at the second-hand book stall at the hospital entrance. I kept an endless supply going. My hunter-gatherer instinct never wavered.

Since I was always there, the other three patients in the room often relied on me for help. 'Nurse Miriam', they called me, and I was happy to be useful. The young woman in the next bed had spent more time in the hospital than out in the last three years. I surreptitiously wheeled her off the hospital grounds to a nearby café to remind her of the world outside.

O ne morning, after Peter had been in hospital for three weeks, I sneaked in the door early with some scented wild flowers. The light was still off, all patients were sleeping and I quietly read my book. Eventually Peter woke up and took his little turquoise towel off his eyes.

'Good morning,' I whispered. 'How was your night?'

I kissed his forehead. He smelled faintly sour. The illness and drugs had robbed him of his natural scent, stolen the smell I loved so much.

He looked exhausted, and his eyes were red. 'I never sleep deeply,' he sighed. 'They wake me up in the middle of the night to measure all sort of things. Patients press the alarm button to call the nurse. I'm so desperate to sleep, I'm utterly ... utterly, exhausted.'

He spoke slowly. His voice was croaky. It was the first time I had seen him on the verge of crying.

'I'm wilting away,' he said. 'I wish I could sleep outside. Even just for one night.'

Then a nurse came in. She noted again all there was to measure, and gave him his daily pills—ten different types of drugs. One medicine created side-effects that were treated with the second drug, which created side-effects that were treated with the third. In the end we didn't know what the original symptoms were.

Another nurse came in to take blood. Needle after needle was stuck in. 'Time for a new cannula!' she said. Every three days a new one had to be inserted. It was always problematic, because Peter was still dehydrated and his veins were difficult to find. Every trial was an agony for him.

An hour after breakfast the renal specialist came by on her round. We called her Doctor Bright because of her consistently cheerful and positive outlook. It was the most important moment of each day. When the doctor was in the room it suddenly grew quiet. All televisions were switched off and everyone eavesdropped on their neighbours' good prognosis or horrible predicament.

Today Doctor Bright had not such bright news. She had received more results, and Peter's GFR—the measure of how much the kidneys filter wastes from the blood—had fallen to 7. Healthy people have a GFR of around 90. So, Doctor Bright ordered a biopsy to find out whether he had suffered from chronic kidney failure for a long time, or whether just the dehydration had caused acute kidney injury. The latter indicated the possibility of recovery. Peter went on the waiting list for the biopsy, but it would take another week before it was his turn.

After the doctor had gone, I walked for half an hour in the burning hot sun to the supermarket to buy fresh mangoes, melons and papayas, the only foods Peter enjoyed. I crossed the highway, finding a break in the stream of cars. Nobody ever walked here; there was no footpath. There was rubbish in the bleak, brown grass. Water bottles, plastic wrappings, cans.

I walked to the river, where huge trees were growing on the bank. I touched the bark of one of them, and I cried. Peter was deteriorating. He might even die. I sat down for a long time feeling depressed.

Then I looked up at the tree: one branch was dead, but the other parts were living. Could he not live with weak kidneys? Could the rest of the body help the kidneys? Surely the body could compensate?

hen I returned to the hospital, his bed was empty. In panic I asked the nurse what had happened. He had gone down to Radiology for a scan, she said. I raced down the steps, ran through the corridors, took the elevator all the way down to the basement. Then I spotted him waiting in a designated area in a wheelchair, his hand tethered to the IV hanging from a pole behind him. He was leaning forward and staring at the ground. He looked utterly dispirited and alone. I hardly recognised him. Blending in with all the rest of the patients, he seemed just another sixty-five-year-old male. Another sick, sunken-eyed man dressed in green hospital clothes. My heart broke when I saw him like that. I wanted to take him in my arms and hold him like a small boy so that he could let his tears flow. But Peter had no energy to cry, or to speak. He had only just enough energy to stay alive.

I rushed towards him, and when he saw me he became again the person I knew. After hugging him and stroking his back, I realised that had I not been here in these last weeks, he would have given up.

I found a chair, sat down next to him and held his hand. Blue and reddish patches marked his poor skin. Every day they had trouble finding veins to take blood. I touched the spots on his arm and looked at my right hand. My veins were prominent, pumped up from running through the hospital. I looked so strong and fit next to him, but this time my muscles were useless. This time I could not carry him. It was the saddest thing. All my strength could not save his kidneys.

I told Peter about the recovering tree I had seen. 'For all living beings, the will to live is strong,' I said.

He nodded.

His grey eyes met mine for a split second. There was no sparkle in them, no joy, no hope, no strength.

After the scan he was wheeled back to the ward. Dinner was served, we had a cup of tea and I gave Peter his daily back massage to prevent bed sores. Now he was lying down, holding my hand while I was reading a book. Every now and then he patted my finger so tenderly and lovingly that I cherished the moment. When it was almost dark, I had to go. With much effort he stood up, for he insisted on giving me a hug.

'Thank you so much for all you have done.' He held me tight and patted my back. 'I really mean it,' he whispered.

'I'm just happy you're alive,' I said. 'I love you so much.'

He held me and said, 'I love you too, very much. I always have.'

Tears rolled over my cheeks.

'Why are you crying?' he asked, surprised.

Never had I seen him so loving, affectionate and vulnerable. We held each other and he opened his heart. I could feel the energy, and it touched me deeply.

'You are opening your heart,' I whispered.

'No, I have no energy to keep it closed,' he said. 'I now see that love is a non-action. If you do nothing at all, you love automatically. When death is near, you become good at receiving and giving. Receiving and giving.'

We hugged silently. It lasted no more than a minute, but it was the most loving moment. There had been some tension between us in the last months, and all that was now wiped away. I cried all the way to the car. I felt intensely happy. And I felt a sense of freedom. That's when I wondered if love and freedom are the same—at the core.

Next morning he was already awake when I came in. His face looked serious.

'How are you today?' I asked.

'In the middle of the night I felt death coming,' he said.

'What do you mean?'

'Death was here. I felt its presence. It was a strong but totally benign entity without a trace of malice. I felt no fear, I just felt relieved. I thought, This is it. It will come and take me. It was nothing like what you imagine it to be. Nothing to be afraid of. It was really beautiful and loving. But it didn't come for me.'

'What?'

'A man across the hallway died half an hour after I felt this presence. Different alarm bells went off in the middle of the night, doctors came, nurses gathered and the man was wheeled off.'

'Somebody died? Tell me again what happened? You felt a friendly version of the grim reaper coming and he took someone else?'

'No, no, nothing like that. We're in the dimension of life. But there is also a dimension of death. It's a parallel existence. We separate the two with our mind, but both of them exist at the same time. If you're in life, you don't see death, but it is there. And the surprising thing is, when you're in that dimension, you feel very peaceful.'

'Could that different dimension be called heaven?' I asked.

'I don't know. Heaven, as in a place where you meet people who have died, might be a little simplistic. But I don't know, of course. I will have to investigate this matter at a later stage.' He smiled. 'But one thing was most obvious—that dimension brings about the most wonderful state of mind you could ever imagine.' He took my hand. 'Really, Miriam. Death is nothing to be afraid of.'

After an initial improvement when he was flown to Townsville, Peter's health continued to fail. The lack of sleep ground him down, and his weight dropped fast: one kilo every two days. His face was gaunt, his body skeletal. In the last week, his diarrhoea had gone by itself, but his kidneys seemed to have deteriorated further.

After nearly four weeks in hospital, there was a space for him in the operating theatre, and Peter was wheeled off for a biopsy. A very skilled surgeon took out a tiny sliver of kidney with a long needle, and a little later we received the news. Peter was officially diagnosed with Acute Tubular Necrosis, ATN, which meant an acute kidney injury—not chronic. The difference was life and death. You can recover from a kidney injury but not from chronic kidney failure. The chronic condition requires dialysis and a donor transplant. It was the best news possible.

After the biopsy, Peter's blood test results improved just enough for him to be discharged. The specialist told him he should be able to recover at least eighty per cent of his kidney function but, she added, 'It may take eighteen months or more to fully recover.'

Peter put on his own clothes for the first time in five weeks. We thanked all our nurses and doctors and said goodbye to our neighbours in the ward. I wheeled Peter through the corridors. At the entrance I helped him stand on his own legs, then ran to the car and drove back. He stood waiting for me in the sun. He looked small and weak. His T-shirt sat loosely over his bony shoulders; his hair was dull, his face pale and anxious. But every single day these last five weeks, I had longed for this moment, and my heart jumped with joy to see him out in the fresh air.

Peter stepped in, and I drove slowly across the hospital grounds.

Through the open window I waved at the building I knew so well. Then we approached the highway.

'Mister Peter Raine! Welcome to the real world!' I laughed happily.

T he doctor had warned us: Peter was a butterfly in the rain. One mistake, one moment of dehydration, one stressful instant and he would be straight back in hospital. We had a place to go in Cairns, where Peter could build up his strength before flying to New Zealand. We'd been invited to stay with the daughter of a friend of my mother—my parents had been in touch with her about our predicament. She and I had last met when we were six years old, and I was extremely grateful for their hospitality.

It turned out that even driving was an ordeal for Peter. Stopping and going was painful, a roundabout was agonising, and the four hours to Cairns felt like eternal hell for him. When we finally arrived, he collapsed with exhaustion.

Astrid and her husband's home was in a gated suburb near the beach. The house was surrounded by a patch of tall trees, and had been built for the tropics with air vents and no air conditioning. It was very pleasant for Peter to be back in a natural setting without hearing alarms at night.

During the two weeks in Cairns I organised all Peter's medical documents and referrals, sold our car online after filling out forms and obtaining warrants, and organised the journey back to New Zealand. In the past we had always trusted randomness and never booked any accommodation beforehand. Now I planned every inch of our travel, for any freak event would be a disaster for Peter. I paid for an expensive airport hotel in Sydney and ignored the costs.

Money had become irrelevant. After sorting through a mountain of official papers, I realised that by living in the wilderness and being nomadic for most of my adult life, I had evaded a great many of the decisions and administrative chores most people had to deal with every day.

At the end of November, Peter was finally fit enough to travel. We flew from Cairns south to Sydney, then boarded another plane across the Tasman.

The first thing we saw was an estuary and some bush on the coastline. All the green colours sparkled. Everything was crystal clear; the clouds were white, the light was bright and the air clean. The country looked empty of people, the vegetation vital and healthy, and I sighed with relief. After eighteen months away, I felt had I had come home again.

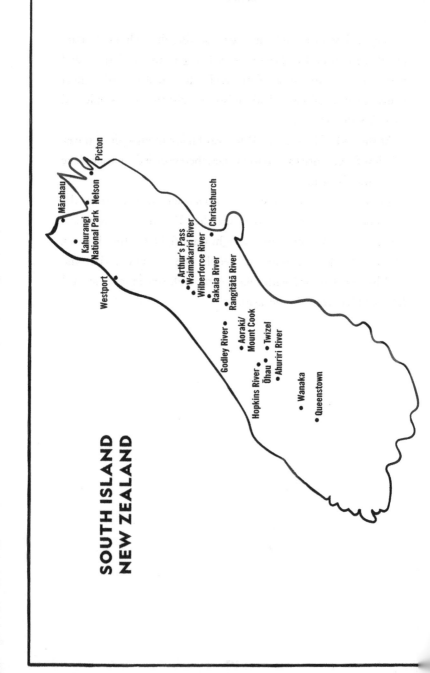

SOUTH ISLAND
NEW ZEALAND

Mārahau
Picton
Kahurangi
National Park Nelson
Westport
Arthur's Pass
Waimakariri River
Wilberforce River
Christchurch
Rakaia River
Rangitātā River
Godley River
Aoraki/
Mount Cook
Twizel
Ōhau
Ahuriri River
Hopkins River
Wanaka
Queenstown

CHAPTER 10

NEW ZEALAND
AN EPIC FEMALE EXPEDITION

Shortly after our arrival back in Auckland, I bought a car and drove Peter south to Whanganui, where we stayed with our friend Nick Maverick. A few weeks later, it was time for my long-planned expedition. I was so looking forward to being in the mountains but I felt horribly guilty for leaving Peter behind, seeing he was still quite vulnerable. But Peter knew how long I had been preparing. He said he felt a lot better now and encouraged me to go. 'It's midsummer and the mountains are calling,' he said. 'You should go, my sweetheart—this time you have to walk for both of us.'

During the weeks in Whanganui, I had a lot of contact with Tamar, my fellow expedition member. Since I had not found another experienced hunter, it would only be the two of us. She understood my situation and was happy to break off our journey if Peter's situation became worse. Peter promised to let me know if he needed me, and Nick would look after him in the meantime. Tamar had a GPS-inreach, and they could send us a message if there was an emergency. I could be back in a few days if need be. But it was with a sinking heart that I said goodbye to Peter that summer afternoon in December.

We kissed goodbye, we hugged, I cried, and I went.

Despite my two dangerous looking rifles and the rain, I made it successfully across Cook Strait and onto the West Coast, where I met up with our old friend Daniel. We had met him eight years ago in the wilderness, and he had taught me many skills, including how to fire a rifle. It was great to see him again.

And there was Tamar. She had not changed much in the six months since we had seen each other in Bulgaria. She looked fit and healthy, and it was a delightful reunion. We talked for hours about all that had happened in the last months. We were excited and a little apprehensive about the journey ahead of us.

I unpacked the rifles and explained to Tamar what she needed to know about our most important instruments. I had just bought a new .223, and my old gun was for her. By law she was allowed to hunt with me, as long as I was with her at all times.

Daniel took us to the rifle range to shoot on a target. He was meticulous, and helped me adjust the scopes to ensure the gun was shooting dead straight. Had it not been for the fact that it was a female expedition, he said, he'd have loved to join us. He'd have been great company, but I knew that if he came with us he would naturally lead. He was stronger, fitter, more skilled than us, and from the first minute we would follow him. He would suggest the routes; he would shoot and carry the animal on his back; by the time we reached camp he would have already set up the tents, gathered the wood, lit the fire and cooked all the meat.

This time it was my turn to take the lead.

Ever since I was a teenager I had dreamed of an expedition. We would set off with not much more than rifles and a rod. We would survive on hunting, fishing and gathering plants. We would have to ford countless milky rivers, and find our own way over many mountain ranges—without following any tracks or routes.

We were going to walk south from Arthur's Pass to the Ahuriri River, to be among the high glaciers. I wanted to be in the toughest places to test my abilities to the maximum. I wanted to discover what I was made of and how I would function in a team. There was also a small question lingering in the back of my mind: who was I without Peter?

Apart from the hunting equipment, I carried many of the same items as we had in Europe. My rifle, scope, silencer and forty rounds of ammunition weighed more than five kilos in total. Tamar's gun and bullets were four kilos, but she carried her fishing rod as well. I had a lightweight four-seasons tent that we would share. We both had air mats and sleeping bags suitable for -25°C. I would eat out of the frypan, and Tamar out of a big plastic plate. We had two metal spoons, my big billy-pot and Tamar's small pot. We had a good supply of waterproof matches and planned to cook on an open fire—there was no fire ban in the high mountains, where it often rained and snowed. For emergencies we carried a first-aid kit and the GPS-inreach. We had a compass, paper maps of the whole region, and a cellphone to take videos and pictures, as well as a small solar charger. We took three kilos of flour with us, some salt and two kilos of rice. Tamar had made some pemmican—meat, berries and fat, an old Inuit recipe for preserving meat—which we planned to keep for emergencies. When we set off, our packs each weighed over twenty-five kilos.

We hitchhiked the five hours from Westport to Arthur's Pass. The further we drove into the mountains, the fouler the weather became. Fog was drifting through the tops and the temperature fell to about 15°. The driver dropped us off at a small roadside parking place under the trees, looking out over the Waimakariri valley. When we sat down at a picnic table, the sun came out and we ate our last civilised meal: rice, vegetables and an omelette that we had cooked that morning.

As Tamar shouldered her pack, I pulled two little white beans out of my pocket. They were just normal beans that you can cook and eat, but they're called angel beans and are imprinted with a pattern that resembles two wings.

'This is our good-luck charm,' I said, handing Tamar her tiny bean. 'It's very light. Let's survive the next ten weeks,' I said solemnly.

'Ah, let's *thrive* the next ten weeks!' She grinned, and gave me a hug.

Our angel beans stayed in our pockets for the rest of the journey.

We followed a little path into the forest, where trees waved their branches above us. Beams of sunshine lit up patches of gold on the forest floor. After a while, we came out in the open where a great wide river valley stretched out in front of us, and I thought: I am back in the wilderness, back in the land I know so well. I felt at home. I was again in a huge landscape where people were small and insignificant. I was in the mountains and the valleys, without fences and boundaries, where everything was living the way it was supposed to.

Following the river for hours, we meandered through the long grass while listening to a skylark as it sang high up in the sky. While resting on a boulder, we were delighted to see two hares running with the wind. We drank from a creek, and paradise ducks flew overhead with much commotion. In the late afternoon we set up camp under the beech trees and lit a fire to boil some mānuka tea. When the twilight gently took over the valley, we went for our first hunt. But we saw no more hares, no deer prints and not a sign of a goat. When we returned in the dark, Tamar rekindled the fire and I took my notebook and pen. From the moment I had left him, Peter was never far from my mind. I began the habit of writing him letters that I would send once we were back in civilisation.

Dear Peter,

When I entered the old beech forest, with the warm sunshine bringing beautiful patterns on the floor, tears were in my eyes, because I miss you so much. You and I have walked in countless valleys like this. You would have loved to be here.

Tamar is enthusiastic, kind and very knowledgeable about edible plants. She is the best companion I could imagine, but it will take time to adjust to being with someone other than you. I have to get used to speaking Dutch again. It feels strange to sleep next to a stranger in a small tent. Tamar seems more open to me than the other way around. I feel like a little dog, being brought to a new home, looking shyly at the room from a corner. I do not know why it takes time to get used to her. Why can I not instantly adjust, the way she seems to?
Miriam

The first days were most difficult. Our bodies were accustomed to a regular diet and now it was going to be either feast or famine. We also had to adjust to a hunting life: to large amounts of meat and relatively few carbohydrates. For three days the hunting was unsuccessful. Apart from some chapatis and edible plants, we ate little. We started to feel very hungry, but could not afford to eat up all our rations so early in the journey.

On the evening of the fourth day, feeling lethargic and with hunger pains in my stomach, I picked up my gun. I was dreading another failure. The sun had set behind the mountains; there was pink and red in the sky and a little breeze moving the tussocks. I wanted to explore the other side of the valley, so I waded across the glacial river. The water was milky and ice cold but did not reach much higher than my knees. I could not see my own feet in the water and I used my walking stick for balance. Slowly I waded through, and on the other bank I stepped on rocks to avoid making any sound. Standing still behind some bushes, I gazed into the distance searching for signs of an animal. I looked for a long time but eventually I came back to camp empty-handed again.

Fortunately, Tamar had collected some edible plants. We

stripped the skin of the Scotch thistle and ate the stems. We sucked the sweet nectar out of flax stalks, and Tamar found astelia plants. I had never tasted them before; the stem of the green vegetable was good, buttery even. But it didn't really cure the gnawing hunger.

Next morning, it was still dark when I crawled out of my sleeping bag. I guessed it was no later than five o'clock. I felt tired, but intuitively I sensed deer out there.

A little moon lit up my way as I put on my clothes. I took my rifle that every day felt a little heavier, and carefully slipped into the forest. I stepped on soft ground—not touching dry sticks. I ducked below branches, stood still behind trees, stepped slowly over big logs. I listened. A little breeze touched my face. The first bellbird began to sing and soon the whole forest came alive with birdsong.

I followed my nose, tracking the scent for a long way. My hearing, sight and sense of smell were heightened. I stayed hidden in dark shadows, looking at the grassy clearings on the side of the river. Then I saw a group of deer moving from the water back to the trees. It was a wondrous sight. One hind stood still and waited for the others. In slow motion I lifted my rifle. The barrel rested on a branch. When everything was still, I pulled the trigger.

An almighty boom echoed between the mountains, and I saw the hind falling to the ground. I ran to her as fast as I could. When I came close I could see the life flowing out of her. I felt sad when I stroked her warm hide, light brown with a dark stripe. I touched her soft nose and looked at her long eyelashes. She had lived a free life and never knew what happened this last morning.

I looked up at the mountains and experienced an immense sense of gratitude. The sky had turned blue and slowly I began to feel joyful and very relieved, for this hind was the end of our hunger.

Hunting in New Zealand is different from hunting in Europe. The native birds evolved on these islands without predators. When the first European settlers brought possums, geese, deer, tahr and many other mammals, the endemic flora and fauna suffered greatly. For years now the government has spent much time and effort trying to eradicate the introduced species, and hunting is encouraged.

I carried the animal to a tree, tied my piece of rope onto a branch, and with all my strength lifted her off the ground. I made an incision around the ankles and pulled the skin off with my hands. After I sliced open the stomach, I took all the intestines out. With my small and sharp Swiss pocketknife, I was swift. I had not skinned an animal for two years, but the ability had stayed with me. I laid out the offal in the open for the hawks to collect later and brought the carcass back to camp.

Tamar woke when I arrived and couldn't believe her eyes. She hopped up and down excitedly and asked all about the hunt. Where was the animal? From how many metres did you fire, where was the wind, did you shoot from the shoulder, was it heavy to lift the animal into the tree, where are the organs? What shall we eat first?

We cut off the head, split the skull and spooned out the brain. Tamar pulled out the tongue with such vigour that it was both frightening and comical. She had no trouble with gruesome tasks. She had eaten the strangest things on her travels in Central Asia, and nothing could deter her. While she fried the brain in the pan over the fire, I washed all the blood off my skin in the river. When I came back we began the eating.

Deer brain is my favourite dish in the world. Tamar agreed. After the whole brain was in our stomach, I was tired from the early hunt and went back to sleep. Tamar spent all morning around the fire and when I woke up, we ate boiled eyes. They were nice too—tasted like oysters. Then she fried up the back steaks. Everything Tamar the Michelin-star chef made was delicious, and every dish was presented with purple clover flowers for decoration and nutrition.

I was feeling happy and proud that we had endured the most difficult part of the expedition: the beginning.

Our first mountain pass over the Shaler Range was covered in permanent snow and ice. High mountains show many faces. Sometimes we saw it moody, aloof and disapproving; at other times it felt inviting and open. Timing was the most important element when climbing high passes. We had to have the mountain on our side; it was entry by invitation only. Reading the land and acting accordingly was paramount to survival.

When the sky was blue and the snow-clad mountain tops looked friendly, we set out. It was an arduous walk from the forest into the stony gully towards the pass. We followed the creek until the water disappeared and we were left with tussock grass. The landscape felt extraordinarily remote. In the distance we spotted a chamois: elegant, confident and fast. We were very well fed, so made no attempt to hunt it, and just enjoyed the wonderful sight.

Then we climbed higher, entered the snow and sank in to our shins. Tamar made a track, I followed her footsteps and halfway through we changed roles. Sometimes we had to walk over an ice-bridge; we went carefully, one by one, for fear of the bridge collapsing.

We felt so small in that huge landscape, like two little ants crawling up the icy mountain. Once we reached the tops, we saw the glacier. The blue ice was astonishing. There were layers and layers of ice, revealing tens of thousands of years of mountain history. The glacier seemed to have its own unique identity, and I understood at once why each one has its own name.

We sat down to rest. Tamar pulled out a plastic bag. 'What do you think this is?' she said with a big grin.

'A tongue!' I laughed. The thing resembled a penis.

Tamar had boiled the tongue for hours the previous day—the result was delicious. It tasted like a sweet sausage. The second course was patties. We had collected dandelion and pūhā—native sowthistle— which we had mixed with flour and deer organs. The patties were a little crumbly without the required egg, but were tasty and filling.

After the food we watched the view from the pass and saw another chamois: this one was walking on the glacier. He was very visible on the white ice. We saw him taking a little run, jumping in the air as if to catch a fly and then jumping a little pirouette. He hopped on, turned around and ran again, this time to jump 180 degrees. It was like watching a circus show. He repeated this act many times before he disappeared again into the vertical rocks. He was marvellous to see the sheer joy of play in the young chamois.

From the pass, we descended into the mighty Wilberforce Valley. Its river was vast and braided; the side creeks came down through deep gullies and untouched forest. All around, the mountains were huge, and the wind was magnificently powerful here. With each mountain pass, we felt further away from civilisation and closer to the heart of the wilderness.

After a couple of sunny days in the Wilberforce, the wind changed into a northerly and it began to rain—hard. The falling water was like a curtain and the former trickles on the cliffs turned into spectacular waterfalls. With mist all around the tops, the mountains looked taller, more distant and aloof. During the day we sat in the tent, told stories about past adventures and played chess on the little tin chessboard I'd brought. In the evening we went out in the rain. Tamar went fishing in the river and I went hunting.

The warm wet weather magnified all subtle scents. Even the smallest flowers had become fragrant. The long wet grasses hugged my calves and their seeds felt soft on my skin. I stayed on the banks of the river until I reached a patch of tōtara where it was still dry underneath. Most animals like to shelter from the rain, and it was clear that deer were living here—I could see their pathways, where they had rubbed their antlers and left their droppings. A little fantail followed me all through the forest, but I didn't see any deer. I came back to camp empty-handed, and so did Tamar. Fishing was difficult in the milky glacial rivers, she said, because there were no pools and she could not see the fish. We spent the rest of the evening picking and eating tōtara berries—they were tasty but a little acidic.

Next morning we woke to a bright blue sky, so I took my rifle and went out again. Every animal would be determined to enjoy and dry itself after a long rain, and I was sure I could find a hare sunbathing. I lay for a long time on my stomach on the high banks of the river until I saw one. I kept very quiet, lined up, breathed out and shot.

We lit a fire from dry bark, and when the hare's meat was soft from long cooking we pulled it off the bones. Tamar piled it all on our big plastic plate, along with some boiled pūhā that tasted like spinach.

'We can eat!' she said, and placed the one plate in front of us.

In Mongolia she had grown used to eating from one dish. To me this was a little unhygienic and unfair, because I ate much quicker than she did. But Tamar was not concerned and I adjusted. It was indeed very practical.

We walked for a week down the long Wilberforce Valley, and by crossing the river multiple times we turned into the Rakaia Valley. On our way we hunted possums. The white meat was tasty and tender when boiled for a long time. One morning we woke to see some streaks of blue between the puffy clouds. We quickly lit the fire, had some meat for breakfast, made possum patties for lunch and packed our bags. By the time we set out, however, the little bit of blue sky had disappeared. Instead of unpacking and pitching the tent again, we decided to make what progress we could towards the next pass, so we followed the river up.

After an hour we were caught between the main river and a steep landslide. We could not cross the water and were forced to climb onto the bank, which was covered in tangled thickets. We wrestled through wet bushes, got caught by vines, ducked underneath low branches. Then, just as I was climbing over a big log, my gun got stuck behind a branch. I tried to turn around but instead fell backwards. The hollow of my knee was caught behind a stick and I screamed with pain. Tamar rushed over and clicked my hip belt loose so that my pack would not pull me backwards. I got out without injury, but I was soaking wet.

The going was slow. We crawled with hands and knees beneath the vegetation. It was like being caught in a terrible jungle. My pack and gun hooked on every passing branch. We could manage barely a hundred metres an hour. Eventually we slid down a gully that was just a narrow chute, and jumped the last two metres onto the stony river bed. We were immensely relieved to be out of the thick forest.

After that we stayed close to the river. We climbed over square black boulders that sat solid in the foaming waves. The sound of rushing water was almost deafening. When the rocks were too large to climb, we we were forced to descend into the water. Even on the river's edge I could feel the pull of the massive current. The river was merciless that day.

A lone black-backed gull flew low over the valley. I stood still and looked up. 'He-he-he-he,' it laughed. The gull disappeared in the mist. Shortly after it began to rain. I regretted breaking up camp that morning. Peter would never have left the dry tent. He would have refused to move. Above us, dark clouds crawled over the tops and drifted down the valley. The mood of the mountains was hostile. Since the pass was out of the question, we studied the map and located a hut. We would aim for there.

We walked for an hour upriver until we were obstructed by a huge cliff. To our surprise there was a wire swing-bridge over the river. We did not really want to cross, because it would put us on the wrong side for the hut, but we had little choice. There was no other way around the cliff. With the help of fixed ropes, we climbed twenty metres to the beginning of the wire bridge and crossed the roaring river. On the other side there was no track either, and we were among gigantic boulders and thick leafy vegetation. We needed to find a way back to the other side of the river again, but there were no more bridges. The rain worsened and the temperature dropped. I began to feel anxious.

The landscape started to feel more and more like Mordor. Mist was hanging low, touching the black stones. All signs told us the mountains wanted to be left alone. In a desperate attempt to get back to the right side of the river, I tried to cross the raging milky water. It was so cold it felt as if a thousand needles were stinging my bones. After three steps I tumbled into a hole and was suddenly up to my hips in the water. Gasping and shaken, I retreated to the bank.

'How on earth are we going to cross?' I shouted in half panic.

'Further up the river!' said Tamar. 'The volume will diminish. Surely!'

Even though I was moving, I began to feel very cold in my wet shorts. When we stopped to eat our possum patties, I took my pack off to get to the food—and foolishly left it sitting in the rain. The pack had been keeping my back warm. I began to shiver almost uncontrollably—not only my arms and legs, but all over, from deep in the chest. I quickly put my pack back on and started walking, but I knew I was in danger of hypothermia.

'I'm very cold!' I shouted over the wind and rain. Tamar was concerned when she saw my pale face and blue lips. 'Can you do this?' She moved her thumb to her index finger, middle finger, ring finger and pinky.

With difficulty I managed to move my white fingers. I vowed not to take my pack off again. I had to keep on walking and avoid a fall into the icy water.

As we marched onwards, my blood slowly began to circulate again. We should have pitched the tent and gone into our sleeping bags, but the prospect of a warm hut on the other side of the river was so appealing that we never thought of camping in the wind and on the stones.

We kept hiking up the valley for an hour or more, thinking the water level would drop. Our map only covered the middle part of the valley, where the hut was situated. We had no idea what was at the top—until we came around the corner and found ourselves confronted by a huge glacial lake. We were horrified. To go around it would take hours, and the glacier at the top would be difficult to negotiate without an ice-axe and crampons. Dispirited, I looked up at the grey rocks and foggy cliffs. Whatever we decided to do would be dangerous.

We looked closely at the lake outlet, and noticed that with all the silt the water level seemed relatively low. I realised that this might be our only chance.

'I'm going!' I said, after looking for the best place to cross.

'Okay!' said Tamar. 'Be careful!' She took her emergency beacon out of her hip pocket and tied it around her neck.

I took a few deep breaths and slowly entered the liquid ice. The cold caused an instant headache. The river was moving very slowly and it felt like walking into a lake. When its level reached my hips I became very nervous, but I had to proceed if we wanted to get to the other side. It was unbelievable, almost surreal to be there. I moved slowly and stared at the bank. My feet had to find the way, for I could see nothing through the milky water. I focused on my breathing, ignoring the freezing cold river. When I had crossed safely, Tamar entered the water. She followed the direction I had taken, and when she finally reached the bank she looked frightened.

'We've done it!' I hugged her, and the expression of horror on her face turned into relief. 'We survived!'

'Yes, we are very alive!' she cheered. 'Woo-hoo!'

Our cries of joy were swallowed by the clouds, and we felt even smaller. Two little dots on the side of a glacier lake in Mordor. The planet felt infinitely vast and wild.

Eventually, we made it to the old hut. Nobody had visited it for a long time. There was an open fire, and a possum had moved in via the chimney. Every surface was covered in possum urine and droppings. I looked at Tamar, who simply turned over the mattress and rolled out her sleeping bag. Unlike me, she was not worried about her gear. Whether her socks in her sandals were muddy, whether her pack got wet, whether she had a wash before crawling in her sleeping bag, none of it concerned her. We once shot a hare while hiking with the packs and Tamar tied the animal on the outside. When I asked her if she didn't mind a bloodstain on her pack, she looked at me in surprise and said, 'But Miriam, you can wash it out!'

It was crystal clear when we climbed over the next pass a few days later. To our surprise a stag had had precisely the same idea that same morning. He was a long way ahead of us, but we could see his fresh hoofprints. By following his marks, I felt we were traversing a world that was ruled by animals who were completely at home. For them, humans were a rare and irrelevant species.

We camped and hunted in beautiful places. We found our way over the mountains and came out at stunning valleys. Each one was different from the last. There were narrow valleys with shrubs holding up steep slopes. Others were bony and barren with a red glow. Some were wide and forested. It was always a surprise what we would see from the top.

One day we hiked up to a pass. The higher we climbed up the creek, the steeper it became. In the end we were merely mounting a roaring waterfall, hanging by our fingers from rocks that were sometimes disturbingly loose. Our boots slid on rock faces that were always wet from the spray. At one point we found ourselves stuck in a chasm and we could not see a way to proceed—the rock faces all around us were sheer and slippery. The only solution was to take off my boots and climb barefoot. Once I could feel the surface and knew how much grip I had, I felt completely safe.

We found many animals to hunt, and gathered as many berries and edible plants as possible to gain all the nutrients. Tamar was always creative with cooking and taught me how to make empanadas, momos and dumplings from our little store of flour. Slowly, I became better at cooking and Tamar became more successful with hunting. After hiking long distances, eating was a great pleasure. We were losing weight, gaining muscle and feeling very fit. We were as strong and agile as the animals we were eating.

Dear Peter,

The further we are going into the wild, the more intense everything becomes. It feels as though everything is more silent, but not a mere peaceful serenity. There is an intensity here, like electrified air—as if everything is waiting for something. It is a silence with expectation. It is like being in an audience of a thousand people, and everyone is waiting for the first spoken word.

When I'm hunting on my own this intensity is very tangible. I walk slowly. I'm looking, listening. Then all thought subsides and I move just with the silence, for the silence itself seems to be a movement.

When the sun sets behind the peaks, a soft orange glow takes over the valley. I look at impossibly angled rock structures, perfect peaks and remarkable spirals in the distance. There are flowers and insects I've never seen before, and it feels as if the creator is at work at this moment: I am among the process of creation. The mountains and

plants are growing, the river is shaping the land. Today is different from yesterday—everything around me is continuously evolving. I feel as if I am looking through the kaleidoscope of the gods. It is a fascinating miracle that this movement of life exists. And, what's more, like everything around me, I am part of it.
Miriam

The weather was favourable and we made great progress. After four weeks crossing mountains and rivers, we descended into the Godley Valley. It was one of the wildest places I had ever seen. It looked as if a big hand had thrown a giant stone from the skies. Upon hitting the earth, the rock had broken into smaller chunks, and the scattered pieces lay about forlornly.

We took our rifles and walked towards a glacier lake at the top of the valley. The closer we got to the lake, the icier the wind became. In the end it felt as if we were being catapulted into winter. Even with all my clothes, it was unbelievably cold. We sheltered from the gale-force wind behind some rocks where we found many Mount Cook lilies and countless big white snowberries. Delighted, we fell upon the berries; they tasted beautifully sweet.

There were more than a hundred Canada geese and paradise ducks floating serenely on the lake's surface. The scene was breath-taking. All were quiet, until one goose warned the others of two dangerous women. Soon the whole flock was honking. Then one began flapping its wings, and slowly all the geese began to depart. The sky was full of wings and feathers and the calling of birds.

I thought we'd missed our chance for hunting, but to my surprise I saw Tamar looking at something nearby in the grass. She lifted her rifle and fired. The shot echoed around the mountains. We stood and watched the goose die graciously. First she spread her wings on the ground. Then she looked up at the sky and very slowly bent her neck, almost bowed down, until her head reached the ground. It was very touching. Strangely enough, it was almost as though she knew her fate—as if she had stayed behind to sacrifice her life.

Tamar walked over and lifted the goose off the ground. It looked enormous. It was sad to see the bird die, yet at the same time I felt so grateful to have something to eat. When we gutted the goose we found many whole snowberries in its stomach. It had eaten the same things as us. We plucked the bird, and ended up in a bed of down feathers. Tamar put it on a stick and roasted it whole over a fire. It took a long time and still it was a little chewy, but it gave us enormous energy.

From the Godley, we had to find a way over the ranges into the next valley. That night we looked at our options on the map and gazed at the 2000-metre mountain above us. We had the best route in our minds, but were waiting for the right day to set out.

Next morning, when darkness was diluting into a grey sky, I collected some wood and lit the fire. By the time Tamar had heated up the goose stew, the sky had become clear blue. We decided to climb the pass. Instantly we grew nervous with anticipation, for pass days always revealed many unknowns.

As the first rays of sunlight entered the valley, we began our climb. The grassy spur became rocky and turned into a shingle slide. With every two steps up, we sank one down again. It was like walking in soft snow. For hours we ascended till we reached the ridge where it was wind-still and unusually silent.

We stopped to drink some water and admire the view, and spotted a large number of Himalayan tahr. It was astonishing to be in one of the most hostile places on Earth, yet to see so many animals living there. A big group of them was nibbling a few blades of grass on a faraway slope. Nearby we saw some scattered individuals wandering the vertical rock faces, resting on tiny ledges and narrow shelves above crevasses and ravines. The tahr were confident among the rocks and peaks. They were not scared, and watched us with interest.

We continued over the ridge and as we came closer, the tahr moved away. Except for one. A large tahr stood on the rocks and jumped down in our direction. It somersaulted off a five-metre cliff, landed awkwardly on more boulders and jumped back and forth in total panic. Then I saw his eyes were glassy white. The poor animal was blind. It was a dangerous place to be unable to see. The animal disappeared for a few minutes. When we saw him again nearby, I clipped my gun off the pack. With the wind in my face I climbed silently up a rocky tower. I shot the tahr in the head from two metres' distance. We heard a boom and the echo, then the sound of the animal falling—and rocks clattering down. Then it was silent.

I had hoped it would land on a little platform just below me, but unfortunately he had tumbled hundreds of metres down into an unfathomable abyss. I was devastated. I replayed the scene in my mind, cursed myself for shooting him from the wrong angle. I felt terrible that we could not eat the animal, and that he had died needlessly. Tamar consoled me, saying he was suffering because he was blind. But he had survived this long; it was not my duty to put him out of his misery.

I tied the gun back on the pack, wet my dry mouth with a sip of water, and followed Tamar up the narrow ridge. We had to climb hands and feet around rocky peaks that resembled castle towers. Each step was dangerous and arduous.

We were very relieved when we finally came to the pass. Exhausted, we sat down to eat our goose meat and take in our surroundings. The other side was a dry and rough valley with nothing but sand and stone. A thousand metres below was the first vegetation. I pointed out a possible way down. 'Shall we stay on the true right,' I said, 'until that triangle cliff, then we sidle to the left, around that big boulder. You see the boulder . . . ?'

'Shall we check where we are?' asked Tamar.

'Check where we are? We've come from the Godley and that is clearly the stream leading to Cass.'

Ignoring my answer, she took out her GPS and a minute later said, 'This stream leads back to the Godley, not to Cass. This is not the pass: that is!' She pointed at a higher mountain above us.

I was already dead tired; to have to climb even higher seemed unbearable. We stopped eating and stowed the leftovers back in our packs for later. Slowly and painstakingly we climbed up the side of a steep slope. I kept slipping down the gravel, and planted my walking stick in as far as possible. My whole weight was hanging on my right arm—it was extremely tiring.

But we made it. We threw our hands in the air and congratulated each other on our achievement. Below us was a stony valley.

'Shingle slide!' I called over the wind, and hurtled my way down. The key was to move with the top layer of stones and keep the movement going. It was like skiing an easy six-hundred-metre slope.

We made fast progress, and at the bottom of the valley we rested, drank a lot of water and ate the remainder of our food. I changed into my sandals to walk leisurely down to the creek. Without a worry in the world, we climbed over boulders, made our way through little gorges, and crossed and re-crossed the stream—until we heard the roar of a distant waterfall. We had not anticipated this, because only waterfalls over twenty metres were noted on the map. This one must have been about fifteen.

'What do we do?' sighed Tamar. She looked very worried.

If Peter had been there, I would have sat down and cried because I was exhausted. But Peter wasn't here and crying would not have helped. We had to find a solution.

I cleared my throat. 'We have to find a way,' I said. 'Let's have a look.'

We moved a little closer, but the sight of the ravine gave me the shivers. The surface of the wall looked hard. If we went down, we would gradually gather speed and eventually crash to our deaths at the bottom. I felt the fear rising in my legs.

Tamar turned around. 'We have to go up there!' she said resolutely, pointing at the other side. 'Up that spur.'

'Impossible! It's vertical wall! That's for mountain goats!'

'If there's vegetation, there's a way!' said Tamar. 'It takes longer than going down the slide, but it will be much safer.'

I looked up again. The wall was covered in speargrass. The tips were so sharp they could draw blood, but if we could grab the base of the plants, I thought, it might hold our weight.

Since we had no other choice, apart from going back the way we came, we began to climb the speargrass wall. The rush of adrenaline gave me renewed energy, and I hurled myself and my heavy pack up the slope.

We climbed the first hundred metres without major problems. Then the vegetation disappeared. We were on a cliff with nothing to hold on to. The wall was only sand and stones hardened by the wind. But fifty metres away was a small animal track leading towards a little outcrop. To get there we needed to cross a near-vertical slope.

'Do you think we can reach that track over there?' I asked Tamar, who stood behind me.

She looked up and nodded. 'Yeah, I think we can do that,' she said casually, as if I had asked whether her car could fit in a parking space.

The situation was absurdly precarious, but I turned around and began inching towards the safety of the animal track. I held on to rocks that sometimes felt frighteningly loose. I shuffled along the side of the slope—relying on my wooden walking stick. One mistake and I would fall. Below was a two-hundred-metre abyss ending at the bottom of the waterfall. I had seldom been more scared of sliding to my death.

Then a voice in my head said: Miriam! You've been doing this for ten years. You know these rocks, this sand, these animal tracks. You know this country like the back of your hand! You have done this many, many times!

I looked up instead of down. Careful, I thought. No mistakes. Slowly, slowly.

When I stood for a second with shaking legs on a stable foothold, I looked at Tamar behind me. The sun had disappeared behind the tops; the air was still.

'You going all right?' I called out in a calm voice.

'Yeah, yeah, all good!' she said in a similar tone, lifting her pole up to show a thumb. She smiled quickly, and redirected her gaze at the terrain in front of her. She took two steps, and for a few seconds she did not seem to know where to go. Then she reached with her right foot towards a big stone. When that came crashing down, she jammed both walking sticks into the sand and simultaneously changed the weight to her left leg to stop herself slipping.

'Are you okay?' I shouted.

'Uhm.'

There was a moment of silence.

'I think I'll go over there!' She pointed uphill.

It was horribly dangerous. With my heart in my throat I watched Tamar until she was in a safer place.

When I reached the goat track, I followed it to the top of the spur and sat down to catch my breath. I wondered if this had been unusually dicey, or whether my perception of danger had magnified a few times without the presence of Peter. I had followed him into many perilous situations and never been overly scared.

By the time Tamar turned up I had regained my composure. We rested a while longer, then discussed possible routes down. In the last light of the day, we followed the spur to reach the valley floor.

In the half dark we pitched the tent, gathered some dead branches from scrub and lit the fire for a cup of tea. We didn't have food for dinner, but we weren't hungry. Wrapped in our sleeping bags, we talked about how terrified we had been. Both of us had wanted to cry when we saw the waterfall, yet neither of us wanted to show our fear.

We were tired at the end of a long day but had such a feeling of accomplishment.

'We've done it, Tamar,' I said at last.

She didn't reply, but even in the darkness I saw her smiling.

Hello my dear Peter,

Expeditions are by definition hard. Trying conditions and tough circumstances. I have read stories of expeditions where people end up fighting with each other. If there is danger and tension, it is understandable that one gets stressed and irritated. Luckily, Tamar and I cooperate extremely well. We never argue, and we have only grown closer. She feels like such a good friend now.

In the last ten years our nomadic life has prevented us from building many long-term friendships. Having a good friend apart from you is rather a new experience to me. I discover that when living in close proximity, one becomes a little bit like the other. We become the people we surround ourselves with—I guess that is how a culture gets formed. Mostly, we are aware of the differences, and so often unconscious of the similarities.

I value my friendship with Tamar a lot, but every day, my dearest, I miss you, and wonder how you are coping with weak kidneys and so little energy. I wonder how you are surviving in a house, in a town—without the forest and the mountains around you. How can you live without the wilderness?

Miriam

We had been away for more than four weeks when, one morning, we were breaking up camp and Tamar said, 'Miriam, you've got a message from Peter.'

I was busy rolling up the tent and looked up at her. It was the end of January, and I knew the message would be about the outcome of a blood test.

'What does it say?' I said, my heart in my throat.

Tamar handed me her orange device.

I read: *Creatinine still at 450, not better or worse. Doctor says kidneys might not improve. Love, P.*

Kidneys might not improve. What did that mean? Does he now have chronic kidney failure? Will he need dialysis to live? Does he need a donor kidney in the long run?

I stared blankly into the distance. Tamar put an arm around me, but I felt numb. I didn't collapse and I didn't cry. I couldn't think of anything to say or do, so I continued rolling up the tent.

We silently ate a big breakfast of hare stew. After the meal, I found a little place to sit out of the wind to write a letter to Peter. When I could think of nothing more to write, I looked up and Tamar was gone. I called her name but there was no reply. Panic gripped me like a claw. Tears came to my eyes. I jumped up, ran frantically around some bushes to look out over the river. When I couldn't see her, a horrible feeling of loneliness came over me. I felt like a child left without a mother. I ran to a higher viewpoint. After a long minute I saw Tamar in the distance. She was strolling back with some washed clothes in her hand.

Ashamed of my panic, I wiped the tears from my face and continued packing. When she arrived I said in a croaky voice, 'Where were you? I couldn't find you!'

She looked at me, saw my moist eyes and hugged me. 'Just over there,' she said softly. She stroked my back and I cried silently. 'Just over there.'

A little breeze came down the valley, gently moving all the golden hairs of the tussocks. A flock of a dozen geese flew overhead. When we heard the honking, we both looked up at the sky.

'Would you like to send something back to Peter?' asked Tamar eventually.

I sat down with pen and paper and thought long about a reply. I practised a few lines on paper. I had only a limited number of characters, so every letter counted. Eventually I wrote:

My sweetheart
We need a miracle now.
Let my love be the divine wind
that can heal you.

The message from Peter meant the end of our life together in the wild. We had hoped for full recovery, but if the doctor suggested dialysis, then we needed to live in a real house with a roof, electricity, phone and internet. We needed to live in town, close to a hospital. I would offer my kidney to him and hope our blood and tissues would match. This winter we could be organising his transplant.

I felt so sorry for Peter. My instinct was to abandon the expedition and return to him. In the worst-case scenario, we would not have much time left together. I was also concerned about myself. Knowing I'd had half a panic attack when I couldn't see Tamar for a minute, I began to doubt whether I could deal with the misery that was coming. I could ford rivers, climb mountains and hunt animals, but I felt I could not survive without Peter.

My dearest Peter,
Since I received your message, I do nothing but cry. My world has changed overnight. My cheerful self is vanishing and tears are never far away. I am losing all enthusiasm for the expedition; I would rather go hungry than take an animal's life. The expedition feels like nonsense. I am running around the mountains, while you are thinking of dialysis and transplant. I should come to you. I can't find the right words to talk with Tamar about it and I am often silent. Actually, I am not good at sharing my sorrow. What are we going to do if you don't get better? Dialysis and transplant? I will give you my kidney, my dearest.

I wish I was with you now. I am thinking of you all the time and miss you. I miss you so much that it hurts.
Miriam

For a long week I walked with a dark cloud over my head. I felt depressed. I was silent and I was dreading everything. I climbed the ranges like a zombie and was only thinking of Peter. A day after the first message, he had sent another one saying there was no need to break off the expedition, but I wanted nothing more than to talk to him. So, Tamar and I agreed to go to the town of Twizel to ring Peter and buy a kilo of flour and oats.

We walked down the valley and after two days came out at a dirt road that led towards a beautiful turquoise lake. It was a clear day and we could see New Zealand's highest peak, Aoraki/Mount Cook. It looked magnificent, but I could not feel it. I only felt pain in my heart.

After hours of walking in the harsh sunlight on a dusty road, we were picked up by a camper van. The driver dropped us in town, and I was able to ring Peter.

'Miriam, listen,' he said. 'You might never do this again. I do not need dialysis yet. Maybe in a few months' time. Then we can talk about a donor transplant. My brother Mark has already offered his kidney, and our friend Hone too. Miriam, you are my hero. Don't turn back yet, you might never do this again. Relax, enjoy yourself.'

The moment I put the phone down, I felt better. If this was my last trip in the mountains for the foreseeable future, I would make sure to fill my heart with wildness. I would have to make it last for the years to come.

Because of the unassailable Ben Ōhau range, we decided to re-enter the wilderness again via Lake Ōhau. The Hopkins River valley is broad and spacious, with bush on the side of the mountain. We had not seen big forest for some weeks, and

I realised how important it was to live near trees. The intense sorrow of the previous week seemed to dissipate beneath them. The branches waved softly like big arms over my head. I felt safe and protected. Trees are immensely strong and stable; they know how to love their fate. Their strength flowed over into me.

Because it was such a beautiful valley, we decided to walk all the way to the top. On our map we saw there was a rock bivouac underneath the glacier where it would be wonderful to spend the night.

The river was braided and easy to cross in the lower areas, but the more we ascended, the more it changed into a roaring torrent. Without a track, everything was a mission. We walked in the river bed, and were forced to scale big boulders. Sometimes we had to pull ourselves up on overhanging branches to get through, and sometimes we had to wade through the water that came as high as our hips.

After several days we reached the glacier. It was incredible. On our left was the dividing ridge of the Southern Alps, parting the country into east and west. We watched a constant stream of little clouds that looked like yellow candyfloss climbing over the ridge. As soon as it reached our side, it dissolved. It was a magical spectacle.

Most weather comes from the west in New Zealand; the clouds hit the main divide and fall down as rain. Over the years Peter and I had learned to stay on the east side of the main divide. We could handle snow and ice while living in a tent, but we detested rain.

Tamar spotted the rock bivouac first. It was a vast boulder that had fallen onto some smaller rocks, creating a little space underneath. People had built up the sides with flat stones. We fitted in it exactly. Around the bivouac, rocks lay scattered in the valley floor. We were surrounded by huge walls with incredible patterns and shapes. The rocky crust had been pushed up by the movement of the earth, now showing myriad vertical stripes. A little further was the glacier itself. The cold wind brought stories of what the world looked like in an ice age.

That evening we were tired. We had eaten the last of our possum the day before, and had not been lucky with hunting since. In the morning we had eaten a handful of oats; in the afternoon we found a lot of small red tōtara berries. We had some oats and flour left, but we were reluctant to use it up when we had another three weeks to go.

We put all our gear inside the rock biv and went hunting. We climbed the boulders and walked up the hill for a viewpoint. We saw hare droppings—but no hare. Had we not been so dead tired, we would have climbed further up the spur to have a wider view. But we had no energy, so we returned to our cave and ate more tōtara and snowberries for dinner.

It was marvellous to sleep under a rock, but I was a little on my guard; if it rained, we would get quite wet. If there was a storm, stones could fall in on us. If there was an earthquake, we would get buried alive. But nothing happened during the night, and in the morning we woke up relieved. After a cup of tea we went hunting again. We weren't very motivated to go far and we ate more snowberries until our stomachs were full. The peculiar thing was that we didn't feel hungry. We were just a little tired. Normally the brain knows that a lack of energy is linked to lack of food, but over the weeks our hunger signals were suppressed; we had no energy, but no hunger either.

We ate watery porridge with snowberries, packed our bags and walked down the valley. In the evening we found a flat spot underneath tall black beech trees. There was soft fern between the trees and we put the tent close to a small stream. A little wind tickled the bright green foliage, making a beautiful whispering sound.

I picked up my gun and followed a side river, looking for animals. I saw a hare, tried to creep closer to secure a good shot. By the time I tried to locate it again, it was gone.

'Will you eat grasshoppers and crickets?' asked Tamar when I came back from the hunt.

'Not sure,' I answered, while taking the bullets out of my magazine.

'Will you eat it if I make a patty?' She showed me a little bag full of grasshoppers and crickets. It must have taken a long time to collect them. She poured them into the plate. We both bent over to have a closer look.

'What do we do with them?' I asked.

'I'll pull out the wings and fry them. It's not difficult.'

I was astonished. 'Have you eaten them before?' I asked.

'No,' she said, 'but people do cook them and I've heard they're very nutritious.'

She fried the insects in the pan, cut them in small pieces, mixed them with flour and herbs and little salt, kneaded the mixture into shape and fried the patties. She had her tools spread out on the moss. She had a thin plastic chopping board, her big knife, a cup full of insects, a plate and frypan. Working on the stones was rather impractical, but she was in her element. She sat cross-legged and chopped everything as quickly as if she was standing at a kitchen bench. The way she prepared those grasshoppers was like she'd done it a million times. It was a joy to see such competence.

The patties were small but delicious. The insects had a nutty essence, and although they did not quite fill the stomach, we felt proud to have secured another food source.

We slowly explored the valley, not making much progress, mainly eating kilos of snowberries.

'Are you hungry?' I asked a few days after our meal of grasshoppers.

'No, not really,' answered Tamar.

'Do you feel like going for a hunt?'

'No, not really, I'm tired. You?'

And instead of hunting we ate more snowberries.

Without realising, we were losing weight fast. We had burnt up all of our fat in the last six weeks and now our bodies had no reserves. Our metabolisms had tricked us; we didn't feel hunger anymore. Rationally we knew that we could not live off berries when hiking long distances through the mountains, but we had simply no energy to go out hunting. We grew more and more lethargic. We were tired and slow, we had to rest often, we slept in the afternoon, and each day we spent hours eating snowberries. We never ate the emergency pemmican that Tamar had made before the expedition, because, strangely enough, the situation never felt too dire.

After a week of eating one goose and kilos of snowberries, we came across two hunters. Luckily for us, the men had just shot a stag and were happy to lead us to the dead animal. They took the head with the antlers and one leg; we took the brain, heart and another leg. The old stag was so huge that most of it would go to waste.

We spent days cooking the meat and eating as much as we could stomach, starting with the brain. On the third day we made ten big hamburgers with fat, heart and a little flour, and put them aside for later. When we finally started hiking again, we took a billy of raw meat and a bag of cooked meat for the days to come. For lunch we ate our hamburgers with relish. I had already finished mine when Tamar said, 'Look at this!' She opened her patty and it was crawling with maggots. 'This is the first time I'm feeling slightly uncomfortable,' she said, slowly putting the patty back on the fire.

The maggots were revolting, but Peter and I had come across this before. Living off hunting without a fridge in midsummer was often problematic. The first time we discovered we were eating maggots we were really alarmed, but after a while we realised that you cannot taste them and they are in fact very nutritious.

After eating so much meat, Tamar and I smelled like deer. Our skin, sweat and clothes reeked of it, and I had the feeling we were turning into deer ourselves. Even our stool looked like that of an animal rather than a human. We passed something that looked like pebbles, solid and pitch black. It was the result of eating vast quantities of dense protein.

All that venison gave us a lot of energy and we felt ready to climb our last pass—the V-notch pass into the Ahuriri Valley. It was a very steep and toilsome climb, especially the last hundred metres, but eventually we made it to the top. It was a beautiful day, and the landscape around us was pristine. This land had not changed for millennia. It was like looking into the past and into the future. I was so overwhelmed by the beauty of the mountains, tears came to my eyes.

Six years ago Peter and I had lived in the Ahuriri Valley for three months, and many wonderful things had happened here. I remembered all the parts of the valley we had explored, the little lakes we discovered on top of the mountains, all the windstorms we endured and all the insights we gained. The memories were wonderful, but also a little painful, for I felt Peter's absence acutely.

Dear Peter,

I am writing this from our beloved Ahuriri valley. The last nine weeks have been extreme. I am more quiet, there is less thought. I don't consider the future, because that seems so far away. I breathe, I walk, I hunt. I lost so much weight that I feel more vulnerable. I have hardly any fat left to protect myself and without protection there is much more sensitivity. My lungs feel every deep breath of fresh air, my skin feels every little cool breeze and ray of light, my feet feel every surface because they lead the way. This sensitivity is extraordinary. It feels as if many layers of the onion have come off, and now the light shines onto my primordial self.

I shot a goose some days ago. When I ran to it, the animal was still alive and I had to twist the neck with my bare hands. It was awful and cruel but I could only think of food. We ate crickets and grasshoppers. We saw maggots crawling in the meat—and it didn't even matter. Nothing matters in the heart of the wilderness. We are far away from civilisation; we have moved beyond good and evil. Artificial morals and rules seem to form a barrier between humans and nature. Without all the rules, I am as raw and savage as all other predators in the animal kingdom. I feel as if we have gone back in time and tapped into a primeval consciousness. Strangely enough, this state of mind feels, above all, very honest.

Miriam

We spent some leisurely days at the top, then walked down the valley. When eventually we came to the dirt road we felt we had entered civilisation again. We saw hikers and mountainbikers fresh from town, smelling of fabric softener, clean clothes, clean dogs and clean four-wheel-drive vehicles. Our clothes stank of smoke, our packs showed years of travel, our guns had bloodstains on them. The leather straps smelled of possum; my wooden walking sticks were shiny with oil from my hands.

We had been in the wind, snow, ice, strong sun and the warmth of the fire. Our bodies were tanned and muscled. Our faces were bony, our noses a little burnt and our eyes were bright. We reflected all we had seen during our ten weeks in the wilderness.

We walked for a couple of days down the dirt road that followed the Ahuriri. At night we found a sheltered space to camp between the trees. For the first time we were far away from the glacier, and the water in the river was clear. Now Tamar had a chance to catch a trout in one of the pools. We smoked the fish over a fire and ate our last supper.

The following morning, we woke early.

'This might have been my last night in the wilderness for a long time,' I said as I lit the fire for breakfast. 'From now on Peter and I will live in a house. *A house!* Can you believe it!'

Tamar sighed and shook her head. 'What a cruel end to a beautiful life,' she said. Then she laughed and said in a funny Kiwi accent that made me laugh too: 'You'll be all right, mate!'

'Don't know,' I said. 'I've almost forgotten what it's like to settle in a real house with electricity.'

'My father always says, the worst suffering is the fear of suffering,' said Tamar. She was balancing the billy between two logs on the fire. 'You cannot always choose what happens in life, but you can choose your own attitude. I'm sure you'll find happiness wherever you are.'

'If I don't find it,' I said, 'you'll have to help me look.'

Soon we would have to say goodbye. Tamar would fly to the Middle East to walk the six-hundred-kilometre Jordan trail. I had grown so fond of her. I admired her great enthusiasm to explore more countries and cultures. Her excitement about food was contagious. She taught me many new recipes and to enjoy every spoonful of food, slowly.

'You can learn anything in the world,' she always said, and her words stayed in my head. Her elegance and softness overflowed into me and her optimism became mine. In the end we smelled the same, talked the same and laughed the same. Tamar was part of me, and I felt sad when I thought of saying goodbye. I discovered why it always takes me time to open up. Once my heart was open, separation was almost unbearable.

We walked the last few kilometres side by side. The forest became tussock, the tussock became grass and with the grass came the sheep. Then we heard the noise of cars and trucks.

'There is the road,' said Tamar. I could hear the dread in her voice. 'It's a pity our adventure is over. I could have walked on for years.'

I looked at the asphalt ahead of us. After many weeks in the mountains, it felt as if I saw the road for the first time. I was back on the straight and narrow lane that sooner or later would lead to quiet desperation.

We hitchhiked to the east coast, to Christchurch airport, where it was warm and summery and where cicadas were chirping in the leafy trees. I would fly to Peter in the North Island and Tamar to Jordan.

We hugged goodbye.

'Bye bye, my good friend,' I said. 'Go strong, go safe and don't forget to look after your angel bean.'

'Angel being?' She smiled and hugged me again. 'Yes, you too, my dear, look after your angel being.'

She followed the footpath to international departures. She walked with a little spring in her step. Anybody looking would notice she was as strong as a tahr, fit as a hare and wild as a hind. She turned around and waved with both hands. I waved back and dropped both arms sideways to imitate a flying goose.

'Fly high!' I called.

I saw her laughing. She waved her arms like a bird too, until she was around the corner.

CHAPTER 11

NEW ZEALAND
WALKING ON
THE EDGE

Peter looked frail when I first saw him back in Whanganui. He was anaemic, his hair had begun to fall out, and he moved slowly, like an old person. He spent a lot of time in bed or sitting on the couch. Every now and then his arms were too heavy and flopped back into his lap. He had so little energy that smiling seemed an effort.

But seeing him again was wonderful and hearing his soft voice was a delight. We sat down with a cup of tea in the back yard and Peter pointed at the flowers, shiny capsicums, fresh basil and the potted eggplant that had grown so well over summer. I realised how much I had missed him in the last ten weeks. For me, he brought an element of rest and therefore wonder at the world we live in. Even though he was terribly weak with kidney failure, his mind was still phenomenal. Talking to Peter was like stepping into an airplane and taking off into the vast unknown. With him I could fly into the land of mystery. There were no limits. We talked about life and death, science and politics, humanity and the nature of thought. With every conversation something sparked; he lit my inner fire, he ignited pure happiness. I now knew that if I had to choose between Peter and the wilderness, I would choose to be with him. He was my sense of home. I didn't care that we could not travel physically anymore; we would explore the next frontier with our minds.

 week after my return, I went with Peter to see his renal doctor. Peter had seen him twice since I had been away. 'I'm Peter's wife,' I said, shaking his hand. 'Miriam. Good to meet you.'

The doctor looked at me with slight surprise.

He sat down behind his desk and leafed through the latest lab results. Eventually he said to Peter, 'The blood tests show that your kidneys have not improved.' His tone was matter-of-fact. He seemed to value honesty above pretence.

'How long has it been now?' asked Peter.

'Almost four months since you were discharged from hospital.

The chance that they will recover now is very, very low, I'm afraid. Less than three per cent.'

We had expected to hear this, we knew it, and yet it still hit me.

There was a silence for a few seconds. I looked up at the doctor and saw his sad eyes. He seemed tired, tired of always being the bearer of dark news.

'So,' he said, 'we are measuring your kidney function with what we call the estimated Glomerular Filtration Rate, the GFR. If it's below fifteen for a long time, then we start talking about dialysis.' Providing medical knowledge seemed his way to comfort his patients.

'What is mine now?' asked Peter.

He turned a couple of pages. 'Twelve. The biggest side-effect of renal failure is high blood pressure, which in turn deteriorates kidney function. I'll prescribe medication for that, because high blood pressure is very dangerous. And I recommend you attend a hospital information meeting to learn more about dialysis.'

Five days later Peter drove us to the meeting. One strange side-effect of his illness was the loss of spatial orientation. Whanganui is only a small town, but he was confused and drove the wrong way. So the meeting had already started when we came in. 'Sorry for being late,' said Peter. 'We got lost.'

Lost indeed, I thought.

It was a small room with twenty people sitting behind tables in a big U.

'The reason you are here, ladies and gentlemen,' said the doctor, 'is because your specialist thinks you will soon need dialysis.'

The slide-show began and the doctor explained haemo-dialysis. Then he invited a woman of about fifty to speak about her experiences. She pointed at the fistula on her arm. The skin was black and blue. I stared at what looked like a matchbox under her skin. It was one of the creepiest things I had ever seen. The matchbox was the place the needles went in, every second day, to get her blood cleaned.

'The hospital days are awful,' she said. 'It takes all day. I have to drive an hour to the city, wait for a dialysis chair, then five hours on the machine. All in all, it takes me more than eight hours, and I am exhausted at the end of it all. But the days off are fantastic,' she added with a wry smile.

I looked at Peter and crossed my eyes.

'Most kidney failure in New Zealand is due to diabetes,' said the doctor. 'Since the number of diabetics is increasing with disturbing speed, hospitals are overburdened and there are not enough chairs for dialysis. The government is advocating doing dialysis at home. It's called peritoneal dialysis. Five times a day, one-hour dialysis on a machine. Or, alternatively, all night, every night.'

'We can do this!' I whispered to Peter. Five times a day for one hour was not much worse than collecting firewood, lighting a fire in the rain or trying to wash clothes in an icy river.

'Nothing is straightforward with any intervention,' said the doctor. 'There are always side-effects with dialysis. Peritonitis, blood clots, infections, aneurysms and a bleeding fistula or graft. Then you need medication, antibiotics, sometimes even surgery. If you're at home and your fistula or graft starts bleeding, you have to ring an ambulance straight away.'

'A kidney transplant is definitely the best,' said the transplant nurse. 'You want to put yourself on the waiting list as soon as possible.'

I smiled encouragingly at Peter.

'Unless it gets rejected,' she continued, 'a transplant should last about fifteen to twenty years. The donor and recipient must have compatible blood and tissue types. After the operation the recipient can almost live a normal life, and the donor can lead almost the same life as before.'

Almost? That didn't sound too promising.

'One problem with a kidney transplant is that you need to take immunosuppressive drugs to prevent rejection,' said the doctor. 'This means that you have little resistance against flus or bacterial infections. Moreover, if there is one cancer cell in your body, it will go rampant. This is particularly true for basal cell carcinoma and melanoma skin cancer.'

Peter had had a lot of problems with his skin from all those years in the strong New Zealand sun. 'Imagine you give me your kidney,' he whispered, 'and six months later I get skin cancer! Then you lost me and your kidney!'

'Can you not just live on dialysis forever?' asked a woman next to me.

'Nobody lives forever,' said the doctor in all seriousness, 'but people live on average about five years on dialysis.'

'If you need dialysis, but choose not to, how long will you live?' asked Peter.

'It varies greatly,' answered the doctor, 'but the chance that kidneys will recover by themselves is less than three percent. You might live between six months to five years if you refuse treatment. Some people in their nineties refuse treatment.'

Everybody looked at the very old man in the right-hand corner. His wife sat next to him. He was staring at the floor. I wasn't sure if he had put his hearing aid on.

'I won't do it,' said Peter as we slowly walked back to the car. 'I refuse,' he said. 'I simply refuse. I am not going to be dependent on machines.' He shook his head. 'No, not me.'

'But . . .' I was choked up and couldn't say, Then you are going to die.

He turned around and put his hand softly around my cheek. 'Not after the life we've led, my sweetheart.'

He got slowly into the car. Before he switched on the engine he leaned on the steering wheel. He was exhausted from the meeting. I noticed again how pasty white his face was. It was as if he had already resigned himself to a life in the shadows. As if he had been snatched away from the warm sun that made him love the days.

He turned the key, drove out of the hospital grounds and onto the road. We went past boxy little houses, each with their own little mowed lawns.

'Imagine living in one of those suburban houses right here,' said Peter, 'so we are safely close to a hospital. Imagine driving every second day to the city. I can't stand the thought. I would die of depression before I'd die of kidney failure.'

There were trees on the side of the road, but the tops had been cut out of them in case they hit the power line above. 'Why didn't they plant the trees on the other side of the road! Or change the electricity wire?' said Peter.

'The other option was doing dialysis at home,' I said, searching in my notes for the right terminology. 'Peritoneal dialysis. That sounds like the way to go.'

'Five times a day on a machine? Or all night long? So that I will never have a decent sleep again? That sounds to me like sheer horror. No, not me, I'd rather die than be chained to a machine.'

'We can skip dialysis and I'll give you my kidney,' I said. 'Put yourself on the waiting list, in case we're not compatible.'

'Remember what he said about those drugs that suppress your immune system? I can choose between dying of skin cancer or kidney failure. Well, I'll choose a kidney death, because cancer can be a horrible way to die.'

We waited at a pedestrian crossing. On our right was the park where we walked every day. I looked at the lake and saw three swans. One of them was black. They glided effortlessly over the water.

'If you could feel for one second what it is to be in my body,' he said, 'you'd understand what a low quality of life I have. Constant nausea, chicken-shit taste in my mouth, and no energy to walk more than a hundred metres. That blood-pressure medication gives me horrible stomach pain. This life sucks. Look at this: my hair keeps falling out, that can't be a good sign!' He pulled on a tuft of hair, and about thirty long strands came out. He dropped them out the window. 'The last few months have been awful. I don't even want to live this way.'

'If I had kidney failure I would choose dialysis,' I said when we drove on again, 'and learn how to live with it. They say you'll have more energy if you're on dialysis, because the machine gets rid of the toxins.'

'If I were your age I might do that, but I've had a very good life. Since that night in the hospital when I felt death coming, I know that it is not something to be afraid of. I don't want to live at any cost. Life is not a prison, you know,' he said. 'We should be able to leave at any time, for any reason.'

'Yes,' I said softly, and took his hand.

'I don't want to be a burden to you,' he said. 'Imagine you have to live in a town and drive me to hospital all the time. I wouldn't want to do that to you.'

'Don't refuse medical treatment for my sake!' I felt a surge of panic. 'I'd rather look after you the rest of my life, than not have you!'

We went home feeling wretched. Our friend Nick also tried to convince Peter to go on dialysis and try a transplant. But to no avail.

Now that Peter had decided to refuse all treatment, I had to accept that his death could be a real possibility. I had no experience with dying people. My grandparents had passed away a long time ago; no one else close to me had died. But over all those years in the wilderness I had learned that even with a blue sky, a turn for the worse was always possible. Rain, snow and ice could come at any time in the mountains. Being prepared is paramount. Now that I could see grief coming, I wondered if I could prepare myself in some ways.

I talked with our cancer-surgeon friend, Celine, who dealt with terminally ill patients almost on a daily basis.

'Yes, it's like preparing for an expedition,' she said. 'Some things will remain unknown, other things you can plan. The more prepared you are, the better you'll go through all of this. Consider practical things like his last will, but also where you'll find emotional support, and where you will live once you're on your own.'

I took her advice seriously and figured everything out carefully. When I felt calm and confident, part of me was curious to see how I would handle all this. Would I have strong enough foundations for when the winds of change came along? At other times I was overcome with sorrow. But there was always a voice in the back of my head that reminded me to stay in the present. Because I could not turn the clock back once he had passed.

I wanted to make sure I walked these last months carefully, to tell him the things that matter. Every step, every word, every gesture would be with attention. I could not afford a mistake, because there might not be a tomorrow to say sorry.

I f he only had a few more months, perhaps a couple of years left, we decided that we should be in the most beautiful place we could find. For the first time in nine years, we would rent a proper house. For the first time we would have electricity, a hot shower, WiFi, bedrooms, a kitchen, firebox and a sunny yard with garden chairs, so that Peter could be as comfortable as possible.

In April, we found a furnished rental house on the hills above the sea at the small settlement of Mārahau. It looked out over the renowned Abel Tasman National Park and was only two kilometres from a beautiful beach. We felt lucky: it was a place many could only dream of visiting, let alone living.

It was a long journey south. Peter was exhausted when we arrived, so he sat quietly on the couch while I unpacked our bags and boiled the electric jug.

We sipped our tea while looking out over the bush-clad hills and the sea. There was a little island close to the shore. It was a very pretty sight.

In the early morning hours, I began writing down our story on our new laptop, with one ear open for Peter. It had been a week since he had taken any blood-pressure medication. He thought risking a stroke or heart attack was better than living the rest of his life with the side-effects of the drugs. Peter was walking on the edge of a ravine, and could fall off any time. He always preferred the edge, but this time he was so weak, it could all be over in a flash.

If he was still in bed around half-past nine in the morning, I started to worry. Had he died in the night? Should I go and look? I had a doctor's brochure pinned on the wall with all the emergency telephone numbers. Each day when he came down, I was relieved to see him.

I loved life, I loved all there is to life, and I learned to accept death, for the possibility of losing Peter had made our life very intense. One moment with him felt like an eternity. Death stretched the time. The number of days and weeks didn't count any longer. Whenever I forgot about my attachment and sorrow, death gifted us a moment of grace.

I felt good and healthy, but life was very difficult for Peter. He was suffering. He often complained about the bad taste in his mouth, the nausea, the lack of energy. The only thing he enjoyed, he said, was sleeping: in his dreams he had plenty of energy and was still walking across the world.

The days became shorter, the nights colder. We lit a fire in the firebox and we were warm. The weeks glided by. Almost every day we walked down the road. Past the weeping willows and magnolia tree. Past the tall poplars, whose leaves slowly turned more yellow. They fluttered in the breeze, like a thousand butterflies that want to fly away but could not quite tear themselves loose. We picked some figs and feijoas to eat along the way, patted the horses and talked to the sheep. After half an hour, we'd come out at the beach and sit on a log.

'It is strange to think that everybody has to go through the process of dying,' said Peter one day in June. 'Yet most people never believe they will. Peculiar. Do you think about your own death?'

'Me? No, not really. Mostly I think of your death, not mine.'

We looked at the surface of the sea moving smoothly like a silk sheet in the wind.

'The main thing this kidney failure has taught me is that the body rules,' he said. 'I always believed the mind is independent of the body in some way, that the mind can influence or override the physical. Now I realise that it doesn't matter what I think. The main thing is to listen to the body. The body indicates when I should rest or sleep, what and when I should eat, and if my body is not well, I am on the way out.'

We walked slowly back through the bush, and followed the river up.

'You see this willow here?' Peter pointed at the trees on the bank. 'If I break off one branch, what happens?'

I laughed; I knew what was coming. I had seen the same outside the hospital in Australia. 'It heals itself.'

'Yes,' he said. 'All creatures constantly heal themselves. The will to live is so inherent in all living beings. Maybe my body can heal,' he went on. 'Maybe I just need more time. Kidneys seem to heal extremely slowly. In New Zealand the doctors have been very pessimistic but they deal mostly with diabetics. In Australia they see more desert victims like me. Remember one specialist in Townsville said that it could take up to eighteen months to fully recover. The kidneys have not started to repair themselves yet, but it might still begin.'

I glanced at Peter and noticed that his eyes seemed a little brighter.

O ur hope of recovery grew. Slowly, over the months, the feeling that Peter could die at any time ebbed away. With hope, we no longer lived only in the present. With hope we were now looking at the future and needed to plan for it.

Peter needed a secure home, with access to medical care. Travelling was out of the question for him—even the twenty-minute drive to the nearest town was too exhausting. Bulgaria and our little village of Miliva became a distant dream. We thought about buying a small property near Mārahau and making ourselves a more permanent home.

So I went to town, strolled around in second-hand shops, looking for teapots, nice bowls and other kitchenware. I bought running shoes, and every day I ran ten kilometres to stay fit. I bought some wall hangings for our future house, and some dumbbells so I could do weight training on rainy days since I was losing my strength by not living in the wild. I found a yoga mat to stretch my body that had become more stiff and sore from sitting on chairs and lying on a soft mattress. Ever since we had left the wilderness, my body felt less clean, and I bought organic food to reduce the build-up of toxins. My mind was restless too, and I felt the need to do some meditation every morning. Slowly my day became a sequence of activities to stay healthy—something I had never even considered in the wild.

After the initial novelty, our comfortable house began to feel like a prison. I felt locked into an artificial reality. In the last decade, we had never stayed more than a couple of weeks in a modern house, and during that time I had always been busy preparing to go back into the wild. I had forgotten what it was like to live in a house. I was astonished to see how much time I wasted in the kitchen. I seemed to be spending hours and hours cooking, cleaning, doing dishes, cleaning, cooking. More dishes. Life in the forest had been so simple with a frypan to eat out of and one spoon.

Our good friend Celine gave me her old phone. I had resisted owning one ever since I had thrown mine away in India fourteen years earlier, but now we needed to be able to ring out in a medical emergency. In the beginning I kept forgetting where I put the thing, but slowly I adapted. The more communication with others, the more important the phone became; the more it interfered in my daily life, the more restless I grew. The pace of life seemed to have increased significantly with the arrival of the phone, and it felt as if the rest of the world was now coming to us. Journalists rang and television crews turned up, wanting to know what had happened to us since the release of the book in 2017. They wanted a piece of the product called Woman in the Wilderness, the woman who was now living in a house, talking about the good old days in the wild, and who was slowly fitting into normality.

I had become a person I had never intended to be: someone who spends hours in the kitchen, who checks her cellphone for the latest message, who looks in the mirror and worries about appearance, who goes running in the park with earphones, who spends most of the day working on a laptop, and eats a thoughtless dinner behind the screen while her husband streams his own movie.

The thought of continuing this way of life for the years to come was nothing short of depressing. The house was comfortable; it stored beautiful things, as well as us. By none of it was *alive*. The walls were a barrier between me and the outside world. I couldn't smell the wind, I couldn't hear a river, I couldn't feel the living world.

One day we were sitting on our log on the beach. The afternoon sun was shimmering over the surface of the water. Small waves were lapping on the gold-coloured sand. A hundred oystercatchers calmly surveyed the sea, standing still with their feet in the moving tide.

'I feel as if something is withering away inside of me by living in a house,' I said while drawing patterns in the sand with a stick. 'This is a nice place, but being settled in a human environment wears me down. Don't know why.'

'I feel the same,' said Peter. 'As if I'm slowly drying up like a mussel washed up on a beach.'

'Mussel in the sand?' I laughed. 'Yes, that's a good description.'

'You seem very happy and cheerful though,' said Peter.

'Most of the time I am very happy,' I said. 'But I don't think happiness is the ultimate goal. I'm happy when I am with you, when I have a good sleep, enough food and no conflicts. A happy dog wags its tail, but a happy pet is wholly different from a wild wolf in the mountains. No, I don't think happiness is my ultimate aim. There is more to life than just happiness. I want to feel alive, I want to feel intensity, rawness. I want clarity and the feeling of having a powerful fire inside me that makes me face fear and danger. For me, it feels as if the security of a house takes away that intensity. Buying a property might not be the right thing to do for us. In the beginning we would be excited, planting trees and gardens and all, and after a while we might feel imprisoned. Our cheap holiday cottage in Bulgaria is one thing. Settling down forever in an expensive property in New Zealand is another.'

'Of course I agree,' said Peter. 'I'd much rather live in a tent in the wilderness. But if I don't get better, we might not have a choice.

I'm so sorry, my sweetheart. I'm so sorry to put you through this.'

I put my arms around him and we said nothing. A seagull spotted us and swooped down to see if we had something for him to eat.

Although Peter had gained some weight and his hair stopped falling out, he still had very little energy. He often complained of a bad taste in his mouth that constantly reminded him of his predicament. On the slightest hill he would become breathless, and his heart would beat alarmingly. Every time I heard him breathing so heavily, I thought of the high chance of a heart attack.

Peter watched news and movies, and avoided reading too much about chronic kidney failure, for it was nothing but depressing information. We kept talking positively and making plans for the long-term future. We kept pretending that he would get better, but we knew the chances of recovery were slim.

After four months in the house, a letter from the nephrologist to the local GP arrived, confronting us with the grim truths. It said that Peter had non-resolving ATN—chronic kidney failure—and should contact the specialist as soon as possible to begin dialysis therapy. To read it in black and white was again a bad blow. In between the lines we read that if he refused medical treatment he would not have long to live.

'Maybe this is it,' Peter said. There were tears in his eyes. 'Maybe I will die soon. Or worse, I will live with this poor health for years to come. What will happen to you? I don't want to hold you back. You should live a life of adventure—in the wild. Not a life of an old person in a house. Civilisation and technology are brilliant if you're sick, but soul destroying if you're young and strong.'

I looked at him with pain in my heart. 'Don't ever worry about me. Being with you is the most important thing in my life,' I said, and I clung to him like a joey to its possum-mother. I wanted to hold him tight. Forever.

I never talked with Peter about how I'd live if he died, but I did sometimes think about it. Where should I go? Be among other people? Go back to Bulgaria and sit in our cottage on my own? Move to a town in New Zealand? Live in a house, rent a room, have a day job to pay for it? That thought was both scary and alien.

My home was with Peter. If he passed away, then my home was not in a house. It would be in the wilderness where I would live intensely. Where the forest was growing, where the rivers were flowing and the wind was allowed to roam freely. But could I handle the solitude, the lack of human contact and even the sheer power of the wild? Had I learned enough to survive on my own? I needed to find that out.

When the first signs of spring appeared, with lilies on the side of the road and blossoms in the trees, I decided to spend some time on my own in Kahurangi National Park. I would take little more than a kilo of flour and bit of salt and would rely on hunting. I knew it would be tough, but I was sick of living in comfort. I wanted to live rough again; sleep on the ground, feel my body, be hungry and tired. I longed to go to the edge and be in touch with reality.

Peter assured me that he was safe and happy on his own for ten days. So I hitchhiked for an hour up the road, and walked with my pack and gun into the park. I followed the track to a little lookout. I sat down on a fallen log and could see the blue-green river down below. It was so beautiful, and I missed Peter intensely. Wouldn't it be wonderful if he could be here, even just once? I cried a little, until I thought: I am going to learn how to be alone, and see what happens.

I looked around for a straight mānuka sapling. With the saw on my pocketknife I cut a new walking stick, as I had thrown my old sticks away after the expedition. I was hot and sweaty when I shouldered my pack again. I zipped open the little pocket to find a hair tie, and found my good-luck charm, the angel bean. I had forgotten all about it. Angels supposedly come from heaven, I thought. Heaven is supposedly the place where dead people go. So death is protecting life, I concluded with a smile.

At lower elevation the vegetation was lush and thick, like jungle. The supplejack vine had made an almost impenetrable web and only the native wood-hen, the weka, was able to navigate through it successfully. I followed the path. When I stood still, it was quiet: there were no footsteps or voices. Just me. It felt a little peculiar, but wonderful to be alone. I hiked up the mountains for two days, and when the bush became more open, I left the track behind and climbed up the big boulders of a river. There was no path, no hut and no sign of humans; I had to find my own way.

Under a large tree, I found a small grassy clearing for my tent. For days I quietly explored the forgotten valley. The place was so full of life, so incredibly beautiful and wild that I never felt lonely. In the morning I woke up with a brilliant dawn chorus of bellbirds. In the twilight, I sat for hours under bushes, spying into clearings, looking for deer or goats. When I finally shot a young goat, I sat around the fire to cook and eat the wild game. I felt strong from eating meat. It felt so natural. The animals and I were just there, we were all gathering food, wandering, resting, eating and sleeping.

One evening I was watching the dancing light over a bed of glowing embers, while the forest slowly grew darker. A morepork hooted in the distance; another owl close by answered. Then suddenly, in the absolute stillness, I saw that I had no goal, no focus or aim and, precisely because of this, I had stepped into a kind of consciousness where there was no sense of passing time. I felt as if the past and future had disappeared and I was left with the natural rhythms. This generated an immense sense of peace.

In the last months, I had been running with the clock, looking at my diary. I had been projecting into the future, based on concepts from the past. I had identified myself with the past, and time— *chronos*—had become part of me. I realised that if I wanted to live in that consciousness outside time, I needed to leave technology and security behind, and go back into the wild. But without a journey from A to B and without a goal. The most simple thing would be the most difficult undertaking.

Except—we had done it before. I remembered the day we'd moved into the mountains, nine years earlier. It felt as if we had stepped into the void, with no future. We had no communication devices, we said goodbye to family and friends, and left the past behind. It had felt timeless. We gathered wood, went for walks, and I hunted, but there were still many hours in the day when we had nothing to do but be. It took weeks for the mind to slow down, but so many insights had flowed from those years of contemplation and reflection.

'She who rides the tiger cannot dismount,' Peter once said. Would I be able to dismount this tiger? The tiger called Time? Or would that tiger eat me if I was to step off?

While quietly roaming the valley in the following days, I remembered Peter's words. He had said he would rather die than live a life he didn't want to live. Never in my life had I seen that kind of powerful determination. His strength had generated so much energy that it had flowed over to me. Now I could say the same. I would use all my attention, strength and awareness to dismount the tiger to live a sane life. I resolved to return to the timeless wilderness, either with Peter if he got better, or without him if he died.

U pon my return, Peter decided to see a doctor for a blood test. He wanted to know whether his kidneys were improving. For six months he had dreaded car travel, the doctors and all the bad news. But then one morning in October he was ready.

The doctor studied his file, looked very worried and murmured something about blood pressure. Then he sent us to the lab. One needle filled up many tubes with dark red blood. When it was all done, we drove home.

A week later the phone rang.

'The doctor,' I said, and panic shot through my body. My heart was in my throat.

Peter picked up the phone. The doctor gave him numbers and the results of the blood test.

'And the GFR?' asked Peter. 'Twenty? Are you saying *twenty*?'

I looked at him incredulously. His kidney function had improved from twelve to twenty. It was a miracle. After all those months of slow deterioration, the kidneys had made a turn and begun to repair. Tears were rolling over my cheeks. He had far surpassed my hopes. He was now in stage four kidney failure, not stage five. There was no need for dialysis. It was a recovery that, according to doctors here, was statistically almost impossible.

Peter put the phone down and stood up. He looked perplexed.

'Miriam, my sweetheart. I will *live!*'

'It's unbelievable,' I whispered, as more tears came.

'I will *live!* The divine wind did come! My body is recovering!'

'It's wonderful,' I said, and kept kissing his face.

'We will go back to Bulgaria when I am able to fly, and see all the old people in Miliva. We will walk to our little cottage in the mountains. When the winter comes, we'll go to warmer places like Greece, or even Oman, and in the spring we'll sail across the Black Sea and travel to Georgia, find a little cottage to rent in Russia, perhaps, who knows. We'll stay nomadic, and just follow randomness. We'll be free as birds, flying away from a constrained life.

'But I won't be able to fly just yet. First we'll live in the wild places here.' He turned around, looked out of the window at the mountains. 'Soon as I am able to, we'll go back to live in the forest. We will set up a camp, sit quietly around the fire, watch the kea fly over. Hear the wind through the beech tops while a robin comes for a visit. We'll sleep in our tent under the possum duvet, and you'll hunt a goat to eat. Our hair, clothing and all we own will smell of smoke again. When it's sunny, we'll go for a little walk. Not far of course, because I'll be weak for a long time. But we will retreat from the fast world. Yes, we will return to the wilderness where I can heal further.' He softly touched my arm. 'You want to?'

I laughed and I cried and I held him for a long time.

EPILOGUE

I t took another five months, but eventually Peter recovered sufficiently to begin to think about living in the mountains again. In February 2020 we started preparing. We gave our household belongings back to the second-hand shop. We found our old gear, repaired our tools and equipment, and bought enough ammunition to last for a year.

In March, as we were about to head away, the Covid-19 pandemic began to spread across the world with frightening speed. The country was locked down and the land became quiet. I had the feeling the end of the age of abundance was in sight, and new times were coming.

With Peter's kidneys not yet fully recovered, the need for self-isolation became urgent. He did not want to risk catching the virus, so we completed last chores, bought food supplies for six months. And we left.

Where we are now is a mystery.

We left the town and roads behind, and followed a small goat track that led into the high mountains. We found our way to the rocky tops where the wind blew fiercely. In the mist and rain we climbed over the pass and descended on the other side into a hidden valley. We pushed through the tūpare until we reached the mountain beeches with a carpet of moss underneath. We followed the creek down until we reached an old tree that was bathed in the afternoon sun. We pitched the tent near the stream, gathered some branches, lit a fire and rested. We found ourselves in a very quiet place.

ACKNOWLEDGEMENTS

had no intention of writing a second book, until my publisher suggested it. Her kindness and positivity has helped me enormously. So, once again, thanks to Jenny Hellen this book is in your hands.

I also want to thank the whole team at Allen & Unwin: particularly Abba Renshaw who dealt with media and Maggie

Thompson who put in much effort to get the books into foreign territories. Special thanks to Jane Parkin for her editing expertise. She carved the text of this book into a smooth story.

I'd like to thank Peter for his encouragement to keep on writing, my sister Sofie, my parents, Jean François Robert, Dr Phil Carter for critical proofreading, and Marilyne Fouquart for her generous contribution of the pictures from Bulgaria.

I am very grateful to all the doctors, nurses and social workers who cared for Peter, and me too. One touch, one loving word kept my heart soft.

I am immensely grateful to our good friend Nick Maverick, who looked after Peter while I was on the expedition with Tamar. He encouraged me to go to the wild mountains to find the essence of all wisdom.

I would like to thank Ben Fogle, and the team of *New Lives in the Wild* for making a beautiful documentary about us in Bulgaria 2019, as well as Floortje Dessing who made another touching episode for *Terug naar het einde van de wereld 2020*.

And thank you for reading the book.

Kia kaha, Kia māia, Kia manawanui.
Be strong, be brave, be steadfast.

www.miriamlancewood.com